My Philosophy of Life,

plus a few handy tips

My Philosophy of Life, plus a few handy tips

Nita Micossi

My Philosophy of Life,

plus a few handy tips

My Philosophy of Life, plus a few handy tips

My Philosophy of Life, plus a few handy tips Copyright © 2010 by Robert Zises
All rights reserved without written permission.
The Zises Group
PO Box 394, Tivoli, NY 12583 / 845-757-2727

ISBN: 978-0-615-35271-8
Library of Congress Control Number: 2010923321

Cover design and illustration: Steve Jennis, www.stevanjennis.com

For Nita

There are those who say that Nita Micossi has squandered her PhD. Her mother, for one. But Dr. M believed that thirty years of scribbling for all sorts of national and international rags—some sitting in your dentist's office, others known only to electrical engineers—has not only utilized her considerable skills, but entitled her to write anything she damn well pleased.

Introduction

For ten years, from 1998 to 2008, Nita wrote a monthly essay for a local publication "Hudson River Sampler" -- the date of publication follows each column. In this body of work, Nita lampooned her own life, politics, and the drama of her community through her unique perspective.

You won't be able to read a single essay without being touched by her wit and wisdom, educated by her relentless fact-checking, and taken by the effortless prose that only painstaking re-writing could produce. You won't find a single trite, corny or hackneyed phrase on these pages.

Her talents were legend; her exploits prodigious. A PhD from Berkeley led her into teaching college courses in Sociology to prisoners at a maximum security prison, but at one time or another, she was a professional cabaret singer, a radio personality, an investigative reporter, a community activist, a journalist, a friend, daughter, sister, wife, mother...and always…always… a humor columnist. It's hard to know which she loved more: the teaching or the humor writing. At the end she had both.

Nita passed away in December 2008, but through this book, her humanity and compassion, insight and warmth, love and levity live on.

Enjoy.

Bob and Sofia

Table of Contents

Chapter 1. Ya-Ya Sisterhood Under the Red Tent   Page 1

Chapter 2. I'm not now, nor will I ever likely be ready for the 21st Century   Page 20

Chapter 3. My Philosophy of Life, plus a few Handy Tips   Page 55

Chapter 4. Stuff   Page 93

Chapter 5. Keep the Red Socks away from the Yellow Towels: Lessons in Domesticity   Page 116

Chapter 6. Marriage, Kids, Pets: The Whole Catastrophe   Page 138

Chapter 7. Hooray for the Holidays!   Page 166

Chapter 8. Who the Hell is Running this Joint, Anyway?   Page 189

Chapter 9. Next in Line   Page 225

Chapter 10. Health, Wealth, and the Hereafter   Page 246

My Philosophy of Life, plus a few handy tips

1.
YA-YA SISTERHOOD UNDER THE RED TENT

NO JANE, NO PAIN? Poor Jane Fonda. To reach peace of mind in her mid-60s she's had to go through hell. I just wish we didn't have to go with her. Page 2

THERE SHE IS. Yes, I confess. I watch the Miss America contest on TV. But no one ever won my vote without qualification until this year's Miss Alabama revealed that her secret ambition in life is to be a Humor Columnist. Page 5

YA-YA SISTERHOOD UNDER THE RED TENT. Within the space of five minutes I had communed with two women I shall never see again, trading cosmetic secrets, marital woes, drug doses, and glimpses of one another's self-image. Think of what we could have done with a 20 minute coffee break. Page 7

I'M LOOKING FOR TWEEZERS AND A TURKEY BASTER. What you find inside a woman's purse may save the world. Page 9

IN PRAISE OF DIFFICULT WOMEN. Today, when every other teenager dresses like a hooker and wants to be a gangsta rapper, "difficult woman" means little more than cheap costuming and a superficial pose. But in 1934, the year Claudette Colbert starred in *It Happened One Night*, "difficult woman" described Character -- strong, confident, and resilient. Page 11

SEX AND MY CITY. Between the ages of 18 and 36 I lived in Berkeley, California and had my own girl gang. Page 13

MEN WE LOVE. For the novices, the befuddled, and those men out there who still don't understand why a woman might get up in the middle of the soup course to go to the powder room and never return, I offer the following list. Page 15

A LESSON IN REVENGE FROM THOSE DESPERATE HOUSEWIVES. We all have a short but bitter list of people who have done us wrong and wounded us deeply. Page 18

NO JANE, NO PAIN?

SOME YEARS AGO I was reading the story of a burley, black-bearded biker who became a quadriplegic in a motorcycle accident. As a result of his life-altering mishap, the man became a poet.

"As a quadriplegic, what do you want most?" asked the interviewer.

"A quadriplegic wishes he were a paraplegic," was the deadpan reply. "A paraplegic wishes he were able-bodied. And the able-bodied wish they were Jane Fonda."

So many wanted to be Jane Fonda, at one point, for her obvious perfections and advantages.... Everyone, it seems, except Jane herself.

In her recent autobiography, MY LIFE SO FAR, Ms. Fonda reveals decades of self-loathing and insecurity. Her first husband, Roger Vadim, forced her into humiliating group sex; her 2nd husband, Tom Hayden, held the movie business in contempt while cheerfully taking money that Jane earned from movies to support his political causes; and her third husband, Ted Turner, started cheating on her before the wedding bouquet had wilted. Her mother committed suicide when she was twelve. And her father, the famous Henry, was so remote from and unloving to his daughter that even Katharine Hepburn, herself no cuddle-bunny, called him "cold, cold, cold."

Jane was prone to depression her whole life, suffered from bulimia since high school, and, get this, always hated her body! Jane, who replaced Brigitte Bardot in Vadim's fantasies. Jane, who gave us all but the full monty in BARBARELLA. Jane, of the infamous WORKOUT that launched ten thousand aerobic gyms. Jane Fonda hated her body.

This piece of news, somehow, did not surprise me. There was always something manic about Jane's tapes that, like all of her public displays, hinted at subterranean goings-on. I never knew before what they were but, I confess, that for years I have resented this woman. Not for her pedigree. Not for her politics. Not for her Oscars. No, I blame Jane Fonda for upping the ante on female self-maintenance.

It's one thing to be healthy and fit. But when Jane, pushing 50, stretched and boogaloo-ed that tall, thin, tiny-waisted figure with legs up to here on those video tapes, the rest of us were finished. WE never looked like that at 20 and here the norm was being recalibrated so that we were expected to look like that post-menopause!

As she speaks of the WORKOUT phase of her life (Janie has gone through more phases than the moon), there is not a trace of irony in her report of the consequences of her crusade to get us all into shape. In her bio she shares testimonials from women who "poured their hearts out about the weight they had lost, self-esteem they had gained" by using her tapes.

Not a word, however, about what women who do not have a Barbie doll figure and face felt like trying to keep up with one who does. I wonder how many became bulimics in the attempt?

She notes that JANE FONDA'S 1982 WORKOUT tape is not only the biggest-selling home video of all time but that it helped to launch the entire home video industry. Not a word, however, about the cosmetic surgery business that has likewise exploded in the wake of the fitness craze. What's the point of having 20-year-old thighs if you have a 55-year-old neck wattle?

Jane, Jane, Jane. What have you done to us?

I have a nine-year-old daughter, a tiny, trim athlete, who stands in front of the mirror and critically assesses her "fat". It's leached into the groundwater of the culture, this obsession with the body. And Ms. Fonda is in no small way responsible.

Jane describes how her own young girl body disappointed her father: "Dad had an obsession with women being thin... (And) once I hit adolescence, the only time my father ever referred to how I looked was when he thought I was too fat...The truth is that I was never fat." (She's right. I've seen the photos.)

Jane, nevertheless, learned to hate her body, and she collected an armory of neuroses, compulsions, and addictions to protect her from Daddy's displeasure. (No blame. Don't we all?) But she has been in a singular position to project her responses to those neuroses onto the American female psyche. "I'm a gorgeous bulimic addicted to aerobic highs... maybe Daddy will love me now... follow me down the Yellow Brick Road." And so we did.

....There is in my house a copy of one of those original WORKOUT tapes. It belongs to my husband a fan of Jane Fonda and her physical-type.

I look at the picture of Jane on the tape box, her dark brown hair piled on top of her head and those impossibly long limbs stretched out in every direction. I always thought that the mega-watt smile was just a bit forced, the eyes maybe a wee bit sad. Poor Jane. To reach peace of mind in her mid-60s she's had to go through hell. I just wish we didn't have to go with her.

Nita Micossi never wanted to be Jane Fonda, but would have enjoyed having dinner, just once, with her three husbands.

July 2005

THERE SHE IS....

YES, I CONFESS. I watch the Miss America pageant on TV every year. Although I've never competed in anything remotely having to do with beauty, I have a very special attachment to this event. It goes back to my childhood in Santa Cruz, site of the annual Miss California Pageant.

Grandpa Tony was the stage manager at the Santa Cruz Civic Auditorium where the pageant was held, and my cousins and I always got free tickets to sit in the audience and watch the show. I'll never forget Miss Bakersfield doing a comic monologue about how mortified she was at a baseball game when everybody in the stands jumped up and shouted that the Red Sox had a run. "But I wasn't going to let them get away with it," she said with a cocky toss of her curls, "So I stood on my seat and hollered, 'I don't care if my red socks do have a run!'"

We little 9-year-old girls were dazzled, and, after the performance, went back stage and asked all the mostly 19-year-old contestants to autograph our souvenir programs. I still have that pageant program.

I know what you're thinking. Miss America is hokey and, worse, reinforces an oppressively narrow definition of beauty and the concept of women as virginal objects – look at Miss 34-22-34 in a bathing suit but do not touch. But my pre-pubescent sister, cousins, and I were so captivated with the pageantry, talent, and grace on stage in the Santa Cruz Civic Auditorium that we made putting on Miss America shows of our own in the backyard a favorite game. And I always delivered the Red Socks monologue for my turn at the talent competition.

This year my daughter and I watched 24-year-old Deidre Downs of Alabama crowned Miss America 2005. With shoulder length chestnut brown hair, lucid blue eyes, and dazzling teeth, Miss Downs (I think we can use "Miss" in this context) more than earned the title by strutting down the runway in a string bikini and spike heels without looking like she was holding in her stomach – by singing the pop tune "I'm Afraid This Must Be Love" without embarrassing her mother – and by knowing that "government of the people, by the people, for the people shall not perish from the earth" are the final words of the Gettysburg Address. Deidre, who plans to become a pediatrician and cure childhood cancer, can do it all.

She was already on MY finalists' list (everyone on my couch keeps a running list of favorites) when Deidre revealed to the emcee that her secret ambition in life is to grow up and be a Humor Columnist. Well, that did it. Darlin' Miss D, you are a winner no matter what the judges say!

Now, it's not too often that I find myself in a position to give advice to Miss America. But, having earned carfare for the past 6 ½ years as…. yes, a Humor Columnist, I feel it my patriotic duty to humbly offer Deirdre Dawn a few tips.

- When writing a humor column, shamelessly use your friends for material.

- Be prepared to lose friends.

- Use your family for material; it's the most satisfying way ever to settle old scores and they can't divorce you.

- Turn every disaster into a funny bit; instead of seeking professional help, make that pain pay.

- Don't worry about running out of ideas for your column. On a dry day, simply do a Google search on "male enhancement surgery." If that doesn't get your funny bone vibrating then watch a presidential press conference.

- Get a website to let the world know how terrific you are and to make it easier for the editor of the New Yorker to find you. (I myself have never gotten it together to set up a website which is, no doubt, why the editor of the New Yorker hasn't yet called.)

- Finish med school and keep your day job. There are three people on the planet who actually make a comfortable living writing nothing but humor columns and two of them are Dave Barry.

And, Miss America, wherever you are, if you can laugh at yourself wearing that silly crown, you can rule the world.

October 2004

YA-YA SISTERHOOD UNDER THE RED TENT

I'M AT MACY'S LAST week returning two pairs of size six trousers to a clerk named Joyce. "I love these pants. I have two more pair at home. But," I lower my voice conspiratorially, "shortly after I bought these, the doc changed my meds and – wham! before I could say Kirstie Alley – I put on fifteen pounds and am lucky to get into a size ten."

"Oh, dear," coos Joyce sympathetically. "The same thing happened to me when the therapist put me on antidepressants after my husband ran off with his Pilates instructor. Isn't it just awwwful!" she moans pulling up her sweater and grabbing a pitiful inch of fatty flab between her thumb and forefinger. I figure she means the fat, not the Pilates instructor.

As I head to Macy's exit through the petite section, I notice that they now carry nothing remotely like the trousers I just returned. Joyce is off on break so I flag down Myra and whimper, "I'm having seller's remorse here." I point to the pile of pants on her returns desk and recount my story about why I had to return them. "But now I'm afraid that when I get my figure back – we must believe – they'll have stopped making this style and I won't be able to find any I like as much," adding sheepishly, "can I buy them back?"

"Of course, darlin'. No problem."

"Don't you just hate that?" I ramble on as Myra taps figures into the cash register, revealing to me that my trousers now cost half of what I returned them for a few minutes earlier. "I mean they do that all the time. You finally find a brassiere you love and then, without even asking, they discontinue the style."

"Tell me about it!" barks Myra flicking her blond page boy with a free hand. "I've been using Clairol's Sunburst on my hair for years and then, all of a sudden I couldn't find it at CVS. So I called Clairol and some fifteen-year-old gum-chewing twit tells me that they've stopped making it. Just like that." Myra's self-esteem clearly depends on how artfully she conceals her graying hair and, as a fellow sister over 50, I identify with the crisis. "So I go and buy some other color and damned if it didn't turn my hair yellow! I looked like a freak."

"But it looks lovely now," I offer supportively.

"Well," she charges on while swiping my credit card, "After this unpleasant episode I'm at Eckerd's and, guess what?"

"What?" being the appropriate response to my comrade's litany of woe.

"Eckerd's still carries Sunburst! I could've rung that little twit's neck for putting me through all that grief."

There it was. Within the space of five minutes I had communed with two women I shall never see again, trading cosmetic secrets, marital woes, drug doses, and glimpses of one another's self-images. Think of what we could have done with a twenty minute coffee break.

This experience, which turns a mere commercial transaction into a bonding ritual, reminds me of book I dearly love, THE RED TENT by Anita [no relation] Diamant. THE RED TENT is about tribal life from the point of view of Dinah, little known daughter of the Old Testament Patriarch Jacob and sister of Joseph and the other eleven who-eventually-became-the-tribes of Israel.

Diamant tells us that much of women's culture developed under the Red Tent, a place where females were exiled during their time of the month. There, unclean and unfit for intercourse with men, social and otherwise, they enjoyed one long coffee klatch. For three days during the lunar cycle all of the women in the tribe (for as I learned living in a commune, the bodies of women who live together do eventually cycle together) gleefully gathered in the Red Tent to eat delicacies, drink beer, tell tales, and swap all the down-and-dirty gossip.

The men, Dinah revealed, thought that the women spent their three days languishing in the straw and stoically enduring their menstrual discomforts. Not true. In the Red Tent girls learned the female body's secrets of pleasure, power, and procreation. They listened with unconditional sympathy to each others' stories about life's daily nuisances and traumatic defeats. And they created an enduring sisterhood that allowed them to foil the boys when they got a little too full of themselves.

We ladies no longer have a Red Tent to flee to, alas. But the chatty and mutually supportive ways of women live. And wherever two or more of us gather together, no matter that we are just introduced, problems are shared, intimacies of the body are revealed, and pains of the heart are tenderly exchanged.

But don't tell the guys.

October 2006

I'M LOOKING FOR TWEEZERS AND A TURKEY BASTER

REMEMBER THAT GAME SHOW with Monty Hall called Let's Make a Deal? In the early years of the show, Monty would find his contestants by going through the audience and asking women if they had some exotic item in their purse. A jar of Noxzema, let's say, or a meat thermometer.

Of course, when it comes to the contents of a woman's pocket book nothing is really too exotic. Occasionally too large or too wet. But bring together a dozen women of various ages, and chances are not utterly remote that they will be able to collectively produce an egg timer, a guitar pick, pinking shears, and a package of parsley seeds.

My grandmother, for instance, always carries a Sherlock Holmesian sized magnifying glass in her purse -- the better to inspect canned peaches at the supermarket. Aunt Lena, who was a U.S. Marine sergeant during WWII packs a hip flask filled with Four Roses -- a social lubricant for all occasions. And my friend Susan never leaves home without her kazoo.

And drugs. Women are a veritable pharmacy of first aid remedies. Walk into a public restroom and complain loudly that you have a headache, and at least three women will simultaneously produce a bottle of Tylenol Extra Strength. On a playground no self-respecting Mom would be without a supply of Barney band-aids even if she's wearing no more than a fanny pack.

It's a habit we girls get into at an early age. Unlike boys, we're given little purses to match our Easter outfits. We watch what Mom, prepared for any crisis, carries in hers (a supply of crackers and fruit, a medical kit, travel Bingo); and we stuff a plastic stethoscope into our little purse in case Betsy-Wetsy has coronary during Mass.

By the time we're in high school we're carrying purses that defy the carry-on luggage limits. But, like Mom, We Are Prepared.

Of course, the precise contents of any woman's handbag depends on her particular age and life circumstances. A young lady going out on date that may or may not end up in an overnight is equipped with certain gear unnecessary to a mother of two toddlers on her way to a Musical Munchkins class. But we women are constantly learning from one another and discovering new ways to be prepared for life's unexpected events.

For example, one warm afternoon last April I'm lying on the grass outside Bard Hall next to a gaggle of college students listening to a Klezmer concert going on inside the building.

I can't decide whether I'm going to clip my nails, read a book, do a crossword puzzle, or crochet my niece a pair of booties. I've got the equipment for all these activities in my purse. But I decide to just lie back and take in the music, so I pull out the over-sized scarf I always carry and roll it up into a little pillow. Then I get hungry and pull a two-point Weight Watcher's candy bar out of my bag. When I get melted chocolate on my chin I pull out a package of unscented baby wipes to clean up.

Up till this point the female students around me pay no mind to what I'm up to -- they have their own purses at hand to cope with contingencies. But when I grab the baby wipes one young lady stares at me with awe and envy. She realizes, as I did when I had a child in diapers, that baby wipes are good for more than fannies. Where, she asks sheepishly, can I buy some of those?

Men make fun of women's purses and the stuff we carry in them. Even though they are as likely as children to benefit from the largesse of their contents. My husband assumes that I will produce on demand your ordinary paper, pen, Kleenex, Maalox, toothpick, and lip balm, as well as the odd bit -- an Ace bandage, Hoyle's Rules of Backgammon, beef jerky, and a New York City subway token. I try never to disappoint. It's a matter of gender pride.

Why, even the Queen carries a purse. She never has to deal with money and I'm sure her lady-in-waiting can supply a lipstick or hanky as needed. But there she is, royal Elizabeth always dangling a stout, dowdy English handbag over her arm. I like to imagine that she carries one of those tacky Grandma's Foto Albums inside… or maybe a turkey baster.

October 2002

IN PRAISE OF DIFFICULT WOMEN

IT WAS 1973 AND I was in L.A. with my buddies Kent and Maddy. With a new clutch in the VW van and an afternoon to kill, we headed out to Hollywood with our "Homes of the Stars" map.

Kent drove, I navigated, and Mad hollered out the sightings. "My god, there's Loretta Young's dog! – Hey, guys, over there…. It's John Wayne's house! Can you believe it? He's got a white picket fence!!" We trolled the lovely suburban streets of Hollywood oohing and aahing. Lucy and Ethel had nothing on us.

"Up ahead, one block," I shouted, "it's Barbara Stanwyck's place." The ever-so-conspicuous hippie van slowed to a crawl as we approached an unassuming ranch house. A few yards ahead of us the postman carrying a large canvas bag was walking to the mail box. And then it happened! The front door swung opened and out She came. Barbara Stanwyck in a pink sweater and black capri pants walked down to the box to get her mail.

Maddy was shrieking, "It's her! It's her!!" Kent was trying to catch a glimpse without running the van up onto the sidewalk. And I was yelling, "Back it up! I wanna see how her hair looks."

Now, I have been up close to the likes of Al Pacino, Michelle Pheiffer, Susan Sarandon, Mick Jagger, and Jeff Bridges, to name a few. And I have always maintained my dignity and cool in the presence of movie stars. But Barbara Stanwyck was an altogether different order of Being.

I think of her and that drive-by spotting in Hollywood 30 years ago because Katherine Hepburn died on June 29. And she was the last of the Great Difficult Women of the Silver Screen.

They're all gone now. Barbara Stanwyck, Bette Davis, Rosalind Russell, Miriam Hopkins, Claudette Colbert, Carole Lombard, Jean Arthur, Joan Crawford, Greta Garbo, Myrna Loy, Norma Shearer. They played strong, audacious, self-reliant, smart, and witty women in those great films from the late 1920's to the early 40's. These were women who knew what they wanted out of life, and they went out and got it.

I call them "difficult" – from the Latin root of the word which means "not easy" -- because they played women on screen who flaunted the social mores of their time. Who can forget Greta Garbo as the lusty bisexual QUEEN CHRISTINA? Or Miriam Hopkins in DESIGN FOR LIVING flipping her blond curls and pulling off a ménage a trois with Fredric March and Gary Cooper? Or Roz Russell giving as good as she got and then some as the only female in the press room in HIS GIRL FRIDAY? And, of course, there's Barbara Stanwyck, making a lap dog out of Henry Fonda in THE LADY EVE. Tough, smart-talking, self-assured, sassy dames.

Today, when every other teenager dresses like a hooker, puts on street-girl attitude, and wants to be a gangsta rapper, "difficult woman" means little more than cheap costuming and a superficial pose – something my eight-year-old daughter is already being exposed to on the cartoon channel.

But in 1934, the year Claudette Colbert starred in IT HAPPENED ONE NIGHT, "difficult woman" described Character -- strong, confident, resilient.

And the women stars of this era often displayed the same independent moxie off screen as well. We all know of Kate Hepburn's 25 year adulterous affair with Spencer Tracy. But how many remember that Joan Crawford adopted three children while unmarried and ascended to the Board of Directors of Pepsi-Cola when the chairman and her husband, Alfred Steele, died? Or Bette Davis' battle royal with Warner Brothers over artistic control of her roles?

These women were, no doubt, considered "difficult" in the negative sense -- as in contrary, inconvenient, or spoiled -- by the men who couldn't manipulate them, break their spirits, or force them into narrow, dependent roles. Difficult? "That's what a man says when he meets a woman he can't handle," several female friends told me.

From the point of view of other women, however, "difficult" means complex, challenging, high-spirited, and gutsy. The Great Difficult Women of the Silver Screen were icons of self-possession and courage. And how few we have today, now that "liberation" is taken for granted and anything goes.

If you ask him why he married me, my husband will reply that it was because I am a difficult woman. I give him a long, affectionate look when he says this and say, "Bette Davis as Margo Channing fighting for her life in ALL ABOUT EVE – now that's a difficult woman! I'm just an amateur."

August 2003

SEX AND MY CITY

I BECAME A FAN of HBO's Sex and the City in reruns. I love the fashion, the hot guys, the love, betrayal, and redemption, the fabulous shots of Manhattan, and the cocktails and endless brunches that obviously aren't calculated in anybody's Weight Watcher counts.

But most of all I love the relationship between the four women: audacious Samantha, conflicted Miranda, upright Charlotte, and Carrie – the lynchpin of this loving and loyal sorority.

I love it because it's a bitter-sweet echo of the best relations I've ever had and whose loss I've never stopped mourning.

Between the ages of 18 and 36 I lived in Berkeley, California and had my own girl gang.

We experimented with drugs, sex, and rock'n'roll. We learned as much about men as we'd ever know. We made some whoppers of mistakes, though nothing fatal. And we grew up.

There was Nell [names changed because we were all guilty], the sexual adventuress and loving it since the age of 13; Brenda, the drama queen who lived High Camp on the West Coast while Andy Warhol was filming it on the East Coast; Elaine, the entitled prom queen who was an alcoholic and drug addict, before she became 180 degrees clean; Angela, the whiskey voiced beauty who confused us all by giving up men and becoming a social worker. And me.

During our 18 years together two of us got married; one birthed a couple of kids; another adopted a child as a single mom; a fourth snatched the single mom's boyfriend and insisted that he have a vasectomy; and the fifth found the love of her life only to lose him to a self-inflicted bullet wound. Joy and giggles, pain and shock. Collectively we did it all.

And then, shortly before my 36th birthday, my first marriage stopped abruptly against the side of a mountain. To clear my sinuses I left California for what was meant to be six months. I never returned.

Nell got a tenure-track teaching job in New Orleans where she bought a house. Elaine moved to the upper Napa Valley where she paints over-sized acrylic canvasses. And Brenda took a civil service job in Sacramento. Only Angela stayed put in Berkeley where she's still living in the same house she rented in grad school.

Our little community, which had kept us laughing through the tough times and which provided ballast during our escapades, scattered. We continued to send birthday trinkets and exchange Christmas cards, but phone calls became less and less frequent, and, before we knew what perimenopause was, we were no longer in each other's day-to-day lives.

My first divorce was unpleasant, as they usually are, but the loss of the man was no where near as consequential and ultimately painful as the loss of this posse of women.

In the years since, I've lived abroad, in Boston, in Manhattan, and now in this pretty valley, and I've made some good friends along the way. But I've never been able to gather in a group of women again like we had in Berkeley.

So when I watch Carrie, Miranda, Charlotte, and Samantha toasting each other with Cosmopolitans [Serves five: 5+oz vodka; 2½ oz Triple Sec; 2½ oz lime juice; 2½ oz cranberry juice; shake with ice and serve in martini glasses] I remember one of the last times we five sat in a restaurant and clinked glasses and laughed ourselves silly. I miss us all together more than I miss any man I've ever known. And life hasn't been as fun or comforting since we flew out of the nest.

I cherish those reckless, tender, and communal times. And I hope that every woman has, at least once in her life, a tribe of women pals to help keep her glued together and on track.

July 2008

MEN WE LOVE

THOUGH RETIRED FROM THE hunt and resigned to spending New Year's Eve with the family, a pizza, and a PG-13 movie, I still on occasion, over a watermelon daiquiri, share ideas with my single girl pals on how to pick The Perfect Man. Or at least An Acceptable Guy.

I find, in these late night chats, that some women select a man the way they pick a pineapple. They want a tough, prickly exterior that will intimidate burglars, yet a sweet, juicy interior.

Others use the tomato technique, simply selecting the prettiest piece of fruit they can find and hoping it won't rot before they can enjoy its delights.

Still other women rely on such time-tested deal breakers as eliminating any prospect who cancels a date with you to drive his mother to her weekly Mah Jong game, who thinks that squeezing your nipples is a form of foreplay, who decorates with empty beer cans, or who thinks farting in a restaurant is a hoot.

We, who have been through the process more times than O.J. Simpson has been fingerprinted, have refined to a science the criteria for Picking the Right Guy. For the novices, the befuddled, and those men out there who still don't understand why a woman might get up in the middle of the soup course to go to the powder room and never return, I offer the following list. Ladies, know that you've got a keeper if....

1. he puts down the toilet seat without being asked (you'd be surprised how many women chose to ignore this obvious red flag thinking they can "train" a man who isn't already properly trained. Girlfriends, you are deluded.)

2. he's willing to go out in the middle of a blizzard to buy you a box of tampons

3. he has one of the following hobbies: cooking, old movies, Scrabble

4. he has gay friends

5. he has female friends

6. he leaves the last piece of chocolate in the box for you

7. he only eats onions on his burger if he knows you're going to eat onions on your burger

8. he doesn't hate your mother

9. he makes your mother laugh

10. he owns a suit and wears it with confidence (it's a grown up thing)

11. he understands why you need separate bathrooms or at least two sinks

12. he's a great kisser (aka the Norma Rae Test)

13. he rubs your feet without being asked

14. he thinks a pregnant woman's body is magnificent

15. he thinks your body is magnificent (no matter what condition it's in)

16. he adores the way you smell

17. he comes home, sees you're tired, and, without prompting says "honey, let's go out to eat"

18. he discreetly leaves gift receipts for all presents that he buys you in an envelope on your desk, just in case

19. he knows how to tell the difference between real and fake pearls

20. he insists on wearing a wedding ring

21. whenever he gets up from the TV to get himself something he asks if you want anything

22. whenever you have long dull spaces in your relationship he suggests a honeymoonette to pep things up (First Rule of Happy Togetherness: occasional honeymoons)

23. he's okay with you going on trips without him (Second Rule of Happy Togetherness: occasional separate vacations)

24. he knows how to pick a good restaurant and make a reservation

25. he cleans up after the dog before you get home

26. he does not put those stinky doggie treats that make you want to vomit in the microwave

27. he buys two tickets to your favorite Broadway musical even if he despises musicals

28. he loves to slow dance

29. he loves to fast dance

30. he's a good dancer

31. he smells nice and washes regularly

32. he takes care of his teeth

33. he believes in taking out life insurance to protect his family's future

34. he does not swear around children

35. he gets out and shovels the snow without being asked

36. he takes out the garbage without being asked

37. he does the dishes whenever you cook the meal, without being asked

38. he has no problem changing a diaper (Any man who refuses to change a diaper will likely not engage in any activity that involves copious amounts of bodily excretions, which means that all once and future caretaking will fall on your shoulders.)

39. he laughs at the same things you laugh at

40. he can laugh at himself.

Find a fella that scores high on this list and be kind to him.

October 2007

A LESSON IN REVENGE FROM THOSE DESPERATE HOUSEWIVES

I CONFESS. I TUNE in to ABC's "Desperate Housewives" on Sunday nights. Watching Bree, Lynette, Susan, Gabrielle, and that maddening slut Edie do stupid things while looking fabulous is one of life's guiltier pleasures, right up there with hot tubbing in the snow with a bottle of champagne and a pound of chocolate covered cherries. I love it.

But what I really love about the show is the way revenge is so sweetly delivered. Edie disses Susan; Susan, unintentionally, burns down Edie's house. Gabrielle's mother-in-law threatens to destroy her marriage; Bree's teenage son, unintentionally, runs down the mother-in-law with his car. Lynette's husband scoffs at doing his housekeeping tasks; Lynette, quite intentionally, lets loose a rat in the kitchen to teach him consequences. The wrong-doer is punished, while the punisher remains anonymous.

Of course, there are still a lot of sins awaiting retribution on Wisteria Lane. Like Paul's murder of meddlesome neighbor Martha Huber. Like Paul's murder of Zach's real mother Deirdre. [Paul has a short fuse.] Like Caleb's murder of Melanie Foster. Like Andrew's reckless hit-and-run. So we can be sure that the series will run long enough to balance the books.

Watching Desperate Housewives makes me think that what the rest of us need is guidance on how to right wrongs and teach those louses who have screwed up our lives a lesson. We need a Revenge Consultant.

Think about it. Someone who can carefully plot and execute a well-deserved punishment on your behalf that doesn't result in your being hospitalized or incarcerated. What, for instance, if you could get your two-timing Ex infected with the avian bird flu without anyone being the wiser. Or the editor, who won't return your calls, busted for the dope plants you know for a fact he grows in his basement. Or your sister-in-law, who talked Aunt Rose into rewriting her will, audited.

We all have a short but bitter list of people who have done us wrong and wounded us deeply. Yet unless a felony is involved we have no recourse. The backstabbing colleague, the callous mate, or the false friend walks free. In fact, they often end up with a Pulitzer Prize, a trophy wife, and a Palm Beach timeshare. It's not fair.

I know there are those who trust to Divine Retribution and Karma, but, frankly, these involve an unacceptable lag time between crime and punishment. As Orson Welles so shrewdly depicted in The Magnificent Ambersons, by the time the scoundrel gets his comeuppance, nobody's around to enjoy it.

Evidently at least two other people think that the time is ripe for a Revenge Consultant. That's how many websites come up in an Internet search for same. One is in Polish entitled or written by [I can't tell] Witaj Maturzystko. The other is Safe Revenge, a franchise operation that promises to "work with you to uncover the exact nature of the wrong done to you and determine what action... would address that wrong in such a way that your life improves."

Unfortunately Safe Revenge appears to be no more than a whimsical suggestion at the moment, appearing nowhere else than on a list of other whacky franchise ideas including Urban Donkey [a service that offers "a trained Afghan mountain goat that follows you around the city, toting packages for you in 'tastefully designed panniers'"]; Partial Adoption ["all of the kid, part of the time"]; and Re-Nippling [you don't want to know]. Still, I think the market is ready for professional revenge services. Harry Whittington, Michael Brown, and Jennifer Aniston aren't the only ones who might want someone to settle old scores for them, discretely.

So I'd just like to put it out there for those of you seeking a different kind of job opportunity. You must be cunning, resourceful, physically fit, and willing to work nights and weekends. You can probably name your own price.

Revenge Consultant. I wonder if Tony Soprano is willing to freelance?

March 2006

2.

I'M NOT NOW, NOR WILL I EVER LIKELY BE READY FOR THE 21ST CENTURY

NONSCENTS. While you don't want to wear perfume while motorcycling in bear country or hunting for poltergeist, a daub of My Sin on the wrist is a modest form of self-expression…. No matter what the scent Nazis say. Page 22

FAME&FORTUNE@MICOSSI.COM. My dentist has one. My exterminator has one. Eighty-seven percent of teenagers on the planet have one. But if I get a web site will Fran Lebowitz return my calls? Page 25

HOMO LUDEN. I'd seen insurance salesmen dressing up like the MinuteMen and re-fighting the battle of Lexington on the village green. I knew of Civil War fanatics who dress up in Dixie grey and fight Antietam every spring. But gladiators? Page 27

COMBAT ZONE. As the average family size has shrunk, the average size of a new home has doubled. Even the self-styled "locals' in this rural county dream of a 4000 square foot house with a three-car garage and enough front lawn to field the entire Little League…. And you wonder why Sprawl? Page 29

BIG BROTHER TALKS. Like inhaling secondhand smoke, it's now impossible to avoid the ubiquitous TV toxins. Page 32

WHEN DID MY DUDDY BECOME SO FUDDY? Am I the only one to notice the smut shop at the Mall next to the Gap? Page 34

THE DREAD UPGRADE. To *save* all the time computers allegedly save you, you have to periodically *spend* obscene amounts of time to Upgrade. Page 37

INQUIRING MINDS WANT TO KNOW. For $39.95 you can get the dirt on your ex-wife's new boyfriend at 1800USSEARCH.com. Page 39

JUNKMAIL.DOC. Far-flung friends and relatives who have never written so much as a postcard are suddenly showering me with electronic junk mail. Page 42

CALLER ID -- BUSTED AGAIN. If I wanted the IRS to know who was really calling, I'd just volunteer my social security number and call the agent's mother a foul name. Page 44

SCHOOL UNIFORMS. Accessories? You bet. Belts, purses, scarves, three inch stack heels. Anything your heart desires so long as it involves glitter, sequins, or bugle beads. Page 46

HIT MAN. A nice little web site for "the most dangerous press in America". Page 49

CIVILIZATION AS WE KNOW IT. Lamenting the demise of old-fashioned letter writing. Page 52

My Philosophy of Life, plus a few handy tips

NONSCENTS

    IT'S ALMOST VALENTINE'S DAY and I must ask my Beloved here in front of God and all the neighbors to please cease and desist buying me another bottle of perfume or perfumed hand lotion until further notice.

It's not that I don't adore those lush jasmine, amber, and vanilla scents in the willowy crystal flagons that grace a shelf in my medicine chest like a chorus line from the Ziegfeld follies. It's just that these frail beauties don't get out much anymore.

Perfume -- or haven't you heard? – is the new tobacco. Like No Smoking signs two decades ago, signs that shout "Do Not Wear Perfume or Cologne!" are beginning to sneak into schools, workplaces, churches, and restaurants.

It started, no surprise, in hospital ORs and the offices of allergists. Perfume, so says the Asthma and Allergy Foundation of America, can trigger a bronchial spasm in some 17 million asthmatics or cause the 50 million allergy sufferers in this country to keel over from headaches or hives. This is no laughing matter, or as Coco Chanel would say "qu'ils mangent de ma culotte!"

Some bans do make sense, such as this advice from African Safari Options to avoid wearing White Shoulders when stalking a lion or a lynx: "Wildlife can detect unnatural smells for miles, making approaches difficult." Not to mention that the musk under notes of Tabu can drive rhinos absolutely mad with desire.

I can also understand why the McGeorge School of Law's Career Development Office tells its public interest law clerk wannabes to avoid wearing cologne to job interviews. "Co-workers may be allergic to it." And some judges may still have bad undergraduate associations with English Leather.

The warning from mysticalblaze.com to avoid perfume while on a ghost hunt clearly makes sense since "spirits are known to use certain smells to get our attention so any noticeable scent you may be wearing could easily be mistaken for a supernatural occurrence." Don't want that to happen.

And, of course, you don't have to remind me of the perils of perfume around swarming insects. One sultry afternoon last July, fresh from a bath and wearing nothing but a sarong and a splash of Victoria's Secret's Pear Glace, I settled into my front porch hammock with a wine cooler and Memoirs of a Geisha. Next morning I made an emergency dash to my doctor where she counted 73 mosquito bites on my fanny and wrote me a prescription for prednisone.

Other bans on scent, however, smack of that smug rectitude that transforms personal preferences into public legislation. Think Volstead Act. Take, for instance, the University of Florida's embargo on perfume while delivering your Computer Science Senior Project. "There may be people in the room with allergies that tend to be aggravated by the stress of giving a presentation," brays the tip sheet.

Or the Flow Yoga Center in Washington, D.C. where a sign on the front door warns that doing the Downward Dog while wearing perfume "can be distracting to your fellow yogis."

Or Stratton transportation, a bus service for snow bunnies between New York City and Vermont, that claims cologne "is offensive in an enclosed vehicle."

Okay, perfume in public places may, to some, be aggravating, distracting, and offensive. But I find the sour breath and body odor of other people's pooches aggravating; the chemical smell of a nylon carpet distracting; and the stench of day old hot dogs in the Food Court offensive. I live with it.

According to anti-fragrance activists, however, ye who wear Obsession or My Sin are polluting the environment, killing your neighbors, and encouraging terrorist reprisals. These people treat toilette water as if it were a gateway drug: a dab of Jean Nate behind the ear today – patchouli incense in the ventilation system at the United Nations building tomorrow.

Now I am not insensitive to the power of perfume and have modified my behavior sensibly. I do, after all, work among men in a maximum security prison who have urgent needs, so I refrain from antagonizing the situation with provocative dress or scented soap. And I voluntarily gave up wearing cologne for two whole years when my brother-in-law's diabetes made all sweet smells intolerable to him. Just as I no longer gift my friends at Christmas with liquor [too many recovering addicts] and chocolate [too many people on the South Beach diet], I no longer give L'Air du Temps body lotion. You just never know.

But am I the only one left for whom the intoxicating aromas of fine perfume are triggers of pleasure and delight? One whiff of Shalimar and I'm enveloped by mother's love, for she always wore Shalimar at those moments when she felt most beautiful and happy. And the delicate scent of French milled soap is forever linked to the romance and freedom of my school girl years in Europe and simply opening a box of it cheers me up.

So while you don't want to wear strongly scented personal care products while motorcycling in bear country, hunting for poltergeist, or interviewing with Proctor and Gamble [they may recognize the competition], I say that a bit of Je Reviens behind the knees or a daub of Evening in Paris on the wrist is a modest form of self-expression. Or as Coco Chanel would say "Une femme qui ne porte pas de parfum n'a pas de futur."

February 2006

fame&fortune@micossi.com

EVERYONE SAYS THAT I'VE got to have a web site. It's the only way to get myself invited to parties where I can meet Fran Lebowitz. They've been saying this for years.

It's not that I don't want one. I have, in fact, been paying for the "micossi.com" domain name for the past three years so that my brother won't buy it and make me pay through the nose to use it. No, web sites are cool. My dentist has one. My exterminator has one. The local farm stand has one. Fifteen years ago a computer-wonk pal of mine in California had his first son; right after he cut the cord he went home and set up a web site about the kid. Eighty-seven percent of teenagers on the planet have one.

It's undoubtedly a good idea from a marketing standpoint for me to have one. That's what all the Career Advice Columnists say and they all have web sites and stock in web site development software companies.

But marketing was never my forte. My light is generally quite comfortable underneath this bush here. Nevertheless, my income needs are increasing in direct proportion to my physical decay, so I figure that it's time to start getting serious about a web site.

I call my old friend and colleague Bill for pointers. Bill writes business books out of his home in New Hampshire, has a spiffy web site, and makes more money than I do. "It's the new resume," he explains when I moan why-oh-why. "It's your portfolio, your calling card."

"But do you get more work with a web site?" I ask.

"Plumbers get more work," says Bill, "CPAs get more work. For writers a web site is a fancy resume. You tell an editor to 'look me up' and you don't have to send her a box full of clips. Think of it as a way of saving on postage."

"That's it?"

"Well, you can occasionally get work if the Right Person with the Right Project happens to stumble across your web site."

"And invites to classy events where I can schmooze with A-list agents and the publisher of the Atlantic Monthly?"

"Whatever...."

Motivated by the vast untapped potential for lucre, I go to Google for a role model and type in "writers." In .00002 seconds Google comes up with 194,337,012 web sites for and about writers. Well now. How does a girl get herself noticed in a population bigger than Brazil? Even assuming that 194,300,000 of these web sites are the feeble displays of the hopeless, how can I possibly get the attention of the people who know the difference?

Poking around these Googled sites I see that the eye-catchers tend to have specialties. There are ghost writers, speech writers, animal writers, and wine writers. There are garden writers and automotive writers, financial writers and translators.

Closer analysis reveals that the more specialized one is, the less the competition. Type in "Christian writers", for instance and you get 46,700 sites; "humor writers" yields 2,540. But search for "Christian humor writers" and there are a mere 49 web sites. A small but choice fraternity that even has its own official "Christian Humor Writers Group."

Similarly, there are 14,000 people who identify themselves as "Jewish writers" in web sites, and 18,100 "food writers." But if you want to be known as a writer about "Jewish food" you're only in competition with 960 self-promoting others.

So there it is. I'll create a web site and promote myself as a Christian humor writer who specializes in stories about knishes and bialys. If that doesn't get Random House beating down my door and Fran insisting that we do lunch next Friday I don't know what will.

Now all I have to do is figure out what a blog is and how to set one up.

Nita Micossi, who is most relaxed among the Gutenberg crowd, wants to know if anybody can suggest some any-idiot-can-do-it-yourself web design software.

May 2006

HOMO LUDEN

I COULD NOT RESIST the Gladiator Set -- non-toxic plastic shield, helmet, breastplate, and sword with scabbard -- $9.95 at the Teacher's Closet toy store. It was totally Jeremy, the four-year-old whose birthday I was shopping for.

I wasn't the only fan. The storeowner told me that another woman was in the week before and bought one for her son so he could "copy his dad." Huh? Is Daddy a Kirk Douglas wannabe who marches around the house in his BVDs tightening an old belt around his right triceps and holding off the Doberman pinscher with a garbage can lid?

No. Dad is part of a gladiator reenactment group.

I'd seen insurance salesmen dressing up like the Minute Men and re-fighting the battle of Lexington on the village green. I knew of Civil War fanatics who dress up in Dixie grey and fight Antietam every spring. But gladiators? They don't even teach Roman history in grade school anymore. Could there really be people out there who dress up like Stephen Boyd and try to decapitate each other with Thracian swords?

I went to the Internet, the font of all information weird and wonderful, and typed in "gladiator reenactment." This got me pages of Russell Crowe reviews, a few video game links, one X-rated bondage web site, and a bona fide history page that describes the origins of gladiatorial combat plus a thumbnail of everything you ever wanted to know about the weapons, armor, and types of gladiators. The Secutor, for instance, fought virtually naked with a dagger, a rectangular shield, and a boiled leather greave (looks like a dancer's leg warmer) wrapped around his left shin. Secutors were typically bald. Who knew?

Like Julius Caesar slogging through Gaul, I pressed onward until I finally found web sites for a passel of "reenactment" groups including the Familia Gladiatoria, the Ludus Gladiatorius, and the Gladiator School in Titirangi, New Zealand ("the ONLY public gladiator school in Australasia"). These latter-day gladiators and gladiatrixes (for gender is no barrier to 21st century combat) typically train weekly, wearing nifty (and historically accurate) outfits and using real steel swords. Yes, they are fully insured.

I don't know why I was so amazed at this passion for such an arcane activity. I myself used to spend Sunday evenings with four other people drinking cold saki and fighting over the pronunciation of Middle English poetry.

But, I found during my Internet ramble, gladiator clubs are the mere tip of the iceberg. There are dozens of groups -- from Maine to Macedonia, from Nevada to Norway -- who dress up in full legionnaire regalia and act out entire Roman battles! The Legio II Trajana Fortis in Las Vegas, for example, reenacts the exploits of a special unit that earned distinction during the Dacian War under the Emperor Trajan. The Legio XX Ballistaria in Minneapolis depicts a 2nd century artillery crew. And members of the Legio XXII out of Cincinnati portray Roman soldiers in 1st century Germany. There are enough of these folks to warrant a "Yahoo! Roman Army Chat Group."

Intrigued by the possibilities, I plugged in plain vanilla "military reenactments" and came up with 3340 matches. There is an Entire Universe out there of people who reenact Wars. All wars and presumably all sides.

In addition to countless Revolutionary and Civil War units, there are groups that relive Vietnam, Korea, World War II (from inside the uniform of the Nazi Luftwaffe), Waterloo, and the Battle of Hastings -- with horses. One club in Britain reenacts the guerilla campaigns of 1st century Celts against the Roman invaders, often inviting a neighboring Roman legion group to be the bad guys. There is even a National Association of Reenactment Societies to help you get the lay of the land.

So, I'm on this Internet odyssey, tracking the exploits of these weekend warriors, and I'm asking myself: What's the fascination? What's it all mean? -- Is this grand obsession with battle reenactment an expression of an irrepressible lust after violence? A primeval urge to bond with our ancestors? Leisure time overload?

The Pacific Northwest Historical Group has a rather grand explanation: "We feel mankind owes the hugest debt to these courageous young men, and our way of showing this gratitude is to go back in time and.... (walk) in their shoes on the battlefield. Joining our ranks, you will wear the same uniforms, eat the same food, sleep in the same conditions, and carry the same weapons as these gallant Men once did.... (We are) about time travel. We ARE living history."

A gladiator in Milwaukee has a simpler motive: "it's what I do for fun."

Some people ski down mountains, some play bridge, and some strap on a leather greave and try to knock over another guy with a iaculum while shouting "Morituri te Salutamus!"

Okay. I can dig it. So play, Jeremy, just play. *February 2003*

COMBAT ZONE

WHOA! THERE IT IS! The latest bit of New Jersey sprawl right there along Route 9G. Another 4000 square foot McMansion at the rear of a clear-cut field. Thanks to the marvels of modular-housing, the darn thing can pop up in the time it takes to attend another Smart Growth Planning Symposium.

That's where I was yesterday, down at the FDR Visitors' Center in Hyde Park. Involved, as I am, in my village's designs on growth and development, I have attended several of these events.

Present at the podium were the usual suspects: architects, planners, engineers, and developers. And, oh yes, lawyers. Can't tote that barge without the lawyers.

The afternoon's topic was "How to Work with Developers: Combating Sprawl by Building in Growth Centers." "Growth Center" -- aka "cluster housing" – is a dull synonym for ye ole traditional village.

Remember when you were a kid around here or when, as a visitor, you first laid eyes on this stretch of rural New York? What did you see? Dense little towns, villages, and hamlets surrounded by farmland. That was the way the area developed organically. Dense little villages surrounded by farmland. And that's what we all loved about the place.

Then something happened....

Some old grump might say we sold our souls to the God of Excess, but, truth is, we just got very rich as a nation. No Blame. And with basic survival needs satisfied, we filled our lives with lots of stuff not at all basic to survival. The economic machinery required it of us and we patriotically complied.

We bought vans, pickups, and pop-up campers to keep the family car company; bored with a bowling ball and fishing pole, we bought pricey adult toys like kayaks and canoes, motorcycles and mountain bikes, repro juke-boxes and pinball machines, billiards tables, poker tables, and bumper pool; we bought flocks of color-coordinated professional quality appliances, and enough entertainment and telecommunications technology to outfit

Paraguay. Once considered the perquisite of the aristocracy, such gear has become standard in the average American household.

Of course, we need somewhere to put all this stuff – larger closets, more rooms, bigger houses, four-car garages. And the builders have obliged.

As the average family size has shrunk, the average size of newly built houses has doubled from 1000 square feet to more than 2000 square feet (in some places 3000sf) over the past 50 years, and the median lot size has increased 150%. So along with our SUVs, TV screens, French fries, and prisons, our houses and the lots they sit on have been super-sized.

Back to the local landscape....

People who have lived in this area more than 10, 20, 50 (pick a number) years like to blame the changes in the landscape on an influx of "Outsiders". Yes, they come and they need a place to live. And the next thing you know the last dairy farm in Red Hook is overrun by ever bigger homes, sprouting like mushrooms after a wet weekend.

Folks who style themselves "Locals", however, are just as eager for the Big House on five acres with enough lawn to field the entire Little League on a Saturday morning. Nobody's Dream House is 1200 square feet.

Enter the high-minded Planners. They tell us that, to preserve the magnificence of this area, we need to do what the previous tenants did: live in dense little villages surrounded by farmland. Take, for instance, a model project described to us at the Hyde Park symposium. Intended as a new hamlet with 263 single family homes, this development is encircled by 311 acres of permanently undeveloped nature. It has a central park, a trail system, and a lush village green surrounded by basic retail amenities. It offers a variety of housing types for different incomes, service roads at the rear of homes for garbage collecting, and a design that encourages walking and cycling. The project evokes small town U.S.A. Lovely.

But then the engineers lay out the details. We're talking homes under 2000 square feet on lots of 10,000 square feet with deep back yards purchased at the expense of vast suburban front lawns. We're talking neighbors close enough that you'll have to keep that $4000 TV surround sound system on mute after 11pm. We're talking the subordination of the automobile to detached garages set at the rear of the property and speed limits congenial to a 10 year old on a bike.

So I raise my hand and I ask the developers and the planners: how do you undo the conditioning that makes Americans measure their success and happiness in terms of residential square footage and lawn acreage?

How do you get people to understand that unless they honor the organic patterns of growth in a rural setting that development will Sprawl and consume every inch of that treasured setting?

Like Utopians throughout history they duck the question, preferring to believe that Enlightened Self-Interest will prevail.

I drive back to my dense little village surrounded by farmland pondering their bold plans and trying to figure out how to sell "growth centers" to my neighbors. But Whoa! There it is! Another bit of New Jersey sprawl right there along Route 9G. I swear it wasn't there this morning.

June 2004

My Philosophy of Life, plus a few handy tips

BIG BROTHER TALKS

REMEMBER THE HARRISON FORD futuristic movie "Blade Runner" where there are video screens everywhere and Big Brother isn't merely watching but talking his fool head off? The future is here.

Television has taken over the world. Bad enough that my sister-in-law has a TV set in every room of the house including the toilet. I can't go to an airport, bank, or hospital anymore without being tortured by some dumb Fox News Network talking head or the VH1 all-time-greatest-rapster video. Waiting in line or sitting in a drab office holding pen, I'm no longer left in peace to catch up with the morning newspaper, make headway on the crossword puzzle, or meditate on my sins. I used to look forward to this casual downtime. Like being stuck in traffic, it was an opportunity to fritter away a few minutes, blameless and unaccountable.

But no more. Now I am subjected to the effluvia of mindless programming and silly ads. I fidget and fight it, mostly by imagining medieval tortures for the bureaucrat who installed the dread box. But it's like being in a room full of smokers -- even if you don't participate in the activity, you are a passive victim.

Alas, I seem to be in the minority. Most of my comrades in line -- who clearly would rather not meditate on their sins -- cheerfully surrender to the stupefying effects of Emeril and Eminem.

Still, I make a point of turning off the offending screen whenever I can get away with it or making a fuss when I can't.

For instance, I was at the gynecologist's in November and discovered that since my last visit she had installed a television in the waiting room. During my hour-long sit I was forced to submit to endless medical infomercials blaring between cooking show segments. (Do they custom program these things?) I tried to correct papers, but was thwarted by the bleating of a buxom blond in a lab coat preaching to the confined about the benefits of adult diapers.

"Why," I pleaded with the receptionist, "do we have to put up with this? I can't read. I can't think."

"It allows for confidentiality," she smiled like a Kindergarten aide on Valium. "If there is a TV on, the patients in the waiting room can't hear what the staff is saying."

I considered this. The staff sits behind a glass barrier and two locked doors. I've been coming to this medical practice for eight years and whenever I needed to talk to a scheduling nurse or receptionist behind the glass wall I had to shout and bang repeatedly. I pressed on.

"That doesn't make sense."

"They just told us it had to be on all day every day," she replied sweetly. "It's an insurance thing...."

Ah, well, that explains it all. It's an insurance thing.

I suspect that that is what some crafty salesman pitched to airport security: "Run the TV in the boarding areas 24/7 and passengers will be so zombied out by flight time that they won't notice the rattle in the turboshaft.... It's an insurance thing."

Having come up with the ultimate marketing scam ("the insurance thing" can hypnotize better than a cobra) it's only a matter of time before we can expect to see television in, let's say, grocery stores: Martha Stewart bakes a pie on the Food Channel while guiding you to aisle five to pick up the sugar and shortening; or churches: Father Murphy gives such lousy sermons that, after the gospel reading, he just switches on the big overhead screen to the Christian Broadcasting Network and lets Billy Graham pick up the slack; or funeral homes: reruns of the Partridge Family on Nickelodeon give the bereaved a perky respite before paying the bill and moving on with life; or the United States Congress: personal TV screens at each Senator's desk can keep them awake between votes. But then if the congressional televisions are tuned to C-SPAN wouldn't that be like a TV looking at a TV looking at a TV? Would Big Brother then implode? What a delightful thought.

January 2003

WHEN DID MY DUDDY BECOME SO FUDDY?

IT'S BACK TO SCHOOL time.

Mothers throughout the land confess to their hairdressers that they failed once again to achieve maternal bliss with their children this summer and gleefully sign up for a college extension course on Tuscan architecture.

Teachers throughout the land buy cases of Instant Krazy Glue and indelible ink marker pens, increase their life insurance coverage, and stock up on Valium.

Kids throughout the land threaten to strangle the hamster unless they get a pair of thigh-high snake skin boots.

And retailers throughout the land get to unload the 101 Dalmatian backpacks left over from last year.

Like all conscientious mothers I set out for The Mall the week before Labor Day in search of essential school apparel and classroom accessories. Like all experienced moms I left the kid at home. This gave me a rare opportunity to visit a few stores I'd never before entered, which is how I happened upon Spencer's Gifts.

There was a "Back To School" banner in the front window and a sign billing Spencer's as "a Universal Studios Company". I expected a movie theme store with Jurassic Park logos on spiral notebooks and pencil cases. Surprise, surprise.

Directly to my left as I walked into the store were shelves filled with coffee cups shaped like bare fannies, various items celebrating flatulence a la the Old Fart Candle Extinguisher, and paraphernalia for so-now-you're-over-the-hill office birthday parties including a crotch washer, a purple tubular bra for sagging tatas, and Oil of Old Lay.

Silly and tasteless, but whom among us doesn't go for the silly and tasteless at times?

As I moved to the middle of the store -- still searching for Crayolas -- I ran into a large display rack of the sort of greeting cards you usually find in a Greenwich Village leather & chains shop. I had to slide past a clutch of pre-teen girls giggling over the pix of DDDD bosoms ("breast wishes!") and full frontal hunks ("he's got something that will make a real Sucker out of you!").

But the real (mostly teenage) crowd seemed to be in the back of the store. That's where the truly irresistible merchandise was displayed floor-to-ceiling: sequined nipple tassels, packages of anatomically correct pasta, and kits for honeymoon lovers including an animal leash and collar with an instructive picture of a nearly naked woman modeling same. Among rather innocent items like lava lamps, whoopie cushions, and plastic vomit are "suck for a buck" tee-shirts and pink satin dice stitched with the words "tease, lips, lick, and blow."

Yes. There, at The Mall, conveniently located next to the Gap, we have our own little smut shop with all the naughty stuff displayed at the eye-level of a six-year-old.

In fact, I found two seven year old boys sitting in a corner and having a whale of time playing with a Penis Erector, Inflatable Boobs, and a C. More Bunz doll that drops its pants when you squeeze an airball.

When I asked the boys what they thought of all this stuff, one pointed to a wall of blood encrusted plastic horror movie dolls like Chucky and Michael Meyers, pulled a face, and said "gross!" But he didn't have any problem with the Bondage Starter Kit (advising users to "show no mercy"), Cumfy Cuffs ("it's fun to play rough"), or Hot Hooters Warming Booby Oil.

Now I'm no prude. Having lived in the Big City for some years, I marvel at the goods people buy in sex shops. Having once researched an article on XXX video rental stores, I am not easily shocked by dirty pictures. Having gone through childbirth, I do not get aroused by fantasies involving bodily fluids.

But I was surprised. Not by the store so much -- down the way is a Victoria's Secret pedaling neo-Frederick's Of Hollywood g-string panties in the front window. No, I was surprised by the fact that mothers pushing baby strollers and daddies shepherding pre-schoolers wandered in casually, as if this were just another Disney store.

A few years back there might have been a gang of moms in hairnets picketing Spencer's Gifts, or a campaign of outraged letters to the editor in the local newspaper, or, at least an Adults Only sign in front of the place.

But in these tolerant times nobody but me seemed to care that their tot was grabbing for a glow-in-the-dark dildo. But, hey, if it's in The Mall I guess that it's passed the community standards test.

So I silently worried about my young daughter (does she really have to learn how to spell fellatio before she graduates from elementary school?) and confessed to my hairdresser that this summer I've become an old fuddy-duddy.

September 2001

THE DREAD UPGRADE

A VERY SMART GUY at M.I.T. named Bob Solow said, "you can see computers everywhere but in the productivity statistics." We know that Bob is smart because he won the Nobel Prize. But even Bob is unable to explain this "productivity paradox". He cannot, for instance, account for the fact that businesses in this country show piddly increases in productivity even though they've spent $1 trillion (that's trillion with a "t") for computers over the past decade.

But I can.

I got a new computer for my birthday this July. My husband told me that it would be faster, easier, and, with its nifty new features like the magic fingers hand massage, more fun. I would, he announced authoritatively, become more Productive. But he was just spouting the campaign literature.

I looked at that new box and all I saw was The Dread Upgrade.

Let me explain: Like car manufacturers (also known to have personality disorders), computer makers change their little boxes ("hard" ware) and what goes inside them ("soft" ware) every couple of years. Actually they change them about every other Friday, but the stubborn user can make do with "obsolete" stuff for three, maybe four, years.

Then you gotta Upgrade. It's a conspiracy. Even if you have a special intimacy thing going with your old accounting program and the coffee-stained computer that runs it, nobody else on the planet is using them anymore. This means you can't communicate messages, transfer files, or have lunch with the boss until you upgrade to the newest version.

So here I am gazing upon an enormous box with a red ribbon around it from my darling husband who loves me and wants to make me happy. "Just plug it in," he whispers in my ear, "install the new software, and you can rule the world!"

Unfortunately, the computer dudes who run companies like Microsoft and Intel are stilled pissed off at the rest of us for not inviting them to the Valentine's Day Sock Hop in high school. They get their revenge with every new hardware/software Upgrade.

The plan is devilishly perverse: Every upgrade includes 435,752 ever-so-subtle, but critical, changes. Thus every upgrade automatically resets the user's knowledge of computers and their programs back to "squat".

Let me illustrate: I sit down at my new computer to write Mom a letter. My quest is a virgin document with a blank screen.

The first thing I see is a screen with little pictures on it. One is labeled MY DOCUMENTS. My old computer had no such item, but it sounds promising so I click. A row of boxes appears with various enticements including FILE, which seems the most logical direction to go – these programs are supposed to be "intuitive", after all. From there I click onto NEW.

Now under NEW I see a lot of tantalizing but vague choices like BITMAP IMAGES, WAVE SOUND, and HYPERTEXT. None of these sounds like a letter to Mom, so I optimistically click on SHORTCUT which, if nothing else, suggests escape. But SHORTCUT is a sly rogue and demands that I surrender a COMMAND LINE, whatever that is. Knowing that I'm in way over my head, I back out of my sequence of clicks bowing and mumbling like a whipped slave.

I spend the next seven hours exploring the byzantine by-ways of my new box and its new software. By the time I get to a blank document page I have entirely forgotten what it was I had to say to my mother.

(I also find that my new and improved upgraded word processing program is preset at the factory with a font size of 8, about the same size as the printed instructions on the back of a bottle of Tylenol. But let's not go there.)

Though I eventually mastered the art of getting a Blank Screen, I still don't understand why it takes 15 clicks to accomplish what amounts to erasing a misspelled word. And every time I want to expand my horizons and learn how to, let's say, "rename" a file, I have to block out three hours and put the Technical Support team on red alert.

Productivity?? To SAVE all the time computers allegedly save you, one has to periodically SPEND obscene amounts of time to Upgrade. It's a wash.

Of course, you can choose to fight the good fight and refuse to upgrade. But be prepared for the consequences. People will stop doing business with you and they will spread rumors that you don't change your underwear. *October 1999*

Nita Micossi

INQUIRING MINDS WANT TO KNOW

SO YOUR EX-WIFE PUT a lien on that waterfront condo you just built in Palm Beach. A bit lax with the child support payments, are we?

Better get a lawyer with a pit bull personality seeing how the lady got a stratospheric judgment against her first husband. What, you didn't know there was a first husband?

And while you're at it, boy, your driver's license expired last month. What's a grown man with three cars and a motorcycle doing driving around without a license?

How did I know about the motorcycle? Why, muffin, I know Everything.

And YOU can too. All you gotta do is pony up $39.95 for the Super Search.

You don't know about the Super Search? It's right there on the Internet at 1800USSEARCH.com. Billed as the "worldwide leader in public record information", they will, for $39.95 (or a topless photo of Miss Monica Lewinsky), spit out information on anyone anywhere.

Listen to this. You can get:

- Driver's license physical descriptions (in case you want to know what her real hair color is)

- The names of neighbors, spouses, family members, and other people at the same address (a first step in finding out if the live-in boyfriend is in drug rehab)

- A summary of assets and their values, including vehicles and real estate (I told you they were slum landlords)

39

- A list of professional licenses (is he a real podiatrist or a quack like you always thought)

And, best of all,

- Details on civil judgments, lien filings, and bankruptcies

Is this legal? It's not only legal, it's one of our inalienable rights. Says so right there on the Home Page: "1-800-U.S. SEARCH accesses U.S. Public record databases used by the FBI, Law Enforcement Agencies and Private Investigators to locate people. Accessing these databases is a privilege!"

It's also a smart idea. Under their FIND OUT ABOUT PEOPLE section, for instance, they ask "do you know who you are dating? are they who they appear to be?" Darn good questions. What with school shootings every other week and Cybill Shepherd threatening to run for president, you can't be too careful anymore. And if you want to be extra vigilant, for an additional $25 they'll do a search of Criminal Records. Frankly, if it were my daughter I wouldn't hesitate to get the total lowdown on that creep she's been seeing.

Do a search on myself? As a matter of fact, I did. For $50 they have a special PROTECT YOUR IDENTITY service. You get all the stuff above plus information on aliases, deed transfers, and aircraft ownership. That way you can tell if someone is fraudulently using your identity or your helicopter. You can also correct errors that you never even knew were in the public domain doing harm to your credit rating and political campaign.

For example, I noticed that my date of birth is on file as July 3, 1898. No wonder I've been getting those odd letters from the Social Security Administration all these years.

They also had me down as owing $37,441.80 on an undergraduate student loan that I know I paid off 17 years ago. Luckily I keep good records that prove the loan was only for $525. But it does explain the difficulty I had getting that Victoria Secret credit card last year.

One error was especially puzzling and it took me several phone calls to figure it out. It seems that I once lived in a loft building in New York City that was owned by a suspected Mafia associate. Who knew? The fella never wore black silk shirts. But he evidently ran an escort service out of the penthouse and, when he was busted, the building's address was red-flagged as a "high risk" residence.

The lady at Citibank explained that no one who lived in that building between 1988 and 1996 was ever granted a mortgage. However, if I agreed to testify at the next anti-organized crime senate hearings they would consider giving me an exemption.

I made a deal with the D.A.'s office to clear my record. I also managed to produce a birth certificate to prove I was born in the 20th century. But I am weary to report that after eight certified letters to the Education Office in Washington, D.C. and 27 midnight calls from the Honeymoon Collection Agency in Bakersfield threatening to "ruin my credit rating" (as if the Victoria Secret rejection weren't humiliation enough), I am still having problems with that student loan.

Nita Micossi's jalopy is worth $1200 and her real hair color is mousy brown; so you can save yourself $39.95.

March 2000

JUNKMAIL.DOC

FAR-FLUNG FRIENDS AND relatives who I could never, in years past, get to write me so much as a postcard are suddenly, inexplicably showering me with electronic mail. Not newsy missives or insightful epistles, no updates on their loves and lives, not a single question about my well-being. What they send me in unwanted profusion are canned packets of allegedly funny stories, reams of one-liners older than Milton Berle, lists of gossip column trivia, and purloined scripts from TV sitcoms -- invariably forwarded to them by an indecipherable lineage of e-mail forbearers.

I've received 101 infamous advertising snafus, a "jolly take-off" on Martha Stewart's holiday calendar, comparisons between the Lincoln and Kennedy assassinations which prove a single trans-historical conspiracy, a parody of Edgar Allen Poe's <u>The Raven</u> about the woes of computer dependency, and eight pages entitled "useless facts" with a caveat that some of the "facts" may be in error. The average length of these unsolicited entertainments is five pages. Here I am, thinking that I'm downloading a nice little note from a pal in San Francisco who I haven't talked with since Christmas and out comes six sheets entitled "Seinfeld: The Final Episode". I never watch Seinfeld.

I try to keep an open and friendly mind about this behavior. I'm a trained sociologist, afterall, and in this age of the isolated freelancer and telecommuter such activity might be seen as the cyberspace equivalent of coffee break banter around the office water cooler. Consider the legions of laboring foot soldiers who are chained to computers in tiny cubicles off the dining room who can't get the latest Monica Lewinsky joke at the office. They pine for a little human contact, a small chuckle, a wee break in an otherwise drab and lonely day.

And, I must confess, once in a great while something comes down the cyber-pipe that is actually amusing. Like the speech presumably delivered by Kurt Vonnegut at the 1997 MIT commencement which turned out to be written by a lady columnist for The Chicago Tribune and in which he/she notes that the secret of success is to "wear sunscreen" -- very funny bit. Or the anecdote about the woman who ate a chocolate chip cookie at Neiman Marcus, offered to buy the recipe, discovered that her AmEx card was charged $250 for said recipe, fought the store's billing department without success, and finally got her revenge by putting the $250 cookie specs out on the net for all the world to eat -- even though my friend Barbara in Sonoma says the tale is a piece of folklore probably cooked up by a mischievous grad student. Yes, there are some genuine entertainments at the water cooler.

But mostly it's all a crashing bore, tired schtick that wastes my time and printer paper. These lengthy so-called joke pages remind me of chain letters -- clearly a hobby for people with time on their hands and little imagination. Or, as is the case with some of my dear old pals, an early warning symptom that lack of exercise is causing the limber wit of their youth to atrophy.

What I really wanna know is how come these far-flung friends and relatives suddenly have time to share this debris and no time for real communication? Is it the novelty of electronic transmission? click a mouse and instantly share trivia with 150 of your near and dear. Is it just another sign of old-fashioned human laziness? Why craft a personal experience into a droll tale to share with friends when you can simply forward a list of obscene elephant jokes.

I shall ponder this further and get back to you. In the meantime, take me off the hit list, guys.

June 1998

CALLER ID -- BUSTED AGAIN

I LIKE MY PRIVACY. I'm the kind of person who uses an alias when I make a restaurant reservation.

So when I heard about the accelerating use of caller ID systems I rushed to have what's called a "universal block" put on my phone line. For those of you who have been living in Upper Niger for the past decade, Caller ID reveals the telephone number of the caller to the recipient by means of a little box containing technology understood by M.I.T. research engineers and Nobel laureates.

A "universal block" is an antidote to this technology. It is like the spinal injection the doc administers to a woman during childbirth to interrupt signals from the lower half of the body to the pain alert center in the woman's brain (ask your mother). It stands like a vigilant sentry between your phone number and the ex-husband's lawyer, the student loan collection agency, or any other rapacious force that would like to snatch your ten-digit telephone address for future mid-meal harassment. If I wanted the IRS to know who was really calling with those "hypothetical situations", I'd just volunteer my social security number and call the agent's mother a foul name.

So you can imagine my panic when I recently telephoned Federal Express, a company with whom I have an account, and was greeted with hearty hi ho "Ms. Micossi how *are* you today and are you still at PO Box 474?"

"Good, lord," I blushed (luckily we don't have picture phones), "how do you know it's ME?!"

"Why we file accounts by telephone number," chirped "Lisa" in that I'd-hammer-a-nail-into-my-nose-to-please-you-dear customer service voice.

"And how do you know my phone number?" I replied, trying to keep up my end of this hail-fellow-well-met exchange, but sensing that I had just been violated by a small digital device trying to suck out my bodily fluids and anything else it could get its smarmy hard drive on.

"It's right here!" she squealed with no small pride, "on my CALLER ID screen."

I immediately hung up and called the phone company to find out why the devil I was feeling labor pains despite the "universal block."

"Oh, my," commiserated "Cheryl", the phone company customer service rep in that this-has-happened-before tone of voice. "This has happened before."

"B-b-b-but..." I stuttered, imitating the Big Bopper.

"It seems," said Cheryl, leaping into my widening breach, "that some Very Big Corporations and Banks and, oh yes, Mail Order Companies now have the ability to override our universal block technology."

"Very Big Corporations and Banks and, oh yes, Mail Order Companies are just the sort of outfits that I do not want to share my phone number with," I gasped. "This has got to be illegal!"

"What's the world coming to?" offered Cheryl.

"This is not Jeopardy!" I screamed. "I don't want a question. I want an answer!"

Cheryl turned me over to "Ken" in marketing.

"Listen carefully, Ken," I said, having encapsulated my rage in a let's-be-calm-and-reasonable tone of voice. "I do not want Federal Express, L.L. Bean, or the Committee to Re-Elect Moynihan to know my phone number should I call. Understand?"

"You're right!" replied Ken, "It's time to go on the offensive. That's why you need to sign up today for our special three month introductory offer to Caller-ID. *You* be the one to know who's calling!"

"Are you insane?" I whispered. Fortunately for Ken he was three counties away or I would have had to sever his jugular vein. Instead I asked to speak to his superior.

Ken got "Rose Louise" on the line.

"Rose Louise," I began with feebly restrained passion -- think of Jimmy Stewart in Mr. Smith Goes To Washington, "let's be reasonable." I recited sections of the Bill of Rights and Brave New World. I quoted Thoreau and invoked the Luddites. I appealed to her humanity and begged for a solution to this outrageous invasion of privacy.

Rose Louise was sympathetic but did not have a solution. When I asked to speak to someone who did, she suggested I call the Federal Communications Commission or the Attorney General's office.

Great, I thought. Then **they** will have my phone number.

September 1998

SCHOOL UNIFORMS

I WENT TO A parochial school for ten years where I wore a uniform. We girls wore pleated wool skirts hemmed to just below the knee (periodically measured by Sister Mary Rectitude), starched white cotton blouses (that taught me how to iron like a professional), wool knit sweaters (that stank when wet), and, for the high school, box cut wool jackets (that made us look quite grown up). Footwear was white bobby sox and brown saddle shoes for the kiddies and ever so stylish brown and white saddles for the upper classes.

I always had two full uniforms with a white dress model for Holy Day services plus a couple of extra blouses – all meticulously maintained. They had to be. These clothes were expensive and replaced only when the sleeves exposed my forearms or the skirt failed to pass Sister Mary R's inspection.

Purchasing a new uniform, available only at the City of Paris, an elegant department store in downtown San Francisco, was always a grand event. My mother and I made a day of it, taking the train into the City and lunching at nearby Blum's on Union Square with its legendary ice cream sundaes. The actual shopping was supervised by a team of elderly women with European accents who did not ask for our opinions, but rather educated us in the fine points of fabric care, seam work, and topstitching. Those uniforms were made to last.

Despite the pity of my cousins who attended public school, I did not mind wearing a uniform. It looked okay and I didn't have to agonize over choices every morning.

Imagine my relief then to discover that my daughter, about to enter middle school, can also enjoy the benefits of a uniform even though she attends a public institution.

Yes, in anticipation of the new academic year, we went clothes shopping the other day. Target, Penney's, Sears', and Old Navy aren't exactly the City of Paris, and the Food Court at the Mall isn't Blum's, but we made a day of it. I came with a mental list of smart ensembles I'd seen in fashion magazines at the dentist's office – a hunter green corduroy jumper with matching knee-high socks and jaunty beret; taupe slacks with a handsome cream-colored cable-knit pullover; or, perhaps, a tartan skirt with a white oxford shirt and a navy cardigan tied around the shoulders. Fabulous.

However, when we got to the store we found racks as far as the eye could see filled with nothing... but blue jeans. Shorts, Bermuda length, clam diggers, capris, gauchos, or hip-hop to the floor; tight, tailored, boot cut, or baggy; belted at the waist, at the mid-hip, or at the pubic bone; and every imaginable degree of wear from factory fresh to rag box ready -- the stores have whatever you might possibly want so long as it's denim.

And tops? There's an endless array of choices as long as you like a cotton jersey and/or polyester blend tee shirt with commentary sprawled across the chest. You have your choice of insolent ("Is there a point to your babbling?"), provocative ("If I said you had a beautiful body would you hold it against me?"), materialistic ("Give me five – support my shopping habit"), or religious marketing ("Jesus is Coming! Look Busy").

Add to this colorful and expressive array of garments a pair of $70 Nike sneakers, and the job is done.

My lifelong ambition to have my child to wear a school uniform has been satisfied. Jeans, tee shirt, and sneakers. Every single kid at Linden Avenue Middle School, and not a few of the teachers, I figure, will show up on the first day of class wearing.... jeans, tee shirt, and sneakers. Despite all the hoo-ha over a kid's right "to express my individuality", the children of America – yeah, the children of the world, have come to a consensus on the Perfect School Uniform. Daily arguments between Mother and Daughter over What To Wear are a thing of the past.

And what about a more "formal" look, you ask, for, say, a wedding or a funeral? Even I, as a kid had a couple of dresses for Sunday Mass in the closet. But dresses are out – and those sweet little plaid dresses with smocking across the bodice and white linen collar and cuffs are as out as a nun's black gabardine floor length habit. Skirts are in and they typically come in three lengths: five inches above the knee; mid-thigh; and your-cheeks-are-showing, dear; also known as slutty, sluttier, and even-Janet-Jackson-is-embarrassed-to-wear-this.

According to the catalogues that clog my mailbox you can top off your skirtlet with: a skin tight spandex halter that exposes the midriff; a skin tight see-through lace pullover; or a skin tight tunic with a décolletage down to your belt line. In sizes 6x to 12.

Accessories? You bet. Belts, purses, scarves, three inch stack heels. Anything your heart desires so long as it involves glitter, sequins, or bugle beads. Imagine the sort of thing that used to be seen only on the vaudeville stage or in the Red Light District.

Thank goodness, my daughter refuses to wear a skirt. We'll just have to avoid weddings and funerals.

So I bought her a bag of new socks at Target and a couple of pairs of almost new-looking blue jeans at Sears'. As for tops, I refuse to pay good money for an article of clothing that screams, "My Mother Mainlines Margaritas". The kid can wear her summer camp tee shirts.

September 2006

HIT MAN

ON MAY 21, 1999 Paladin Press in Boulder, Colorado agreed to stop publishing "Hit Man: A Technical Manual for Independent Contractors". This was part of a settlement to two families who claim that James E. Perry read this manual before killing their relatives.

What's this world coming to?

Books don't kill people. People kill people.

If my arteries harden and I go into cardiac arrest after reading Julia Child's "Mastering The Art of French Cooking" do I hold Julia's publisher responsible? Of course not.

Perhaps "Hit Man" gave Mr. Perry a few helpful tips, but I suspect that the dude who hired him to commit the murders didn't check Perry's summer reading list first. Besides the Paladin book can't be all that helpful since Perry was caught and today sits on death row.

So what's all the fuss about?

I decided to look into this Paladin Press and see for myself.

Nice little website. An attractive logo. And a great lead: "Paladin Press has been called 'the most dangerous press in America.'" They go on to brag about their "outrageous and controversial" library that covers such subjects as weaponry, combat shooting, silencers, sniping, explosives, knife fighting, humor, survival, and espionage. The current pick of the month is about cannibalism.

I was deeply touched that they squeezed "humor" into the pack. Does that mean that they offer all the blood-and-guts stuff tongue-in-cheek? Or is the inclusion of "humor" a diversionary tactic in case the Justice Department starts sniffing around?

Clearly legal issues are on Paladin's mind. Right below their introductory statement is this warning: "PALADIN PRESS DOES NOT INTEND FOR ANY OF THE INFORMATION CONTAINED IN ITS BOOKS AND VIDEOS TO BE USED FOR CRIMINAL PURPOSES."

What a relief! You can't be too vigilant these days.

There's also a lot of conversation on their website about the First Amendment and how if you don't fight for these rights on the fringes you'll have to do so on your front porch, blahblahblahblah.

But the really nifty stuff is on their Best Seller page. They have nine Top Ten Lists covering different areas of interest such as FIREARMS, EXOTIC WEAPONS, COMBAT SHOOTING, SNIPING, & SILENCERS (the whole gun thing), EXPLOSIVES & DEMOLITION (the bomb thing), KNIVES & KNIFE FIGHTING (the West Side Story Thing) and REVENGE & HUMOR -- I guess they figure that just plain "humor" won't get a rise out of their audience without a little savage payback thrown in.

The book titles are playful: "Ragnar's Big Book of Homemade Weapons", "Ragnar's Action Encyclopedia of Practical Knowledge and Proven Techniques", and "Ragnar's Homemade Detonators: How to Make 'Em, How to Salvage 'Em, How to Detonate 'Em!" (Ragnar is really cleaning up in this market). There's also the "Whole Spy Catalogue", "Middle Eastern Terrorist Bomb Designs", and "New and Improved C-4: Better-Than-Ever Recipes for Half the Money and Double the Fun" (I think "C-4" is some sort of explosive thing).

Under the category of ACTION CAREERS you'll find "Secrets of Lock Picking", "The Complete Guide to Lock Picking", and "Advanced Lock Picking Techniques". Anyone with a three-year-old at home will appreciate the need for these books.

Speaking of pickings, they're pretty slim under the HUMOR category unless you're into "The Joy of Cold Revenge" or "Revenge Tactics for All Occasions", subtitle of the book "Screw Unto Others".

I must confess that, however tantalizing these selections, there is really nothing that Paladin has to offer me. I guess it's just a girl thing. I can't lift an assault weapon let alone fire one. Large knives make me queasy. And I'd be in big doo-doo if I tried to throw a hand grenade; they didn't put me in right field on the girl's softball team for nothing.

My husband once took me into the woods and tried to teach me how to use a little rifle that was designed to annoy field mice. It was a thrill, I admit, but short-lived. Some kids broke into the house while we were on vacation and stole that, our only firearm.

So is Paladin Press a public menace?

Are they simply pushing the envelope of the First Amendment for the benefit of us all?

Should people be allowed to order books like "Hit Man"? As long as they promise absolutely, positively, cross-your-heart-and-hope-to-die to never ever do any of the naughty things described in these books for criminal purposes. We're all on the Honor Code here.

July 1999

CIVILIZATION AS WE KNOW IT

Max died in Jerusalem last month. I lost a dear friend and the last of my old-fashioned letter writing correspondents.

About six times a year for the past 18 years our messages would criss-cross the Atlantic in translucent airmail envelopes covered with exotic postage stamps. Those pretty stamps enhanced the thrill of getting a real letter from a far away place.

We both cherished this leisurely and intimate form of communication. And I will miss him terribly.

At the same time I find that I am communicating (in the loosest sense of that word) with more people today than ever before. Folks who could never manage to lick a stamp are enraptured by electronic mail. And I am suddenly on the receiving end of the daily debris of far-flung acquaintances.

Alas, these terse communiques bear little resemblance to the intimate letters of yore (I guess "letter" is now archaic enough to be in the company of words like "yore.") E-mail is evolving into a form unto itself, and, frankly, it gives me a headache.

Take salutations and personal closings. Nobody uses them anymore. That cozy little "Dear", "Dearest", or "My darling" at the top is long gone; and you can forget a sign-off wrapped in "Sincerely", "Tender regards", or "Fondly". Some people are even too lazy to put my name at the top of their message. How am I supposed to know where I fall in the sender's pantheon of affections? Am I his sweet babboo or his business prospect?

I am insulted. I am confused. I feel like the sender has a thought that she is simply tossing into the ether for reception by anyone with a catcher's mitt.

I suppose real letters have always been vulnerable to a sly snoop like Lucy Ricardo who could steam open a suspicious letter to husband Ricky in no time flat. But once you lick that envelope and re-enforce it with a seal or a bit of hot wax, you can pretty much trust that only the addressee will open and read your letter – unless it's wartime or being sent to North Korea. But electronic missives can be hijacked by anybody with your basic hacker know-how.

And what about the e-mail messages themselves? Bland factoids and terse verbiage lacking punctuation, e-mail often resembles a ping pong exchange:

A.   got pkg?

B.   yo – the ring fits

A.   well?

B.   sure

A.   wanna set a data

B.   I've got a non-ref tix to Cancun for spring brk - let's shoot for sometime after that. Priest, rabbi or wiccan?

Billions of dollars and millions of man-hours have been invested over the past 20 years to perfect a global Internet technology so that humankind can communicate thusly.

What's become of the pensive replies to important questions? the lively anecdotes? the imaginative rumblings on an actual idea?

Max could do three heart-pounding paragraphs on Jerusalem's Old City souk in the searing July heat. I could enthrall him with the minutiae of a one-hour layover in Penn Station. We could debate the future of the Golan Heights for years.

But nowadays everyone is too busy for this kind of relaxed exchange. Gotta cruise eBay for vintage refrigerator magnets, beta test the latest all-sound all-homicide video game, and spend half the night jockeying to get through on the Who Wants To Be A Millionaire hotline.

Finally, I really miss the sensual pleasure that comes from reading a handwritten letter. Grandma Dora never went past the third grade and her English-as-a-second-language grammar was self-invented. Yet I felt her warm touch whenever I read a letter written in her wobbly, childlike script.

Long ago I started typing my letters since I can't write fast enough to keep up with what I have to say. But even when I type a letter to a friend I always write a message at the bottom by hand just to make that personal connection.

Which is all I'm asking for here – a little old-fashioned personal connection. E-mail is really nothing more than a fast way to mail a letter; it doesn't have to be the scourge of human communication.

Last year, for example, I rekindled an old friendship with a man in Oregon I haven't seen in 25 years. We compose long thoughtful letters to one another. And a month or so passes between each exchange – as if every letter were being transmitted across the ocean in a slow boat. We send these letters via e-mail but we always write "Dear" at the top and "Love" at the bottom.

May 2000

3.
MY PHILOSOPHY OF LIFE, PLUS A FEW HANDY TIPS

CHOCOLATE AND CHEESE. In the interests of clean living I've given up everything but chocolate and cheese, and, frankly, I'm a bit nervous about it. Page 57

BE HAPPY AND FORGET THE LAUNDRY. It works for my friend Lea. Page 59

JUST SLAP ME, FINE ME, AND BE DONE WITH IT. Pay the gods of mayhem up front and you can go about your daily business knowing you will never have to spend five hours in the emergency room with a screaming four-year-old. Page 61

OF COURSE I MULTITASK. Helpful tips for improving your ability to play the oboe and rebuild transmissions at the same time. Page 63

DO IT! You never visited the top of the World Trade Center? You passed on that ticket to see Billie Jean King play? You missed taking your daughter to the Palm Court for high tea? The most regrettable phrase in the English language has got to be "we can always do it some other time." Page 66

PACKING TIPS YOU WON'T GET FROM MARTHA. Before checking your suitcase, take the batteries out of your vibrator and, remember, it's illegal to ship human remains to Puerto Rico for burial on a commercial flight. Page 68

PUTTING SIN BACK INTO SIN CITY. I was thrilled to read that Las Vegas has finally given up on its foolish flirtation with family values. Page 70

GAUDEAMUS IGITUR. A commencement speech by a failed alumna who still owes the college $729 in student loans. Page 73

IT'S THE THOUGHT. How to get past the no-win misery of gift giving. Page 76

DEAR AUNT NITA… Too fat? First time mom? A zero with the girls? -- some tender Q&A from my mailbag. Page 79

THE ZEN OF BUSY. I've surrendered to my cultural destiny and chosen to make an art out of busy-ness. Page 81

STAYING SAFE ON THE INTERNET: A GUIDE FOR PARENTS. I'm speaking of the easy and inviting ways we simple souls of all ages can get sucked into squandering extraordinary amounts of time on the Net. Page 83

SCHOOL IS OUT. Having spent 21 years as a student in school and another 18 as a teacher, my biological clock is irrevocably set to the academic year.   Page 85

AH! SWEET MYSTERIES OF LIFE. it takes only one celebratory night of margaritas, sour dough bruschetta, and chocolate lava cake to gain two pounds. Why is that?   Page 87

SKI AND ME. For me, winter means jacking up the electric blanket to 22, doubling my intake of Vitamin C, and making a novena for an early thaw.   Page 89

REGRETS ONLY. Regret, it seems, is a part of the human condition.   Page 91

CHOCOLATE AND CHEESE

I'VE GIVEN UP SEX, drugs, rock'n'roll, spike heels, convertible cars, red meat, cigarettes, caffeine, tap water, fried chicken, saccharine, salty snacks, MSG, and root canals. That's right. My friend Ellie says that root canals cause cancer. So I'm down to chocolate and cheese.

And, frankly, I'm a bit nervous about it. It's all on account of Mark Twain. He tells the story of the old lady who is so run down that medicines no longer have any helpful effect upon her.

What should I do to save myself?" she asks him.

It's easy, says Twain, just give up smokin' and drinkin' and swearin'.

But, says the old lady, I don't smoke and drink and swear.

Well, there you have it, replies Twain. No freight. Nothing to throw overboard and lighten the load when the vessel begins to sink.

"Why, even one or two little bad habits could have saved her," he scolds," but she was just a moral pauper."

And that's how I feel. All this Clean Living has got me at sea without any freight. I sense my impending doom whenever I read stories about miraculous cures -- "I gave up tobacco and firearms and my arthritis disappeared overnight" -- or astonishing weight loss -- "just stopped those Jamoca Almond Fudge and pork rind binges and darned if I didn't lose 100 pounds in six weeks!"

Well, here I am with hardly anything unhealthy, dangerous, or sinful left to give up. Gone are the hot dogs, gravy, salami, and malteds. No more summer tan, ultra-amped rock concerts, or riding a motorcycle without a helmet. I sleep eight hours a night, drink four quarts of water a day, work out at the gym, and practice deep breathing relaxation techniques when I'm stuck in traffic. I eat my daily minimum roughage requirement, buy organic produce, and remove the fatty skin from chicken. I floss, gargle, and waterpik every night, stretch my aching back and Kegel my you-know-what every morning.

I've abandoned all the really good bad stuff and already do all the boring healthy stuff. There's no where left for me to go. Should I ever hear the dread diagnosis, I'm a dead woman.

My brother Jim, on the other hand, has taken Twain's advice to heart. Ask him to name the basic food groups and he'll say onion rings, bacon bits, Cheetos, and fried bread dough. He smokes three packs of Marlboros a day, imbibes two six-packs of Miller each night, and – despite being a grandfather several times over – only dates girls too young to remember any president before Bill Clinton. No moral pauper he.

And whenever Jim wants to lose a quick ten pounds, why, it's a cinch: he just jettisons the Mallomars and the sausage and pepper heroes for a few days and he's got that flat tummy back, no sweat. He may not floss or use sunscreen, but the boy is one of the happiest human beings I know.

Compare Brother Jim to an acquaintance of mine who is known among friends and colleagues as "the most knowledgeable alternative health professional" in the mid-Hudson Valley. Before the American Medical Association, before the New York Times, before Oprah, this woman is privy to every hot new health discovery on the planet. And she takes it all profoundly to heart. She jogs five miles a day, sleeps under a pyramid, has had her amalgam dental fillings removed, and eats seaweed and brown rice three times a week to flush the toxins out of her colon.

What has all this clean living gotten her? The poor dear lives alone with seven cats. She has never been caught laughing out loud. And she's always griping about some physical affliction. As Twain would say, the woman has neglected her habits.

I, at least have my chocolate and cheese – the last little remnants of my careless, wicked, and high metabolism youth. I cling to these guilty pleasures as tenaciously as a barnacle sucks rock face. And I am seriously thinking of putting Margaritas back into my daily diet.

Strictly, of course, for health reasons.

September 1999

BE HAPPY AND FORGET THE LAUNDRY

MY FRIEND LEA BROWN has discovered the secret of life. You see, Lea is a very cheerful person and completely undependable. The fact that she is cheerful makes her pleasant to be around. The fact that she is completely undependable means that nobody ever asks or expects her to do anything. And whenever she does remember to reset her clock to daylight savings, get to the airport on time, or show up at her wedding, we are all absolutely thrilled and utterly grateful.

For instance, when my daughter was born Lea promised to mail me a box from California with all her three-year-old son's good hand-me-downs. The box arrived on my daughter's fourth birthday. Nothing fit, but I was pleased nevertheless. Good old Lea! Her heart is in the right place.

I, on the other hand, have always been dependable to a fault. I attend to every detail, cover every base, anticipate every need, and stock up for every contingency. When I make a pledge to do something, I do it. And if I have been struck down by a truck and lie helplessly in a coma in intensive care you can be sure to find a file on my desk with contact numbers and a profusely illustrated backup plan.

College deans count on me to show up to teach my class in a blizzard. Editors know that I never miss a deadline.

When I have to go out of town for a few days I leave my family with a drawer full of clean underwear, a closet full of toilet tissue, and a freezer full of meals. I sign up all my girlfriends for rotating childcare duty so that Daddy won't be inconvenienced. I pay the bills early and make sure that the fuel oil tanks are full so that my dears are assured of uninterrupted heat and light.

Now you would think that taking care of the people I love and meeting every expectation of the people I work for would make me feel good about myself. But being dependable is an affliction.

I am not appreciated. The only time my endeavors are even noticed is when I FAIL to deliver perfection, on time and under budget. And my efforts are not reciprocated. Instead, the more I show up and do, the more often I am expected to show up and do.

When this makes me cranky -- as it does from time to time -- I am scolded by the very people who benefit from my dependability. "Why can't you be more easy going?" asks my husband, "Look at Barry's wife. She doesn't make lists!" The wife of his best friend hasn't filed her federal income tax for the past five years. I guess I could do that.

Actually I have been in therapy for some time to overcome my compulsion to take care of business. My therapist has ordered me to tear up all notes from school requesting bake sale volunteers. She insists that I refuse to cook dinner one night a week whether I feel like it or not. And she's urged me to stop sending out birthday cards to all of my in-laws for just one year, to see if I can handle it.

It's not easy to undo decades of knee jerk responsibility. But Barry's wife does appear less stressed than I am, so I'm willing to tough out the program.

I'm leaving on Sunday for a week in San Diego to help my mother move. Before I go I will file this column, correct my students' final exams, water the geraniums, and leave my daughter's swim practice schedule on the refrigerator.

I have vowed, however, not to make and freeze a 5-day supply of chili, not to leave notes about his overdue library books on my husband's pillow, not to check the batteries in all the flashlights and smoke detectors, and not to ask my daughter's teacher to brush her hair in the morning even though I know that when I return it will not have been brushed in eight days.

I have also tried to get in touch with my friend Lea to see if she has any advice on how to relax and let go of my irresistible impulse to pay the electric bill on time. But Lea never remembers to return my calls.

March 2002

JUST SLAP ME, FINE ME, AND BE DONE WITH IT

FORGET THE INCOME TAX or the Sales Tax or the Sin Tax on imported hooch. In this first election year of the third millenium I am campaigning for the Tax-on-Living Tax. Here's how it works.

Every morning, at say 9a.m., a woman appears at my door. She knocks. I answer. She scowls, spits in my eye, slaps me soundly across the face, and then demands payment of $25 in cash.

I cheerfully pay up each morning. I am then free to go about my business for the rest of the day without any of those pesky interruptions that are always messing everything up. Personally, I would much prefer such scheduled abuse to the haphazard variety.

Take last Tuesday. A typical day. I carpool the kids to nursery school, workout at the gym, meet my girlfriend for lunch, and, there, as I bite into my Monte Cristo sandwich oblivious to the sour breath of the stalking fates, it happens. A hairline crack down the center of my upper left molar suddenly splits open and sends an urgent message to my brain's scream center.

Faster than you can say nitrous oxide, I'm crawling into the dentist's chair, pleading for drugs, and agreeing to a $850 crown.

Two hours later I'm on the phone performing damage control: canceling, rescheduling, and begging forgiveness from all the other people whose lives have been hit by this unforeseen nuisance in a numbing cascade of consequence. They're pissed. I'm pissed. The kids are pissed. My husband, who has to eat canned broth for dinner, is pissed.

How much kinder and gentler to pay the tax first thing each day and be done with it. That way you can actually schedule your day and know with confidence that you will not

- Drive your car into a snow bank and have to wait three hours for a tow
- Dislocate your shoulder in the middle of jazz-er-size class
- Drop your keys down the sewer grate while wearing a white silk dress and pumps
- Spend five hours in the emergency room with a screaming four year old who split open her chin on a rusty jungle-gym
- Listen to your old babysitter call you a filthy capitalist pig for reporting her earnings to the IRS

The pain, the humiliation, the expense – you've already paid your dues. And the gods of mayhem get theirs up front. Everybody wins. That's why this Tax-On-Living Tax idea is so perfect.

Of course, it will require a slight adjustment of the Economic World Order to work properly. I mean think of all the people who make their living off the pain and humiliation of others.

Lawyers are certainly finished. The 37 legal minds who wrote the contract I was asked to sign yesterday ("you give us all rights to everything forever and we'll give you $100 unless you're a half hour late in which case we'll give you $49.95 and a swift kick") will have to learn computer programming at the local community college.

Telemarketers might do well in janitorial service. Loan collectors could swell the ranks of the Peace Corps. While your dental hygienist may want to consider a career in wallpaper removal. The change is not without its opportunities.

But I'm not too worried about these folks. There will be an enormous demand for people willing to get up early and go door-to-door inflicting pain on their neighbors. And there are, as we all know, thousands of qualified individuals out there already.

It's only 11a.m. and Nita Micossi has already had to fight on the phone with the health insurance people (don't ask), price out a new fax machine to replace the one that got fried in last night's lightning storm, and take two Tylenol with codeine for a headache caused by her new $400 prescription eyeglasses.

June 2000

OF COURSE I MULTITASK

YOU THINK I'M WRITING this column. Actually, I'm doing the laundry, auditioning a carpenter, calculating today's Weight Watchers points, launching a multi-level marketing business, AND writing this column.

Last month a lady named Catherine Bush wrote an article in the New York Times Sunday Magazine called "How To Multitask".

Being myself a big fan of multitasking I read Ms. Bush's article -- twice. Once while eating a tuna salad sandwich and balancing my check book, and once while plucking my chin hairs and supervising my daughter's Daisy troop who, being multitaskers in training, were playing kick ball, sucking orange popsicles, and listening to Raffi & Big Bird At Carnegie Hall.

For those of you too busy multitasking to read an article on the subject, allow me to summarize and comment on her main points:

1. DON'T THINK YOU CAN ACTUALLY DO TWO THINGS AT ONCE.

Gee, Cathy, of course not. Only a lazy slut would do only two things at once. A person's got five senses, afterall, and if you cannot chew, chop, listen, scratch, and gaze longingly at your dear progeny all at once you're not living up to your full God-given potential.

I once knew a guy who did only two things – play the oboe and rebuild transmissions – and never at the same time. He became a hopeless alcoholic.

2. PRIORITIZE AND BLOW OFF THOSE TASKS YOU CAN AFFORD TO BLOW OFF.

I totally agree. But I personally have a problem finding tasks trivial enough to blow off.

For instance, I was having one of my periodic screaming lunatic breakdowns last Saturday night in which I enumerate the innumerable jobs on my Essential To Do List between raving chants of Ican'tdoitall Ican'tdoitall Ican'tdoitall Ican'tdoitall, when my husband calmly suggested that I "prioritize".

"What do I NOT do, you stupid idiot?" I gently replied. "Stop the kids from gouging out each others' eyes? Call the fuel oil company and tell them that the furnace is belching smoke? Cook your dinner?" That stopped the conversation but not my problem.

3. DEPEND ON ROUTINES.

Amen. Fortunately, my grandmother taught me to dice onions when I was four so I can make an omelet without ever engaging my pre-frontal cortex.

I never cook without multitasking. It's the only time I have left in the day to nag my mother long distance about her medication, run lines with my daughter for her role in the Purim spiel, and calculate this year's earned income credit.

But where in all these fancy-dancy parenting manuals do we ever hear a word about teaching our little ones those basic routines that will enable them to maximize their multitasking skills as adults?

Children should not only be able to cook on automatic pilot but iron, floss, and blind stitch hems.

4. FOR EFFECTIVE MULTITASKING USE TIMERS.

I would go one step further and say that the real Olympians of multitasking cannot function without timers. I personally could not. The last time the battery in my timer went dead, I fried a batch of rayon in the clothes dryer and lost a valued client.

On the other hand, with the help of a timer you CAN prepare a coq au vin, do 45 minutes on the treadmill, and run a business from home all at once. And that's just your morning.

5. WHATEVER YOU DO, DON'T ANSWER THE PHONE.

This suggestion is somewhat redundant because most multitasking episodes will already have you on the phone arguing with an HMO claims adjuster.

I think what Cathy has in mind here is that you – the multitasker – need to stay in control of this very complex operation. In-coming calls can throw you off your game. Especially if it's your girlfriend begging you to watch her attention deficit disorder afflicted nine-year-old son for three hours this afternoon.

Here's where a second phone line and an answering machine message pirated from an old Lenny Bruce record can help.

6. OLD PEOPLE ARE BETTER AT MULTITASKING THAN KIDS.

There's an area of the brain that is activated during multitasking called Brodmann's Area 10 after Agnes Brodmann who was found in a state of catatonia as a result of trying to put up twelve bushels of sour cherries while arguing with her daughter's bridal consultant over the seating arrangements. Agnes, they discovered, lacked the neurological switch that pumps extra blood into Area 10 during high velocity multitasking events.

Since Area 10 is the last part of the brain to evolve, multitasking actually improves with age. Tots are easily distracted while the rest of us only get better, the older we get, at doing ten things at once. This is a comfort.

May 2001

DO IT!

THE PLAZA HOTEL IN New York City is closing at the end of this month and with it one of my dearest fantasies. You see, ever since I had my first luncheon in the hotel's legendary Palm Court I dreamed of someday taking my daughter to there for tea. And this was a dozen years before I even had a daughter.

An elegant Baroque winter garden where white gloved ladies and little girls in mary-janes gather for English finger sandwiches, scones and clotted cream, and pots of tea – the Palm Court is a unique theatrical pleasure accompanied by a harpist, of course.

But the Plaza Hotel is about to undergo a metamorphosis into a shopping mall and condo complex and the fate of the beloved Court is doubtful.

Alas. Tea with my girl in the Palm Court is about to fall into the bag of Lost Opportunities & Regrets along with that trip across the border into Egypt with a busload of Israelis in 1983. The trip cost $500 which was $450 more than I had at the time. But in retrospect it was a pittance and now it will cost me thousands to fulltime my lifelong desire to see the Valley of the Kings.

I also regret that I let my boyfriend talk me out of going to see Rex Harrison in the road show of My Fair Lady when it came to San Francisco, and that I declined a chance to see Lena Horne in a private cabaret performance before her sold-out Carnegie Hall show because I couldn't get a date.

I didn't make that trip to China before it opened up to the West to see the collective farms for myself. And I didn't let my friend RT do an erotic photo shoot of me when I still have a 26 year old body. Too late now. All gone.

My good fortune, however, is that in this life, for every experience I passed on there were a dozen others that I seized.

For example, I spent a long summer on a Greek island with a man I loved. I went to graduate school when the chance was offered. And I lived on a kibbutz before the movement went corporate.

I got to walk to the top of the Leaning Tower of Pisa, touch the cold marble of the original David in Florence, go eyeball to eyeball with the Mona Lisa in Paris, and ramble through the Athenian Parthenon before they roped off all these sites to visitors.

I saw Ike and Tina Turner every year when they played the small Bay Area clubs in the late 60's. I visited East Germany before it was reabsorbed into greater Germany and Czechoslovakia before it split in half and went democratic. I bought that house in 1998 before the market exploded. And I had lunch at top of the north tower of the World Trade Center where I was informed by the head waiter of Windows on the World that the lamp shade I saw floating in New York harbor was the Statue of Liberty.

But I did not take my daughter to the Palm Court for tea and am reminded once again that you regret the things you did Not do more than the things you did.

And so I'm off to Portugal for the honeymoon my husband promised me 13 years ago. I want to see the megaliths of Evora, the border castles, and the azulejos on the Carmelite church in Porto before the inevitable forces of global capitalism set up golden arches in their shadows. Already the ancient Alfama district of Lisbon sports chic $300 a night hotels, so I'd better hurry.

April 2005

My Philosophy of Life, plus a few handy tips

PACKING TIPS YOU WON'T GET FROM MARTHA

CHARLOTTE WARDLE CARDEZA, ONE of the passengers who survived the sinking of the Titanic in 1912, subsequently sued White Star Line for the loss of her luggage that consisted of 14 trunks, four suitcases, three crates, and one medicine chest. White Star eventually paid Ms. Cardeza $177,352 for her loss which included 70 dresses, 10 fur coats, 38 feather boas, 22 jeweled hatpins, 91 pairs of gloves, and one Swiss made music box.

Now that's the way to travel! Assuming you've got a chamber maid, personal assistant, and ex-longshoreman handyman on call.

When I crossed the North Atlantic in 1962 with my brother, sister, and parents on the largest and most elegant ocean liner of its day, I was allowed to bring along one suitcase. The Swiss made music box had to stay behind.

My father's company had transferred him to Europe, and shortly after my mother got the news, she went out and bought five of the biggest suitcases she could find. "You can bring anything you want," she said as she handed us each a single piece of luggage, "just as long as you can fit it in here."

Since my favorite childhood game had always been "covered wagon" -- an exercise in choosing the essentials to make a new life on the other side of the continent -- I loved the challenge. I'm a born traveler. So who better to share a few insights into packing as we hit the peak of the busy summer vacation season?

First, What to Pack. You all know to bring the camera, some sun screen, and a Spanish-English phrase book. But I've discovered over the years and thousands of frequent flyer miles that there are a few small items that improve what my old pal Mr. D calls "road flex." Before his back went out, Mr. D used to spend his summers working on the Alaska pipeline north of Anchorage and his winters in Las Vegas spending the money he made on the line. He crashed in the backrooms of countless friends on his bi-annual trek between Nevada and Alaska and he developed superior road flex, that is, the ability to adapt to any situation that might arise when one is on the move.

Now among the essentials to enhance your traveler's adaptability are earplugs and an eye mask. Earplugs allow you to remain gracious in the company of the all those shrieking bores on their cell phones who have overrun trains, planes, buses, and ferries. And an eye mask lets you sleep in a hotel room in Times Square that has a blinking neon light outside your window.

Also make sure to slip a kazoo, harmonica, two metal spoons, or some other small musical instrument into your bag for impromptu entertainments. Once, a few friends and I transformed an endless delay at the East German border into a jolly party with nothing more than a ukulele and a hip flask.

Did I tell you to bring the hip flask? Filled, of course.

If you're not the musical type or do not know what a hip flask is, I suggest three juggling balls. Traveling involves long stretches of waiting and nothing kicks the boredom like a little juggling. Don't know how? All the better! You'll have hours of opportunity to learn while standing in the airport security line.

Don't forget the baby wipes. These pre-moistened towelettes are not just for baby fannies and anal-retentive detectives. After sharing a bus seat with a goat in the Yucatan or when you're in that gas station bathroom outside Big Sandy, Montana you'll thank me for it.

Pack Valium. Do I really need to explain?

Next, here are a few tips for the packing process itself:

* Don't fill your shampoo bottle up to the top when flying.

* If you're carrying medicinal marijuana make sure that the permit is on your person at all times.

* Remember, it's illegal to ship human remains to Puerto Rico for burial on a commercial flight.

* Before checking a suitcase, take the batteries out of your vibrator.

Now go have fun and send me a postcard.

August 2004

My Philosophy of Life, plus a few handy tips

PUTTING SIN BACK INTO SIN CITY

I WAS THRILLED TO read that Las Vegas has finally given up on its foolish flirtation with family values.

I knew we were in big trouble when they tore down the Hacienda and the Sands, put up those mega-theme hotels, and ran ads that invited couples "to bring the kids! See our circus acts, magicians, video arcades, and roller coasters! Fun for the entire family!"

Nonsense. The whole idea of Vegas was to have one spot in the country where people could let down their hair and anything else Clark County law would allow. Put it out in the middle of the desert, hundreds of miles from civil society, and let the 24/7 Saturnalia begin. That was the dream of the gangsters who turned a parched little town in the middle of nowhere into a naughty playground for adults with unleashed libidos and lots of money.

I remember the first time I ever went to Las Vegas in the early 70s. The Strip -- with its miles of neon and more marquee bulbs than the Lido de Paris had goose bumps -- was an eye-popping over-the-top glitter and glitz movie set. And visitors went native. Moms from Fresno got to wear their New Year's Eve sequins at noon. Little League coaches from Boise bought Stetson hats and silver money clips to flash at the tables. And mild-mannered grannies from everywhere west of the Rockies put on eye shades and saddlebags full of coins. Everybody was ready to let the games begin!

And did they ever. Music from the lounges kept the collective heartbeat up round the clock. Liquor was served free to anybody who sat at the Blackjack table longer than 10 minutes. And, no matter where you went, from the powder room to the bus depot, from the gas station to the bank, there was gambling: craps, roulette wheels, bingo, keno, high stakes poker, baccarat, and, of course, the one-arm bandits -- those nickel slot machines that could keep my Aunt Minnie hypnotized for a full 8-hour shift.

Weary of gambling? Plush cabaret theaters featured classy faux-French show girls sashaying around the stage in less fabric than you'd find on a baby's behind. Frank Sinatra and Don Rickles were still headlining and you'd better believe that the language alone in those shows broke a few commandments. Tacky chapels offered cowboy preachers or Elvis impersonators willing to tie the knot for $25 and legitimize a weekend of raunchy coupling. Who knew if they were legal weddings? Who cared?

Yep. Every imaginable (and unimaginable, I can only hope) vice was available in Las Vegas. That's what it was built for. That's why parents left the kids with their grandparents and drove the Chevy across the Mojave Dessert. That's why blue-haired widow ladies came by the busload from Los Angeles and Sacramento. That's why college kids like me flew down on the Vegas Special to celebrate their 21st birthdays.

Arriving in Las Vegas was always a kick, but especially so if by airplane at night. In those days, before it became one of the fastest growing cities in the country and had uncontrolled housing sprawl, Vegas was a concentrated jewel of light in the middle of a vast ink-black darkness. Data from a military satellite once reported that, from outer space, Vegas was brighter than New York City, L.A., or Tokyo.

Driving down the Strip at night for the first time was, for me, a life high right up there with strolling the Champs-Elysees and climbing the Acropolis. And to do so was to enter a non-Euclidean universe with its own quirky rules.

For example, you checked your concept of money at the city limits. Everything in Vegas was either outrageously expensive or free. On a jaunt there in the late 70s I remember having a sudden yen about two in the morning for a corned beef sandwich. I flagged down a taxi driver who knew of only one place that could satisfy me -- a small deli in a strip mall at the edge of town. The taxi ride, short but un-metered, and the sandwich together cost me $40. In any other place or circumstance I would have been appalled. But I'd been in town for a few days and by then it was all Monopoly money to me.

That's what Las Vegas was all about: a place where time and money operated on idiosyncrasy, and you could indulge the venial sin, knowing that the straight and narrow was patiently waiting for you back home.

And then something happened -- not in Las Vegas, but everywhere else. In 1976 Atlantic City was the first place outside of Nevada to allow casino gambling. Then in 1988 Congress legalized gaming on Indian reservations. In that same decade state lotteries and Off Track Betting went big time, riverboat casinos returned to the Mississippi River, XXX-rated video stores popped up in family neighborhoods, and dirty movies appeared on cable TV.

Victimless vice -- once the exclusive product of Las Vegas -- was suddenly everywhere.

I guess it was out of self-defense that the Vegas City Fathers decided to turn the tables. If Florence, Indiana is going to offer gambling and dirty movies, then we'll offer Barney Brunches and puppet shows in the casino lounge.

But, I am happy to say, the experiment failed. "The big money is never going to come from people who drink Shirley Temples," wrote a local columnist. And Las Vegas is back to its wicked old ways. The town's new ad campaign says it all: "Sin City Has Found Its Soul" and "What Happens Here, Stays Here." Yeah! That's the Vegas I remember.

Now how about getting rid of the smut on TV and the gambling in Connecticut?

July 2003

GAUDEAMUS IGITUR

FRIENDS, FAMILIES, FACULTY, HONORED guests, and graduating seniors:

It is customary at commencement ceremonies to invite a famous and successful individual to speak to the assembled. These invited luminaries generally talk about the obstacles they overcame to get to the exalted positions they now enjoy.

The idea is to encourage young graduates to follow their good example: to have high expectations and persevere in the face of life's inevitable challenges.

I salute the administration of your school for inviting to this year's commencement an individual who is neither famous nor successful and who, in fact, still owes this esteemed institution $729 in student loans.

It shows both courage and imagination to have one who has failed to scale the highest social, economic, artistic, and/or intellectual heights address this eagerly expectant crowd of young people.

Thank you for your confidence. I shall try to tell it like it really is and give a few useful tips.

First, let me say that I am not bitter over that "C" in zoology from Mr. Ziegler. It did deter me from pursuing a pre-med program and derailed my childhood dreams of becoming a $250,000 a year research oncologist and winning a Nobel Prize.

I am, on the other hand, eternally grateful for getting that switchboard operator job at the Faculty Club that allowed me to pursue a Ph.D. in Finnish Folklore. Even though I have not earned enough money to date to pay off my graduate education, I want to assure you that every limousine operator and building contractor I have ever worked for has been terribly impressed by my advanced academic degrees.

Which leads to my first bit of advice:

STAY IN SCHOOL AS LONG AS YOU CAN. Kids, this is as good as it will ever get. You are old enough to stay up all night if you want and young enough to think it's fun to stay up all night.

Now, I realize that you are graduating today and may already be angsting over getting that first real job. But don't let that worry you. It's not too late to apply to grad school for the fall. And for those of you who have already finished the Ph.D. do not despair. There's always law school.

BE CAREFUL WHAT YOU ARE SUCCESSFUL AT. For those of you who have already taken my first bit of advice and -- at the age of 36 -- stand breathless on the brink of adulthood, allow me to share this cautionary tale:

Upon graduating from college, my Aunt Lucille, with B.A., M.B.A., Ph.D., LL.D., D.S.W., and D.D.S. in hand, decided that her first order of business was to make pots of money which would allow her to retire at the age of 40 (she was 38 at the time) and pursue her dream of sailing around the world on a tramp steamer and writing haiku poetry.

So Lucille got involved in a multi-level tattoo-removing marketing scheme. She hated marketing, tattoos, and any level above the ground floor. But she became fabulously wealthy beyond her wildest expectations. She was the undisputed Queen of the tattoo-removal industry and often featured on the cover of Body Art Weekly.

She tried to break free of this life and pursue her dreams but her husband, kids, and good-for-nothing in-laws refused to give up the 9,000 square foot house in Paramus, the live-in cook, and iced cappuccino on demand.

Lucille died last year -- rich, famous, and still a beauty at 70 (since she could afford all those facelifts) -- but sad and empty in her heart.

Dear graduates, when you go to sign up for that high paying, soul surrendering job at the big corporation, remember poor Lucille.

LIVE IN A FOREIGN COUNTRY. As a kid I lived in Holland where I discovered that on a kid's birthday she does not receive gifts but instead gives everyone in class a gift. At first I thought this was a lousy deal. Then I saw the big pay-off.

Go live in a foreign country and you will find that other people's answers to life's little how-to questions may actually be prettier, tastier, cleaner, or more humane.

STUDY SOME LATIN. Latin used to be the foundation of a good education. Nowadays it's out of favor. Too bad for you. The coupling of Latin and Anglo-Saxon produced the language we speak. Language is power and anyone who appreciates and uses the two richly different roots of English can better wield that power.

Come to think of it, study a little Anglo-Saxon as well.

The last and most important tip I want to leave you with on this auspicious occasion, has, in my own darkest hours, kept me on life's steady path. When faced with anxious choices at those innumerable crossroads with their unknown consequences, I always recall the words of Mark Twain. On the prospect of getting old, Twain observed: IF YOU'RE NOT HAVING FUN GETTING THERE, DON'T GO.

June 2001

IT'S THE THOUGHT

IT WAS MY FIRST Christmas as a young bride just married into a large Irish family. My new husband and I were broke and there was no way we could possibly afford to buy gifts for his seven young nieces and nephews. So, fool that I am, I decided to crochet each one of the kiddies a matching set of mittens, hat, and scarf for the winter. (Don't say it.)

I worked day and night between Thanksgiving and December 24th till my fingers bled and my astigmatism slipped another ten degrees off its axis. But it was worth it! By Christmas morning I had seven little packages under the tree.

The family gathered. My mother-in-law pulled a whistle out of her apron pocket, blew it, and summoned the gods of pandemonium. There was a firestorm of flying ribbons and wrapping paper while everyone opened everything in one mad frenzy. In the time it took me to refill my coffee cup, the living room was covered in mounds of debris and the children were off to the den to fight over the biggest empty boxes.

When I asked my in-laws a few weeks later if the mitten sets fit their children, they looked at me blankly.

I tell you this tale because this July is a big gift-giving month around our house what with a couple of birthdays, an anniversary, and several new babies. And I've been dwelling on the wisdom of my pal Dolores, who believes that gift giving can make or break a relationship. She sums up the dilemma with this tidy Zen koan: "The space between the gift giver and the gift receiver is very great."

Indeed.

The giver SHOULD put herself in the other's place and ask "what would really please this person?" The receiver, no matter how disappointed, SHOULD appreciate the sincere effort. And the whole enterprise SHOULD bring the two closer.

Following this advice, I'd give my 7-year-old daughter a Barbie doll for her birthday rather than two tickets to see a stage production of South Pacific. I would have given my hippie niece a wok for her wedding rather than a baroque cut-crystal vase with the card: "someday you'll be delighted to have this." And I would have wrapped empty boxes for my husband's seven nieces and nephews.

But this rarely occurs.

Sometimes the gift is too much. A young man once gave me a magnificent pair of pearl earrings to soften me up, I discovered, for the diamond ring he had on lay-away at Zales. I bolted from the poor fellow faster than a fox streaking from the hounds.

Sometimes it's too little. On one of my serious decade-turning birthdays my husband gave me a tin of talcum powder. He was clueless as to why I slashed his tires and wouldn't talk to him for a month.

Sometimes it's puzzling. As a wedding gift, an old friend sent us a tiny ceramic snail glued to a square wooden block. My husband and I were confused. Was this a married person's inside joke? Were we supposed to smash it and find the "real" gift inside? Did my friend's wife -- who I was never sure really liked me -- send the snail as a snub?

In all these cases the gift-giving event put a kink in the relationship.

On the other hand, the perfect gift, perfectly given can cement a bond forever. When I was in college my brother Jim came to visit one weekend. As we strolled around the campus, Jim, who had maneuvered behind me, suddenly flung an exquisite silk shawl over my shoulders and shouted "happy birthday!" I'd swooned over this shawl when I saw it in a shop window earlier in the day. "Why don't you get it?" he had asked. "Oh, no," I'd said. "It's much too extravagant." So, when I wasn't looking, my brother bought it for me. What a guy!

I haven't figured out the deep drill psychology of gift giving or why it's so fraught with emotional land mines. But I have come up with a few tips. For the giver:

1. Don't buy anything that you think somebody "needs." That's no fun. And you always get it wrong anyway.

2. Don't buy anything that needs to be sized. Nothing puts the kibosh on a birthday like getting a smashing satin and lace teddy -- that's too small.

3. Stick with a consumable like wine, chocolates, or nice smelling soap. If the recipient doesn't want it at least she can share it with her guests.

My Philosophy of Life, plus a few handy tips

4. For weddings go to Tiffany's. You can buy a lovely objet for surprisingly little money. Everyone is thrilled to get something in a Tiffany box. And you can still return it years later, after the divorce.

5. For kid's birthdays buy books and puzzles by the gross on sale at Marshall's. If you're like me, your child goes to 37 birthday parties a year. The kids at these events already have more stuff than God; and if a mother is sore at you for not buying her darling a $35 American Girl Doll accessory, then the worst that can happen is she won't invite you back next year.

As for being on the receiving end, I take a cue from my sister. No matter what gift Carol gets, she lavishes the giver with thanks and compliments, then discretely returns the item to the store.

Finally, never depend on your husband to get you that special something that reveals how well he understands your inner being and how willing he is to shop. Just buy it for yourself.

July 2002

DEAR AUNT NITA....

MY MAILBAG HAS BEEN filled to overflowing lately. Most of your letters have sought my advice on a number of tender issues. So I thought, dear friends, that I would take this opportunity to answer a few of them. Remember, I am not a certified psychologist or drug rehabilitation expert, just a concerned friend and a mom....

****

Dear Aunt Nita: I'm fat. I'm so fat that I can't bend over to lift a case of Cheetos off the pallet at Sam's Club. I have tried everything including having my jaw wired closed from Thanksgiving to New Year's Day (though I have to say that pureed pepperoni through a straw just doesn't do it for me). My girlfriend says that the June wedding is off unless I shed a few pounds. What's your secret to losing weight? I'm desperate. – signed, Waldo in Poughkeepsie.

Dear Waldo: Despite all the blather about "portion control" and "exercise" (phew! who needs that grief?) there is a secret to weight loss. You think Gwyneth Paltrow really looks like that? Nonsense. It's all done with lighting and lenses. All you have to do, sweetie, is buy yourself a "skinny mirror". That's right. There are actually mirrors that make you look 20% thinner – I've got one on the back of my closet door. The only thing that really counts is how you feel about yourself. And, believe me, you look into a skinny mirror every morning and you'll feel sensational. Let the clerk at Sam's Club do the heavy lifting. And as for your girlfriend, if she can't get past those little love handles then dump her. Hang out in the lingerie department at Lane Bryant's and find yourself a Camryn Manheim wannabe.

****

My Philosophy of Life, plus a few handy tips

Dear Aunt Nita: I am pregnant with my first child and very nervous about being a mom. What can I expect the first few years? Any tips on how to get this kid to be genius who can support me in my old age? – signed, Trixie in Wassaic.

Dear Trixie: There are an overwhelming number of childrearing books out there that describe in great detail what to expect from the various "stages of life". But, frankly, it comes down to this: during the first year of the kid's life you just hope she keeps breathing; the second year you hope she doesn't kill herself; the third year you hope you have the patience not to kill her. Once she's potty trained and can order her own Kiddie Meal at Wendy's, I recommend that you buy your little genius some of those handy "let's play" kits – "let's play" dentist, "let's play" tax attorney, "let's play" old house renovation expert – to encourage her into a financially sensible career path. If you must do Barbie make sure it's the Internet Mogul Barbie or the Nobel Prize Winning Physicist Barbie.

****

Dear Aunt Nita: I need some serious advice about my love life. I know that at your age you've had lots and lots of experience. So tell me, what do girls really want? I am 15 years old and don't have a driver's license yet, so please don't tell me to do anything that involves cars, ok? – signed, George in Red Hook.

Dear George: I'll let slide that comment about my age, but I should warn you right off the bat that girls are very sensitive about age and that you should avoid the subject whenever possible. Next, I advise you to hurry up and become 16 as soon as you can since most of the really good stuff does involve cars. In the meantime, I suggest that you learn how to play a musical instrument. Most guys think the guitar is neat but girls really like boys who can play the piano. Classical music is good, but a little Gershwin sends the message that you are sophisticated, romantic, and old-fashioned enough to pick up the check. Girls love that. Of course, if you can carry a tune, learn all the lyrics to the Fred Astaire Songbook (ask your grandmother) and you'll have to beat the babes off with a stick. Trust me on this.

****

Dear Aunt Nita: What is the secret of success? – signed, Marge in Milan.

Dear Marge: That is one tough question. I myself have pondered it for many years. But, frankly, I've never been able to improve upon my Brother Jim's answer: "just double space."

April 2000

THE ZEN OF BUSY

LIKE EVERYONE ELSE, I grumble about how busy, busy, busy I am. I hear it from working moms, stay-at-home moms, men and women who get up at 5am to catch Metro-North into Grand Central. I even hear it from my childless, retired acquaintances who spend their days gardening and meditating. So much to do, so little time to do it. "Busy" has become the standard 21st century reply to "how are you?"

Our collective obsession with overfilling the cup of time reminds me of a favorite undergraduate read, THE SILENT LANGUAGE by anthropologist Edward T. Hall. Hall writes of striking cultural differences in such unspoken ways of communicating as body language, territoriality, personal space -- and time.

For instance, when an American calls a dinner party for 6pm, there is a limited time of acceptable lateness and each level of lateness conveys its own meaning: 6:15pm is okay, but 6:30pm demands a slight apology; 6:45pm is mildly insulting though still within the happy hour warm-up phase and easily forgiven with a really nice hostess gift; 7:00pm, however, is downright rude and probably the last time you'll be invited.

The Sioux Natives, on the other hand, have no word in their language for "time" or "late" or "waiting". So you can miss the soup course altogether and no one will even notice. And the Pueblo Indians commence events – a dance, a wedding, a birthday party – when the time is ripe and all of the players have assembled. A tribal outsider may arrive at 8pm only to find that things don't get going till 1am. Or maybe the next day.

I had to adjust to Latin Time when I moved to Italy as a child. But I quickly found the idea of closing down in the middle of the day to eat, sleep, and play canasta an absolutely enchanting way to live, and I return to the Mediterranean whenever I can as much for the relaxed sense of time as for the linguini.

In the meantime, I'm stuck with the rest of you in this hyper-rationalized industrial culture where Time is a commodity: we earn it, spend it, save it, buy it, sell it, measure it, lose it, waste it. We segment and schedule time down to the minute and increasingly the micro-minute.

Think of that lawyer you're chatting with on the phone with a time sheet at her elbow divided into 15-minute slices. Think of the phone company ticking off your long distance chat with Aunt Rena in six-second bits.

Scan the dates and times for lessons, practices, meets, holidays, holy days, appointments, lunch dates, and parties that litter the refrigerator door. We're all slaves to the tight-fisted schedules.

And we teach our kids early and often to cut their lives to suit mercilessly regimented schedules. My daughter's middle school day, for example, is chopped into nine 39 minute hunks [7:57am to 8:36am, 8:38am to 9:17am, and so forth]. Learning to sprint from room to room during the two minute intervals between classes is the single most stressful challenge of entering sixth grade. Am I the only one who thinks this is a stupid way to learn?

I'm no role model, of course. Last Monday I programmed a 9am drop off at soccer camp, followed by a 9:30am Yoga class, an 11am echocardiogram at the hospital, a noon lunch date, a 2:30 piano lesson, a 3:50 soccer camp pickup, a 4pm committee meeting, a 7pm dinner-on-the-table, and a 9pm check-for-ticks and three chapters of reading with the child before bed. T.S. Eliot's cri de coeur "I have measured out my life with coffee spoons" resonates as I lie in the dark mentally running through tomorrow's game plan.

What to do? I could go live with the Sioux, but they've all learned how to read clocks. I could find a job in Tuscany, but vast tracts of Italy have gone rational since 1962, alas. I could enter a Trappist monastery and whittle down my daily activities to prayer and mopping the cloister, but the children would object.

So, I've surrendered to my cultural destiny and chosen to make an art out of busy-ness. My wall calendar is color-coded. My daily DayTimer is neatly triaged with contingency footnotes. My watch tells time in four different zones.

And whenever I pull off a day like last Monday -- on time, under budget, and without incurring a single moving violation -- I celebrate by staring at a blank wall for 15 minutes.

September 2007

STAYING SAFE ON THE INTERNET: A GUIDE FOR PARENTS

THAT'S THE TITLE OF a booklet that the school sent home with my daughter. Prevent Child Abuse Publications wants to make sure that we are all aware, in explicit detail, of the Dangers a kid may stumble across on the most innocent Internet cruise.

There are the garden variety porno, violence, and hate sites; the chat room bullies and predators; web pages where any fool can get tips on how to build a thermonuclear bomb or brew methamphetamine in the garage; and -- the latest curse of the college undergraduate – those illicit gambling rooms. Evidently, it will now take the average college grad 15 years to pay off his student loans and another 15 years to make good on his gambling debts to Guido "the'Net" Vincenza.

While every conscientious parent needs to recalibrate their radar to snare these 21st century evils, the booklet omits the most devilish risk of the Internet. I'm speaking of the easy and inviting ways we simple souls of all ages can get sucked into squandering extraordinary amounts of time on the Net.

Let's start with the hypnotic effect of games. There are a gazillion games on the Internet -- card games, word games, board games, puzzles. Something for everyone. Me, I can't resist Scrabble and Spider Solitaire. I first began to play Solitaire while waiting on hold for the health insurance claims adjuster. The distraction kept me from blowing smoke out of my ears, which generally occurs after I've been kept on hold for longer than five minutes. But then I began to play Solitaire while actually talking to the claims adjuster, and then while talking to my girlfriends, and then while talking to no one at all but just as a nice little "transition" between daily computer chores. Since I transit a lot, I'm up to a dozen games a day. They each take seven minutes.

Then there's the Window Shopping. I'm on the Internet hit list for Nordstrom, Macy's, Pier One, Zappos, and the PerfumeMart – just to name a few of the regular offenders. And who can say no to a quickie five-minute flip through this week's "fresh and flirty summer skirts," "25%-off petite sale," "wicker seat savings," or "new arrivals from Naturalizer." Since I never have time to actually go to a store and shop anymore, I figure I'm entitled to this small guilty pleasure.

I'm also a sucker for trivia searches. Like how many episodes of Star Trek: Voyager were there and which ones have I missed during the current reruns on Spike TV? In answering this question, I make a brief side trip to the "where are they now?" cast page. This can take anywhere from 10 minutes to an hour depending on whether or not I succumb to the urge and follow the link to Robert Beltran's Official Web Site.

One isn't safe even in the dentist's office. While waiting for a root canal last week, I came across an irresistible article in Oprah the Magazine on "Killer Shoes" that lured me to a website with a promise of Jimmy Choo sling backs in "C" width. It was, of course, a rotten lie, but it took me 20 minutes of fruitless search through bergdorfgoodman.com to discover I'd been had.

You see how I can easily blow off an afternoon online reviewing the pros and cons of botox injections, sampling jazz&blues radio stations on 365.com, taking a virtual tour of Caribbean real estate, or lying to my South Beach Diet weigh-in counselor.

And this doesn't count the hours I spend on legit work-related investigations, essential health queries, and routine e-mail correspondence.

They say that the average American kid fritters away four hours a day in front of the TV [it took me 11 minutes to double check that factoid online]. But I predict that this statistic is about to be obliterated by the marathon hours that kids spend on the Net playing Sudoku Sniper, shopping for vibrating tongue rings, and uploading slumber party videos to their MySpace pages. I may be an Internet sinner, but I'll always be an amateur compared to the crowd born and bred to it.

June 2007

SCHOOL IS OUT

IT'S LATE JUNE, IT'S 11:30am, it's hot, and my brain is tomato paste. The kid just stormed off the school bus and left a trail of debris from the mud room to the guinea pig cage upstairs.

The third of her four Big Final Exams allegedly "went okay" this morning and I tender a feeble bribe to get her to study for tomorrow's dread math test.

But she is already into summer mode and I can't blame her. Despite commitments, projects, assignments, overtime, and deadlines, I wanna be in summer mode too. Having spent 21 years as a student in school and another 18 as a teacher, my biological clock is irrevocably set to the academic year. Fresh ideas flower, new projects commence, and life is reinvigorated right after Labor Day. Spent ideas fade, old projects conclude, and life relaxes after Father's Day. The fool who decided to begin classes at the local college in August is simply wrong. The brain cannot function properly in August. Or late June.

For years I would come home on the last day of class and boogie around the house while old 45rpm favorites – "School is Out" by Gary U.S. Bonds, "Summertime Blues" by Eddie Cochran, "Palisades Park" by Freddy Cannon, "Summer Means Fun" by Bruce & Terry, "Hot Fun in the Summertime" by Sly & the Family Stone, – alerted the neighbors that School IS Absolutely Out, there are no "school nights" for the next three months, and we just might close down the street tonight and dance till a quarter to three.

Watching my kid look beyond tomorrow's exam to a carefree spell of BBQs and pool parties, croquette tourneys and soccer camp, backyard tents and jaunts to the Jersey shore, I'm crazy with longing for those nearly naked days of youthful silliness and excess and, god save us, No Lists.

Just as my Play Angel is about to lose a wrestling match to my Work Angel, I spy a hand-addressed letter from California in my mail stack. The return address in the upper left hand corner of this letter is a stab from the very same past I've been crooning over all morning.

Julia F. Aptos, California. I went to high school with Julie and haven't seen her in decades.

"Hi, Nita, any chance you can join us in Redwood City on July 7th?" The personal note is scribbled across an invite to a gathering at the "lovely and spacious home" of Kathy G. and Steve A., two old high school pals who not only got married, as they threatened to do on prom night, but who evidently stayed married all of these years.

In the margin Julie has added the names of a small but choice group of people who have said they'd come, including two of my three favorite teachers.

I dig out my high school yearbook and look them up. William G.: wrestling, track, soccer, and tennis; freshmen, sophomore, junior, and senior boards; sophomore and junior class president; legislature; Rotarian Club. Peggy Y.: California Scholarship Federation secretary; Russian Club; Hostess Club president; junior and senior boards; voted "most intelligent girl" by the senior class. Dave W.: football, wrestling, CSF president; welfare board; boys' sports board; junior and senior boards; student court; orchestra; legislature parliamentarian; National Merit finalist; American Field Service exchange student to Italy.

So much achievement, so much ambition, so much promise as we graduated from high school and began our last summer of childhood before leaving home. I remember that summer well -- carhopping at the A&W, boating on the Bay, hanging out at the bowling alley, comparing college plans with pals as we toasted on the beach. If I had worries and lists I sure can't recall.

Not a one of those high school friendships survived much beyond graduation and I'm kind of curious how these kids with the funny haircuts in the year book turned out. What became of them after school was out for good?

I wonder if I should hop on a plane and head out to San Francisco to see if Bill K. is still a rascal and whether Chris M. has kept her figure. Instead, I make an iced coffee, grab a Robin Cook novel, and call dibsies on the hammock. I may not be a school kid, but for the afternoon I'm in summer mode.

July 2007

AH! SWEET MYSTERIES OF LIFE

IT'S MARCH. AND IF you're like me you've been on a diet since early January. And if you're like me you have discovered once again that, while it takes two weeks of no beer, pizza, cookies, and chips to slough four ounces off your hips, it takes only one celebratory night of margaritas, sour dough bruschetta, and chocolate lava cake to gain two pounds. Why is that? I ask my husband for the umpteenth time as I stare down at the scale.

This is one of life's great mysteries, he grunts, calculating his own caloric damage.

MYSTERY: *something that is not fully understood or that baffles; an enigma.*

No matter how much science and reason we use to demystify the human genome or the chemical composition of Pluto, life is littered with inexplicable mysteries. On this frigid morning waiting for the fuel oil delivery truck, I sit and contemplate those pesky things that frustrate my peace of mind and the smooth flow of my days.

Why, for example, when I'm at a friend's house do their cats, who make my eyes burn and my skin itch, make a beeline to my lap where they bivouac for the evening?

Why does the furnace conk out a Friday night in January when my sister-in-law is expected for a three-day holiday weekend?

Why is it that by the time you figure out how the opposite sex ticks you've pretty much lost interest?

Why does my mind go utterly blank when some cretin at the Department of Motor Vehicles insults my pedigree, when, an hour later, while lying on my back in Yoga class seeking No Mind, it is assaulted with a relentless stream of snappy comebacks?

Why do large bosoms look cheerful on young women and unsightly on old women?

Why, no matter how careful, do I always lose my favorite shearling gloves while, no matter how careless, I can't lose those loathsome bargain box mittens?

Why do people like vast lawns in front of their homes that are never used yet require huge amounts of water and weekly mowing from May to October?

Why do so many creeps win the lottery, get the girl, and own a villa in the South of France?

Why do I find that lost CD of Judy Garland at Carnegie Hall as soon as I've bought a replacement for it?

Why is it that if you've got IT [love, money, prizes, VIP box seats, or whatever] then people give IT to you because you obviously deserve IT since you already have IT; BUT if you don't have IT then people refuse to give IT to you because you clearly don't deserve IT or you'd already have IT.... Why is that?

Why do so many "pro-lifers" support the death penalty?

Why, when my husband finally remembers to buy me a birthday present it's a non-returnable silk teddy three sizes too small?

Why does love come when you don't need it while a great need for love drives it away?

Why did my cousin, who squandered millions on liposuction and stuff she never uses, inherit a fortune, while I, who would finance a community radio station, a job bank for the hearing impaired, or a cure for colon cancer, inherited nothing?

Why do the World's Major Religions believe that all the fun people are going to Hell?

....Why, oh, why? Mysteries all. But if you insist on an answer I can't improve on Garrison Keillor's observation that all tragedy is misunderstood comedy. God, says Keillor, is a great joker who's working with a rather slow audience.

March 2007

SKI AND ME

AH, WINTER! FOR THOSE of us above the 40th parallel that means black ice on the highway, unscheduled holidays for our kids, and snow, snow, snow. For some of my friends that also means treks to the slick slopes of New England for the long ski weekend.

For me, winter means jacking up the electric blanket to 22, doubling my intake of Vitamin C, and making a novena for an early thaw. But it emphatically does not include hitting the slopes.

I used to ski. Born and raised in California, snow was a pleasure manufactured in the mountains for our entertainment. And skiing was an annual school field trip to Squaw Valley with Father O'Connell, a slalom champ. I never learned how to stop skillfully, but I could make it down a serious mountain without a spill due to my agility as a dancer and a pair of flexible hips.

My memories of skiing in the Sierras are filled with sunlight so bright on fresh powder that kids could play in their tee shirts. I did not experience the sport's main attribute as being a hostile confrontation with cruel weather.

Then, 22 years ago, I moved to the Northeast where I am cold from Halloween to Easter. And where ski conditions are typically grey, damp, and frigid. The notion of choosing to spend long hours outdoors in February flinging oneself down an icy hill through a bitter wind is as appealing to me as getting a root canal without nitrous.

I am not alone. My friend Amy, a native New Englander, recently had her first experience on downhill skis. "I took a lesson and tackled the baby slope and didn't even panic too much," writes Amy from Vermont. "But in no time my fingers froze and my skin was plastered with sweat to the inside of my ski suit." Amy did the only sensible thing and retired to The Lodge for a hot drink in front of a blazing fire, adding without regret, "at least the instructor was cute."

Cute instructors and flaming après-ski beverages. I can go for that.

But consider the price of these delights. The outfit alone – remember it must protect you from life threatening climate – costs, at the very least, several hundred dollars and, for the money, you get an ensemble that makes you look like a pastel fire hydrant. Pile on the expense of boots, skis, lift tickets, and a night at The Lodge for the family and you're looking at a semester's tuition at the state university. Henry David Thoreau said, "Beware of all enterprises that require new clothes." I say, beware of any leisure time activity that requires expensive gear.

Then there is the physical risk. Yes, I do remember the joy of tearing down a slope at 40 miles an hour. But whereas I experienced a dazzling thrill ride at 25, I now imagine the Emergency Room doctor setting my cracked old bones and writing a script for Demerol.

Finally, there is the commute penalty. To get to the slopes means driving on the worst roads in the worst conditions at the most inconvenient time of day to beat the lift traffic. At many resorts you then have to schlep your equipment from the parking lot to the ski lifts, a prospect so odious to the super-rich that some are spending $250,000 in places like Sun Valley just to get prime parking spots feet from the lifts. Not only do I get to be cold, but I get to leave my house and drive an hour-and-a-half to be cold.

I am grateful to be asked each year by my neighborhood crew if I'd like to join them on their weekly Friday night ski jaunts (NIGHT? Are you crazy?). Please keep asking. One of these days I may just get a reckless urge to come along. Perhaps global warming will transform Hunter Mountain into a tropical spa.

February 2005

REGRETS ONLY

RUMOR HAS IT THAT Edith Piaf, on her deathbed, murmured, "I regret everything." I've had days like that.

I regret buying a quart of chocolate fudge brownie ice cream last November. I regret wearing that little red spandex number to my high school reunion. I regret marrying my first husband.

Regret, it seems, is a part of the human condition.

Witness: A three year old child is taking a shower when suddenly a cry of misery alerts me to great danger. As I turn the corner to rescue her, I hear her tiny voice wail piteously to the fates, "WHAT HAVE I DONE?" She stares at the bottle of bubble soap in her hand, up side down, all the soap spilled onto the tub floor. She looks sadly at me and, in that instant, undergoes a critical rite of passage. My daughter experiences her first regret.

But just what is regret? Where does it come from? Why does it plague us so?

Hoping to rid myself of this mental nuisance, I consulted Herr Doktor Neibold Whymegod, the eminent podiatrist and dream analyst.

Here's what the doc told me:

"First, you make zuh decision. I am not talking about zuh snap decision. No no no. Zis is zuh carefully veighed decision. Zis is a decision you can be proud of, sure about, bring to zuh bank. Zuh kind of decision you make after considering every imaginable consequence of every imaginable pro and con of every imaginable option."

"But what," I ask the good doctor, "about the unimaginable?"

"Aha! You have schtruck at zuh very heart of zuh matter," he notes sadly. "However vise your decision, it usually leads to events zat you did not, could not possibly anticipate."

I nod in agreement. Who, for example, could know that the freezer would break down and I'd have to eat the entire quart of Haagen-Dazs myself?

"Zis is zuh root of regret. You vip yourself for being so schtupid," says Dr. Whymegod, "even zough your decision vas made in good faith based on zuh best information available."

"So who IS to blame?" I ask meekly.

"Zat," replies the doctor, "is zuh secret." I lean in closely. "It is all zuh fault of zuh Unimaginable. It is all God's fault."

"Good Lord!" I gasp, "Do you really mean…."

"Yes, Liebchen," he says in a voice suggesting that knowledge, however painful, is salvation. "Ve are schniveling insects barely able to discern a blade of grass in front of our noses. But He knows Everyzing. He sees all zuh pros and cons and consequences in one single effortless vink. No schveat. HE JUST KNOWS!"

I ponder this brilliant insight. So simple, so obvious.

For instance, I knew in my heart of hearts that giving those orange suede platform sandals to the Goodwill in 1983 was the right thing to do. Yet how could I ever know that platforms would come back into style in my lifetime?

But HE KNEW. Of course, He chose not to inform me. Which is okay. That's His business, to share or not to share. Who are we to question the Grand Schemer of Things?

"So, doctor," I ask, "what shall I do?"

"Don't you see?" he says. "You're off zuh hook! Make zuh smart choices and you are still going to screw up. It's not your fault. So, no more regret."

No more regret. I repeat it like a mantra as I leave the doctor's penthouse suite. I have gone to the mountain and the master has spoken: No more regret.

I repeat it as I write the check to the car insurance company. I swear there was enough room to fit my Subaru next to that Harley parked in front of the diner. But how was I to know that the bike's owner thinks the death penalty is too good for anyone who gets so much as smug on his motorcycle? And how was I to know that the jerk is a lawyer?

January 2001

4.
STUFF

RECESSION OR NO RECESSION, GET THE HELL OUT AND SHOP. I, for one, took the morning off work yesterday to devote myself to a higher purpose. Page 94

STURM UND DRANG AT THE DRUGSTORE. I stand in catatonic wonder before a wall of feminine hygiene products. Page 96

LIVE IT UP! Shopping, consumption, wretched excess. Hey, that's what the holidays are all about. Page 98

STUFF. Dumpster diving, hand-me-downs, tag sales, and mother's basement -- you can live quite nicely on other people's leftover stuff. Page 100

THINGS I CAN'T DO WITHOUT. An extra pair of reading glasses, a radio in every room, my black suede dancing shoes, earplugs. What's on your list? Page 103

MY WORST NIGHTMARE. The ordeal of buying a mattress. Page 105

BURY ME IN MY FOUR INCH SPIKE HEEL RED LEATHER SLINGBACK SEX-IN-THE-AFTERNOON SANDALS. I dream of being so rich that I can pay Manolo Blahnik to make a last of MY foot and custom design for me and me alone the most outrageously fun and sexy shoes on the planet. Page 108

FOR GOD, COUNTRY, AND SAM WALTON. In the words of our Great Leader: shop early, shop often. Page 110

THE SHOPPING FOOL. Monica Lewinsky? She was only living out every girl's fantasy of shopping for the most powerful man on the planet. Page 112

WASTE NOT, WANT NOT. My preteen tells me of a hip hop singer who brags that he wears a pair of jockey shorts exactly once before throwing them into the garbage can. Page 114

My Philosophy of Life, plus a few handy tips

RECESSION OR NO RECESSION, GET THE HELL OUT AND SHOP

I, FOR ONE, TOOK the morning off work yesterday to devote myself to a higher purpose. There was a big sale at Macy's and I was there when the doors opened at 9am, clutching my EXTRA 20% OFF BONUS COUPONS. I've been holding off any serious purchases against the day I had a serious income, believing, as I do, the deficit spending is right down there with checking kiting in the morally reprehensible column.

But the world has changed in these past months — General Motors, for goodness sake, is threatening to go belly up -- and I knew I had to readjust my morals accordingly.

So, with my eyeglasses at a jaunty angle and my credit card raised high, I stepped across the threshold of the department store, determined to do my share to resurrect the economy, push the S&P back to its historical summit, and protect the good old U.S. of A. from those Socialists – or whoever.

I noticed a similar steely resolve among my fellow soldierettes – young moms with tots-in-tow, middle-aged women in polyester stretch pants, and blue-haired grandmas waving their EARLY BIRD ADDITIONAL EXTRA PERCENTAGE OFF CREDIT SLIPS. We were a force to be reckoned with and the Macy's sales staff saluted us respectfully as we marched forth.

Stirred by Whitney Houston keening *God Bless America* over the store's loudspeakers, I felt like George S. Patton on a good day as I advanced to the coat department. This was no brassiere and pantie raid. I headed straight into the Big-Ticket battle.

I wanted a fleece coat to replace the black fleece coat that I'd bought five years ago at the same store and had grown to hate [how much black can a girl take in winter without aggravating an intense case of

Seasonal Affective Disorder?] There, against the back wall, arrayed like the cavalry poised for attack, were row upon row of coats all the same style as the one I already owned, and in all the same drab colors as they've had for the past five years. But I was not to be defeated. I bought one anyway.

I moved on to linens where I purchased a set of sheets for my child's bed even though the top and bottom were from two different dye lots. Would Eisenhower have delayed D-Day just because his khaki trousers were a different shade than his shirt?

My shopping addiction unshackled, I bought like a woman possessed. Boots a size too small; sweaters in kindergarten colors I will never wear; horribly expensive gifts for people I don't like.

Then I got lucky. I found some cotton pajamas for my daughter in her size and favorite color! I felt like Washington must have felt at Yorktown, and bought three pairs – two because she needed them, the third for Ben Bernanke.

Running short of time, I began to pick off small items like a precision sniper. A Waterpik plaque remover attachment, a stovetop spoon rest shaped like the Starship Enterprise, an Al Gore For President commemorative candy dish [deeply discounted] – each little purchase a minor victory, but a clean kill.

On my way out of the Mall I passed through Penney's to return two flannel shirts I'd bought for my husband the week before, even though he never wears flannel shirts. I miscalculated his commitment to the cause. Although the clerk mercifully gave me full return credit on my card without comment, I felt shame falling upon our entire kinship group with this act of treason.

To make up for it I bought myself a grey sweatshirt that I don't need and my daughter a winter jacket that, since I love it, she will absolutely refuse to wear.

It was a sacrifice and there will be hell and about $600 to pay later. But what is patriotism if there's no sacrifice involved? No one ever said that fighting the good fight was going to be easy.

Nita Micossi believes that anyone can wear a tin flag on their lapel, but it takes a real patriot to spend above her credit card limit.

December 2008

STURM UND DRANG AT THE DRUGSTORE

So here I am in a large drugstore, looking for a box of Kotex, a product I haven't used since high school. Actually, the proper name of what I want is "sanitary napkin." But when I was a girl the only choice available was manufactured by Kotex, so that's what we called them.

Following a clerk's instructions, I sight the aisle marked "feminine hygiene products" and find, to my utter astonishment, an entire wall of sanitary napkins.

Old familiar Kotex is there, but so are dozens of other brands and all different size boxes and plastic sacks in boudoir hues. Since I stopped paying attention, the generic napkin has been replaced by the "minipad", "maxipad", "extra thin maxi", and "junior maxi", plus "overnights", "light day longs", and "panty shields", all with or without scent, contours, curves, flaps, stay-put tabs, and quilted sides. I'm getting dizzy.

I discretely motion to a young female clerk who is stocking mascara in the next aisle. "I'm looking for something simple. Just an ordinary pad," I plead, "...like a Kotex. You know." She doesn't and replies blankly, "there's a whole wall to choose from."

That, of course, is my problem. That wall of choice. What is a "maxi" and how does it differ (in length? width? thickness? shape? dare, I say, function?) from a "mini"? And what, indeed, is a "panty liner"? Pictures on the back of packages only confound me further. They all look the same.

Now, a maxi sounds reliable. Except do I want a super maxi for "extra heavy flow"? No, don't think so. Nothing that implies fat and bulgy. (Embarrassed memories of a high school sophomore in a tight wool skirt during "that time of the month" float through my confusion.) What say then to a "long thin maxi with wings"? Wings? Is that the in-flight model? And what's this? A "double plus extra long super with wings". (You think I'm making this up?) Surely if I'm going to fly, "double" and "extra" seem like the prudent alternative. But I'm only driving to Boston for the weekend.

Maybe a mini is better. Breezy, unfettered. Perhaps my body will forget it's even menstruating. Look here what it says on the package.... This, however, proves to be a strategic error since descriptions of the super mini and the junior maxi are identical.

I stand there in catatonic wonder, debating the possibilities, calculating the consequences, trying to figure out if 12 minis for $2.95 is a better deal than 10 maxis for $2.59.

I recall the Harvard professor who ran an experiment on his students. He asked them to choose between two careers, let's say architecture versus medicine. After the decision making he measured each student's level of anxiety and found it to be negligible. Then he offered them three alternatives, then four, then five, and so on. After each round, the professor found that his students' discomfort grew, until the kids had so many choices they went berserk and couldn't make any decision at all.

The moral: The more options one has, the greater the number of roads not taken. Thus, the greater the potential for confusion and regret.

In the drugstore I confront a near infinity of choices. I am deeply confused and regretting my decision to abandon tried and true biodegradable, super absorbent, flushable fit-in-your-purse tampons. And I am whipping myself for not being decisive. I feel low, incompetent, defeated by the cunning of the military-industrial-marketing complex. I can just see those smug product development wonks sitting around a table, fiddling with 3,000 chips of latex paint in digitally enhanced ever so slightly different shades of white and devising next season's consumer decision-making nightmare.

Life's basic choices are daunting enough -- what to do for a living, how many children to have, where to throw the wedding reception. Why must we endure existential distress over trivial choices like which breakfast cereal to buy? Little wonder that Americans are foaming at the mouth with nameless anxiety.

I know you're wondering how I resolved the great Kotex dilemma. Simple. I closed my eyes and grabbed -- a package of ultra thin maxis with side gathers, as it turned out -- and went off hunting for the next item on my list: red nail polish. Now there's a concept.

November 1998

My Philosophy of Life, plus a few handy tips

LIVE IT UP

IT'S THE DAY AFTER Thanksgiving and all through the houses not a creature is stirring, not even the mouses. That's because everybody is at the Mall shopping.

According to the TV newscasters department stores across the country opened their doors this morning as early as 3am. "Everybody's trying to make up for the shortened shopping season this year," noted a blond broadcaster, reporting live from a K-Mart where people were waiting in line, in the dark. One store, already filled to the fire department's definition of capacity, made excess shoppers wait outside in the pre-dawn cold for the real early birds to finish their business; as one customer emerged with packages, a replacement shopper was allowed through the door.

Shopping, consumption, wretched excess. Hey, that's what the holidays are all about.

Well, this year we can perform the sacred ritual of spending money we don't have for stuff we don't need in good conscience. James P. Twitchell, an English teacher at the University of Florida, maintains that conspicuous and completely unnecessary consumption is good for us. In his latest tome, "Living It Up: Our Love Affair With Luxury", Jim notes that luxury items once affordable only by the rich -- think bottled spa water, Russian caviar, and more toys than God -- are now available to Everybody. This trend, he argues, is great since it signals a more democratic America.

Instead of one's social place in the community depending on the accidents of race, parentage, and SAT scores, it is now based on what and how much stuff you've got: You are what you own. And constrained only by one's tolerance for debt, a garage mechanic in Hudson can enjoy the same Martha Stewart bed linens, Ralph Lauren leather jacket, and Glenlivet scotch as a pedigreed capitalist like, say, George W.

You can see this democratizing of social status in action at Saks Fifth Avenue in Manhattan. Once the retail temple of the sable coated grand dame, the aisles are now crowded with scruffy parka-wearing nouveau immigrants with kids in tow. Everybody can buy Fendi!

Like the subway, over-indulgence not only levels us but brings us together. What some may call a gluttonous feeding frenzy, a soul-deadening obsession with materialism, shallow compensation for inadequate mother love, Jim Twitchell describes as a "unifying" trend: "We understand each other not by sharing religion, politics, or ideas. We share branded things. We speak the Esperanto of advertising...."

What a vision for world peace! Buying stuff appeals across religious, cultural, and class lines. It gathers us together into the Great Global Village. And it gives us back the sense of dignity and satisfaction we have lost in the workplace, in our forsaken ethnic identities, and in our crumbled and mismatched families. The delights of luxuries recast by the marketing geniuses as "needs" allow us all, wealthy and humble, to feel like we have a piece of the pie. "I don't own a yacht," chirps Jim, "but I'm taking a Princess cruise."

And he's right, you know. I remember watching the Berlin Wall fall in 1989. Hordes of East Berliners flowed through the rubble that was, for 28 years, the barrier between them and freedom of expression, freedom of religion, freedom of assembly. But did they pour into the West to buy a newspaper, go to a church, attend a rally? Ah, no. They all came clutching their marks to buy, buy, buy.

That's all people really want to do. And Jim Twitchell has the guts to say it out loud.

So take your acquisitive lust out of the closet, march right down to the Mall, and buy yourself a little comforting status. 'Tis the season.

December 2002

STUFF

MY SEVEN-YEAR OLD daughter is studying the American pioneers and reading about how children lived on the frontier. When I asked her whether she thought it was better to be a kid then or now, she said without hesitation, "Oh, now."

"And why is that?" I asked.

"Because kids today have more stuff."

Ah, yes. Stuff. My child is barely on the threshold of reason and she has already grasped the essential nature of modern society.

"In the way we live now," says James B. Twitchell, advertising professor at the University of Florida, "you are not what you make. You are what you consume. And outside of that which is found in a few aisles in the grocery and hardware stores, most of what you consume is TOTALLY unnecessary."

I have observed this evolving excess of stuff in our lives for some time and have reached several conclusions.

ONE. YOU CAN LIVE COMFORTABLY ON OTHERS' LEFTOVER STUFF. Years ago, while visiting a friend in San Luis Obispo, I was invited to join an end-of-semester "dumpster diving" expedition. It was June and the students had just abandoned their apartment complexes near the University. We drove around in a pickup truck and scavenged through the building dumpsters.

I was squeamish at first, imagining filthy, rat-infested garbage cans. But our leaders knew exactly where the affluent kids lived and how they lived -- tidy enough, but wasteful. Eager to get to wherever summer vacation was, they had hastily dumped unopened reams of paper, unboxed pairs of new sneakers, cases of canned tuna, radios, records, typewriters, bookcases, bed linens, clothes, and jewelry. Some had opened their kitchen cabinets and unloaded into large clear plastic bags, bottles, cans, and boxes of food -- most of it still sealed.

A carpenter among us rejoiced at the quantity of lumber he found -- college students make bookcases out of lumber and cinder blocks -- a budding poet grabbed a nearly new typewriter, and a single mother pounced on the food. I was a little timid, until I discovered a lovely straw hat still in its I. Magnin hatbox.

We sneer at the urban homeless scavenging through nasty looking trash bins. But if we turned them loose on curbside refuse in a flush suburb once a month, why, we'd help balance out the inequities of too little and too much all at once!

TWO. SIT STILL AND STUFF WILL COME. Twenty years ago, returning from a year abroad, I stepped off a plane in Boston with one suitcase and an Olivetti portable. I knew a guy in the city who helped get me a room in a house and a mattress to sleep on.

By the time I left Boston seven years later I had a house full of stuff including a dining table, bed, two leather lounge chairs and an ottoman, a maple dresser and bookcase, a TV set, computer, and stereo, and enough kitchen gear to equip a CIA graduate. Except for my linens I had bought nothing.

This has happened to me enough times to qualify as a rule of capitalist over-consumption: People buy new stuff so often that there is a never-ending flow of barely used stuff out there. All you have to do to get it, is to stay in one place long enough and make a few friends.

THREE. BE CAREFUL, STUFF CAN OWN YOU. If "you are what you own" as Jim Twitchell says, then if you lose what you own, are you nothing?

Most of us don't want to take that chance. So we spend much time, money, and emotional capital to protect our stuff: we house it, store it, temperature-control the environment in which it sits, insure it, put alarm systems around it, and hire sitters to watch over it when we go away. We sometimes even risk our lives to protect it.

And we mourn its loss like a dear friend. When the United States Postal Service carelessly destroyed a box that contained 25 years worth of my published work, I felt like a part of me had died.

Now, I like to think that should I ever lose ALL my stuff, I will feel like the poet who uttered: "Now that my house has burned down, I have a better view of the moon." But I doubt it.

FOUR. STILL, YOU CAN WEAKEN THE POWER OF STUFF. We humans probably have an acquisition gene in there somewhere. But we also have a primeval impulse to keep our kit bag light -- for the quick getaway. So I find it good for both my soul and my walk-in closet to periodically divest myself of a quantity of stuff.

Frequently moving is the best way to do this. Second best is to set up a grown child in her own apartment and furnish it with your overstock (my mother frequently used this strategy).

Our annual village-wide yard sale is a good idea, but I find that I use the money I make selling stuff, to buy other stuff from my neighbors. If all else fails, I recommend a crude but effective way to get rid of all that dust-collecting stuff: invite a half-dozen four-year-old boys into your home and leave them unattended for an afternoon.

March 2003

THINGS I CAN'T DO WITHOUT

SCANNING AN ONLINE MAGAZINE the other day I came across the answer a teen starlet gave to a reporter's question: what five things can't you do without?

Interesting question, I thought. Putting aside the basic necessities of food, shelter, and clothing, and the obvious blessings like love and music and the soft of a child's ear, I sat at my desk and pondered.

My desk is covered with jars, bottles, tins, cups, baskets, boxes, and files filled with stuff I think I need. It sits in a small room crowded with filing cabinets, computer equipment, paper supplies, floor-to-ceiling bookcases overflowing with books, and a lifetime's worth of photos and keepsakes. My office is only one of seven rooms in this house and each one of them is full of stuff.

But what can't I live without?

My first thought is Reading Glasses. All of those fine books scattered about in every single room of this house are worthless without my reading glasses. Remember that chilling Twilight Zone episode where a middle-aged misanthrope finds himself, the sole survivor of a nuclear holocaust, in a bunker surrounded by the greatest books of civilization. Not regretting the loss of humanity for a nanosecond, he revels in his future among the books he loves. But as he surveys his treasure, the man stumbles, his eye glasses fall off his nose, and he proceeds to crush them underfoot. The poor fellow's paradise is sud-denly transformed into a mocking hell.... No, reading glasses (with a backup pair) are definitely on the list.

Then there is the Comfortable Pillow. I can't fall asleep on those grim foam rubber things that hotels favor, and genuine feather pillows with just the right amount of stuffing are hard to come by. Once, when I was visiting my brother Jim in Chicago, I had such a blissful nap on his pillow that I begged it off him and rushed down to a department store, before he could change his mind, to buy him the finest replacement money could buy.... I travel with my pillow, which is a clue that this should definitely be on the list.

My husband's snoring puts my teeth on edge as I lie awake trying to think of other absolutely must-haves. To block out his wheezing I put in my earplugs and realize – epiphany! – Earplugs are essential to my day-to-day wellbeing. There is always a pair in my purse for planes, trains, and noisy malls. Last Sunday, for instance, I survived the deafening din of an indoor swim meet by stuffing my ears. Smile a lot and nobody will suspect.

What about electronic devices, you say? We have one 22 year old TV in our house and eight radios including one in the shower and one on the front porch (and not counting the car). When I lived in Northern Israel my prized possession was a little portable receiver that hooked me into the world via the Voice of America, the BBC, and a pirate station in Lebanon's Beka'a Valley. When I recently stayed in a fancy Saratoga Springs hotel, they provided me with a TV, alarm clock, ironing board, hair dryer, and minibar, but I had to bribe housekeeping to score me a radio. I guess it's safe to say that, for me, life without a Radio would be grim indeed.

So I'm down to number five. A Swiss Army knife? A typewriter? My dictionary? Dental floss? If there's room in the get away car.... But if I only get one more pick I have to go with my black suede platform dancing shoes. A girl has to be ready to party anytime, anywhere, doncha think?

By the way, our teen starlit picked her CD-player, Palm pilot, plasma TV, cell phone, and dog.

March 2005

MY WORST NIGHTMARE

OUR NEW MATTRESS WAS delivered four weeks ago. Shortly after, I started to have back pains. Last week the store replaced this mattress which, it turned out, was not the one we ordered in the store. Every night since the arrival of the "new" new mattress, however, I have had insomnia. This might just be a jolly coincidence, but it does not reflect kindly on the mattresses in question.

My present misery however is piddling compared to the process that preceded it. As one Elizabeth Razzi wrote in an article on shopping for mattresses published in Kiplinger's Magazine two years ago: "The worst nightmare you have on your new mattress may be reliving the ordeal of buying it."

It started 16 years. The first time I went to the apartment of the man who I later married, he complained of his mattress and declared that it was time to replace it. At first I thought this might be a ploy to get me to stretch out on his bed (men have used odder seduction tactics). But when I eventually did try it (and, no, I won't tell you how soon was "even- tually") I found he was right. His old thing was not as firm and taut as the one I had in my own bedroom (the mattress, the mattress).

Still it took ten years and a marriage certificate for us to finally get motivated to go out and shop for a replacement. We soon became frustrated and wandered off to the sofa department. Then I got pregnant, got sciatica, and got too busy to shop for anything.

Six years passed, and my husband's nightly wheezing attacks in bed convinced us that we had to bite the bullet and acquire a new mattress no matter what it took.

The first thing it took was two months on the Internet. "If you think shopping for a car is an ordeal," began an article posted on ConsumerReports.org, "wait until the next time you shop for a mattress." It is, added another bedding expert at consumersearch.com "one of the most disorienting experiences you can have." Still we slogged on.

We downloaded pages on the science of coil count and amount. We investigated the current lexicon of upholstery which spans a dazzling array of options including "ultra firm," "firm," "plush," "super-plush," and something called "pillow-top." We scoured the ads for what we came to see as the Holy Grail of mattress buying: the "comfort guarantee" which allows you to actually sleep on a mattress for 30 days to determine whether or not you like it.

All the major brands, we soon found, have several lines and up to a half dozen choices in each line, and are marketed under as many different names as there are retail outlets. We quickly experienced the promised disorientation and chose to follow the sage advice of one Internet columnist and forget comparison-shopping. We threw in our sorry lot with one of the largest department store chains in the area. At least we knew where to find them if something went wrong.

Narrowing ourselves down, however, didn't spare us from the agony of choice. The store had 30 or 40 mattresses on display. George (whose name has been changed to protect me from a lawsuit) invited us to "lie down" and try out each and every one of them.

The Stearns and Foster was the safe luxury-brand choice, but it felt too darn hard. I liked the Spring Air, but the "pillow top" model was too squishy, the "firm" was unyielding, and they didn't have the intermediate "plush" on the floor for me to sample.

My husband liked the Simmons, but I was suspicious of the product's terry cloth ticking. I spend a princely sum to buy my husband, he of the tender skin, 300-count Egyptian cotton sheets and here was George trying to convince me that sleeping on a beach towel is a good idea.

But after two weary hours lying now here, now there, and back again, I cave and let my husband have his terry cloth-covered Simmons. Testing mattresses is like sampling perfumes -- you quickly experience sensory overload. I was 90 minutes past the fatigue threshold and suspecting that most mattresses get sold when people reach the point where they just don't care anymore and want the whole business to end.

Alas, the business did not end when I handed George my charge card. Three weeks later, a mattress ensemble was delivered and assembled in my bedroom. My seven-inch thick mattress was replaced with a 15-inch mattress that rendered my inventory of bed linens suddenly obsolete. I had to climb onto a stool to get into the thing and, when I did, I sunk into what felt like a vat of marshmallows. George had inadvertently sent us the ultra soft "pillow-top" rather than the not quite so plushy "plush."

I agreed to give it a try. But after a week of backaches and the odd sensation of itching (was I imagining it or did I actually feel that terry cloth through the mattress pad and sheets?) I told George to ship us the Spring Air.

He complied. But the mattress that was swapped out felt like Granny's old cotton-stuffed daybed. "Nothing in the store felt like this!" I wailed, recalling another Internet warning that "the floor sample in the showroom could be quite different from the mattress that arrives at your door."

Ever patient George offered to send us a third alternative for a 30-day test drive. But my husband and I have already decided that no matter what it feels like it's a keeper. And, even though the American Chiropractic Association advises consumers to buy a new one every ten years, we have vowed that this will be the last mattress we will ever buy in this lifetime.

June 2002

My Philosophy of Life, plus a few handy tips

BURY ME IN MY FOUR-INCH SPIKE HEEL RED LEATHER SLINGBACK SEX-IN-THE-AFTERNOON SANDALS

WHEN IT COMES TO shoes, my sister-in-law Dolly is my idol. Not only can she never say no to a rhinestone-encrusted gold espadrille or a dyed lizard cowboy boot or a pink suede wedgie, but she has never tossed out a pair of shoes in her life. And since she is into her eighth decade of shoe shopping, that's a closet full. Just when I think I've seen the whole repertoire, she dazzles me with vintage 1940s navy and white spectator pumps or a pair of silver strappies that Marilyn Monroe might have worn in Gentlemen Prefer Blonds.

What's more, the dame still has fabulous gams and, to display them to best advantage, wears only serious heels, the higher and thinner the better. There are no flats or, god save us, sneakers in Dolly's collection.

One of our favorite pastimes together is to prowl the deeply discounted shoe sale racks. Once in a great while I'll find a treasure, but Dolly never leaves a shoe sale empty-handed. Never.

So naturally I think of her as I cross the threshold of the DSW shoe emporium at the Galleria Mall in Poughkeepsie. My heart flutters as I scout a display floor the size of a football field. Two-sided chest-high racks of shoes ripple out in every direction. Black patent leather peep toes to the right of me. Bronze metallic t-straps to the left of me. Turquoise water snake pumps with pointy toes out-to-there straight ahead. I am dizzy. I am gasping for breath.

Now, for the guys reading this, you should know that, as far as women are concerned, shoes are not just something to walk in. Shoes are the primal expression of a woman's deepest fantasies. Shoes are a relief from the tedium of daily life. Shoes are a peephole into the feminine mystique. Shoes are therapy. There's nothing like a new pair of raspberry mules in shantung silk to perk up my spirits on a gloomy March day.

My options, however, have shrunk over the years. First it was the shoe width. Although my heel remains narrow and trim, the widest part of my sole – from years of wearing flip flops? from all those barefoot summers? from pregnancy? -- has spread out to the span of an air craft carrier. And the most alluring shoes Never come in air craft carrier widths. Madam, see the orthopedic clogs in aisle nine.

Then came back trouble and the crushing discovery that if I wear a heel higher than 1-1/2" I can count on three weeks in traction. Like Dolly I never wear flats and at five-feet-and-shrinking I've always counted on that generously stacked heel to make sure that when I belly up to the bar, the barmaid can see me.

I did find a temporary solution to both of these limitations with a glamorous version of the platform sandal. But since I got the vertigo, wearing platforms is a death wish.

As I walk the aisles at DSW I feel like an impotent cowboy in a whore house. Surrounded on every side by shoes too high, too low, too narrow. All out of reach except for those too grotesque for words, proving once again that ancient Fashion Law: if the shoe fits, it's ugly.

Frustrated, I go home and pay a wistful visit to the shoes in my closet that I will never again be able to wear. There're those stunning champagne satin stiletto heel sandals I wore at my wedding; the taupe calfskin pumps with basket weave vamps that carried me into many a corporate boardroom; the camel suede chunky heel sling backs I bought in Rome; the open-toed four-inch green snakeskin slides I loved so much that I bought another pair in lemon yellow.

I keep them in the feeble hope that my eleven year old daughter, who's already a half size away from fitting into those wedding shoes, will one day swoon over them as I do.

And I dream of being so rich that I can pay Manolo Blahnik to make a last of MY foot and custom design for me and me alone the most outrageously fun and sexy shoes on the planet.

In the meantime, I wear over-sized boots in the winter and thongs in the summer, and avoid all occasions that require pumps.

In the meantime, I watch reruns of Carrie Bradshaw's closet for vicarious thrills.

In the meantime, I call Dolly and book a shoe shopping safari to the Westchester Mall.

May 2007

My Philosophy of Life, plus a few handy tips

FOR GOD, COUNTRY, AND SAM WALTON

I TOOK THE MORNING off work yesterday to devote myself to a higher purpose. I went shopping. There was a big sale at Filene's and I was there when the doors opened at 9am, clutching my EXTRA 20% OFF BONUS COUPONS. I've been holding off any serious purchases against the day I had a serious income, believing, as I do, the deficit spending is right down there with checking kiting in the morally reprehensible column.

But the world has changed in the past two months and I knew I had to adjust my morals accordingly. Had not our Glorious Leader admonished us to get out there on the retail front lines and kick some butt?

So, with my eyeglasses at a jaunty angle and my credit card raised high, I stepped across the threshold of the department store, determined to do my share to resurrect the economy, push the S&P back to its historical summit, and protect the good old U.S. of A. from those Commies – or whoever.

I noticed a similar steely resolve among my fellow soldierettes – young moms with tots-in-tow, middle-aged women in polyester stretch pants, and blue-haired grandmas waving their EARLY BIRD ADDITIONAL EXTRA PERCENTAGE OFF CREDIT SLIPS. We were a force to be reckoned with and the Filene's sales staff saluted us respectfully as we marched forth.

Stirred by Whitney Houston keening God Bless America over the store's loudspeakers, I felt like George S. Patton on a good day as I advanced to the coat department. This was no brassiere and pantie raid. I headed straight into the Big-Ticket battle.

I wanted a fleece coat to replace the black fleece coat that I'd bought three years ago at the same store and had grown to hate [how much black can a girl take in winter without aggravating an intense case of Seasonal Affective Disorder?] There, against the back wall, arrayed like the cavalry poised for attack, were row upon row of coats all the same style as the one I already owned, all the same drab colors as they've had for the past five years. But I was not to be defeated. I bought one anyway.

I moved on to linens where I purchased a set of sheets for my child's bed even though the top and bottom were from two different dye lots. Would Eisenhower have delayed D-Day just because his khaki trousers were a different shade than his shirt?

My shopping addiction unshackled, I bought like a mad woman. Boots a size too small; sweaters in kindergarten colors I will never wear; horribly expensive gifts for people I don't like.

Then I got lucky. I found some cotton pajamas for my daughter in her size and favorite color! I felt like Washington must have felt at Yorktown, and bought three pairs – two because she needed them, the third for Alan Greenspan.

Running short of time, I began to pick off small items like a precision sniper. A Waterpik plaque remover attachment, a stovetop spoon rest shaped like the Starship Enterprise, an Al Gore For President commemorative candy dish [deeply discounted] – each little purchase a minor victory, but a clean kill.

On my way out of the Mall I passed through Penney's to return two flannel shirts I'd bought for my husband the week before, even though he never wears flannel shirts. I miscalculated his commitment to the cause. Although the clerk mercifully gave me full return credit on my card without comment, I felt shame falling upon our entire kinship group with this act of treason.

To make up for it I bought myself a grey sweatshirt that I don't need and my daughter a winter jacket that, since I love it, she will absolutely refuse to wear.

It was a sacrifice and there will be hell and about $500 to pay later. But what is patriotism if there's no sacrifice involved? No one ever said that fighting this war was going to be easy.

November 2001

THE SHOPPING FOOL

BY THE TIME THESE words are published Bill Clinton will have been banished from office -- or not. Al Gore will be secretly gloating over his astonishing good luck -- or not. And Hillary will have assumed her maiden name -- or not.

Still, I cannot let this political carnival roll out of town without adding my own invaluable insights into what really happened. No, I don't mean did He lie or not lie, but whether there was anything to lie about. I mean, did Bill and Monica really Have Sex in ANY shape or form -- according to ANYBODY'S definition of sex?

Consider: a recent newspaper poll notes that 97% of American females would rather shop than have sex. Gosh, I know I sure would. So who are the other 3%? And is Monica really one of them? I for one do not think Monica was particularly into the sex thing, no matter what that Tripp woman would have us believe. She may have "admitted" stuff, but boys aren't the only ones who exaggerate their conquests.

No. Miss Lewinsky definitely had other things on her mind. How do I know? It just so happens that and I are pals and that I have a few tapes of my own from phone conversations between old Mon' and me. (Lest you think I'm a snoopy slime bucket like Linda Tripp, let me just say right here and now that we journalists routinely record our phone chats -- it's a well-known journalist thing.)

Take, for example, a little back and forth that Monica and I had the day after one of her so-called "encounters" with Mr. C in a small room off the oval office:

"MONICA: You'll never guess what he said when I gave him the blue tie with the tiny orange Elmos I picked up at Bloomingdale's.

ME: I'm all ears.

MONICA: 'Golly, Monica, you've got the keenest eye for ties of any woman I have ever met.' And when I told him it was on sale at 40% off he was flabbergasted! He said that the General Accounting Office needed someone with my kind of shopping savvy.

ME: But did he know that you got an additional 15% rebate for buying 12 of the ties?

MONICA: Well, I didn't wanna brag or anything, but I did mention that Bloomies has a deep discount policy for quantity purchases.

ME: Was he impressed?

MONICA: Impressed?! He told me that come Christmas he was going to let me do all the gift shopping for the office staff.

ME: Wow.

MONICA: And [on the tape, she is breathless at this point] he asked me if I could find something special within his price range for Mrs. Clinton's birthday. Imagine! I get to buy for the First Lady. I feel like I've died and gone to heaven."

Still not convinced? According to Master Starr's very own tell-all report, Monica bought Mr. C at least 30 items during their 16 month long so-called "affair." (Compare THAT with the measly ten alleged "sexual encounters" that supposedly happened during the same time period.)

Thirty gifts. Think about it. That's one tchotchke every other week. And we're not just talking here about those goofy things like the Elmo tie and the mug emblazoned "Santa Monica" (that girl can be such a hoot!) She went in for antiques and fine silver objets d'art. It took time and effort to find this kind of stuff on an intern's salary. But that's Monica for you -- always going the distance when it comes to shopping.

Nookie? Naa. Monica just wanted the opportunity to shop for the most powerful man on the planet. Who wouldn't? Believe me, I know the girl and she would rather fry her American Express card at Loehmann's than muss up her Victoria's Secret lace brassiere (three for the price of two) with any guy.

Notice that green silk blouse that Hillary wore at Hilton Head last month? That was one of Monica's coups -- a Christmas close-out at Saks.

February 1999

My Philosophy of Life, plus a few handy tips

WASTE NOT, WANT NOT

STROLLING AROUND A LOCAL town main street last week, I passed a drycleaners, hardware store, consignment shop, and barber, a cobbler, seamstress, watch repair, and lamp rewiring operation. You'll never find a cobbler at the Mall.

Remember when shoes were resoled until the top seams split? When socks with holes were mended, toasters with faulty switches were fixed, and buttons were reattached whenever they fell off?

Today, shoes are tossed when the lights in the heel no longer flash, socks with pin holes are history, replacement parts are no longer made for small appliances, and nobody knows how to sew on a button anyway. My preteen tells me of a hip hop singer who brags that he wears a pair of jockey shorts exactly once before throwing them into the garbage can. So much for the solid waste crisis.

It wasn't all that long ago people thought it was prudent to take care of what they had... because you never know. What happened?

Well, it's a lot easier to buy something new than to repair and maintain what you've got. Rich folks know this, which is why the Park Avenue ladies purchase new fashions every season and their husbands flip the 2007 Mercedes for a 2008 model. Buy because you can, not because you need, silly. It's the religion that keeps capitalism chugging along. And the Mall, that cathedral of consumption, has brought the holy word to the rest of us.

"Consume & Waste" is not just for Donald Trump anymore. Everyone can do their fair share of spending what they don't have on what they don't need. And the retailers of the world have made this possible by coaxing us with the irresistible lure of Cheap Stuff. The Mall has nothing to do with variety and choice; it's all about finding the store with the cheapest Puma Speed Cat sneakers.

To make sure that all of us eager pilgrims can have a lot of Cheap Stuff under the Christmas tree, Toys-R-Us, Nike, Best Buy, Target, Sears, and the rest of the gang of global peddlers have relocated manufacturing to Occupied Tibet where the minimum wage is fifteen cents an hour and nobody watches what goes into the sausage.

There are a few hidden costs to this system of democratic abbondanza. Like, we have to give up all those nice manufacturing jobs with the health benefits, we're forced to go to work for Starbucks, and we get to buy radioactive jewelry, lead poisoned toys, and toothpaste laced with anti-freeze.

And unless you can afford to outbid Sarah Jessica Parker for a pair of handmade Italian sandals, quality is a thing of the past. With electronic gizmos designed to break down in 13 months and sweaters unraveling after three machine washings, you have to keep buying new stuff. But that's part of the plan, dontcha know.

I once lived on a Greek island for a long summer and rented a two-room cinder-block hut from one of the local olive growers. Demetrius would come by from time to time to fix a pipe or mend the roof. He never brought tools or supplies, but, eying the property, always found a piece of cord, a yard of lumber, stray nails, and a rock to pound things into place. Demetrius never threw anything away and eventually he found a use for every scrap of material, every leftover.

We Americans, on the other hand, throw away about one ton of old stuff per person per year to make room for the new stuff we buy. But as we wade through the big holiday shopping season this year, I say: rethink this madness! Refuse to buy stuff you don't need with money you don't have. Tell the consumption machine to go to hell. And take a walk down Main Street where the tailor will put new elastic in your winter jacket, the cobbler will resole your boots, the electrician will rewire the lamp, and the hardware store will sell you some stain to refinish your mother's sideboard. Who needs a new one, already?

December 2007

5.
KEEP THE RED SOCKS AWAY FROM THE YELLOW TOWELS: LESSONS IN DOMESTICITY

READ MY LISTS. A compulsive list maker confesses all. Page 117

THE GOOD LIFE. Who needs two weeks in Mexico in February when they can have a beautiful new stainless steel indirect-fired water heater. Page 120

START THE NEW MILLENIUM RIGHT. With a clean, uncluttered living space you will achieve peace, prosperity, and a lower cholesterol count. Page 122

A PENNY SAVED. If American Airlines can save $440,000 a year by getting rid of the olive in the salad, then surely I can save a bundle by cutting out some domestic extravagance, can't I? Page 125

THE OLYMPICS. If the organizers want over-the-top TV ratings they'll add "moms competing in domestic events" to the program. Page 127

KEEP THE RED SOCKS AWAY FROM THE YELLOW TOWELS. No matter how well you teach a kid to do the laundry, one day she will open the washing machine to find – oh, the horror – all of her pants and sweatshirts covered with tiny flecks of white tissue. Page 129

PLAN B. A grim looking doctor on TV says that water, batteries, a portable radio, and an M-16 assault rifle won't be enough if the avian bird flu jumps the border. Gotta stock the basement with a month's supply of food just in case half the truckers in the country get the plague and the food chain goes bust. Page 131

GARDEN PARTY. Plant nursery owners are endlessly optimistic and supportive of experimentation. Full sun required? Give it a try in partial shade! Best to plant in early spring? I put things in the ground all through the heat of the summer! Deer resistant? Never had that problem! Page 133

EMPOWERMENT OVERLOAD. So now we do our own taxes on the computer, cater our own affairs, handle our own divorce paperwork, and research the epidemiology of Lyme Disease online. What began as a sensible take-charge attitude has become a self-inflicted wound.... Enough already! Page 136

Nita Micossi

READ MY LISTS

YOU WANT TO KNOW my most private self? Then read my lists. They reveal my hopes, record my delights, document my commitments, and expose my anxieties.

Start with the fact that I don't have a single list but many, yeh many, lists. I have a list of what to do today, what to do this coming weekend, and what to get done before I leave town in four weeks.

I have a Master List for the year 2001 just as I did for 2000. In fact, the 2001 list looks a lot like the 2000 list since I generally only get two or three things from my Master List done each year. That's a good year.

I misplaced my To-Do-Before-I-Die list but it doesn't matter. The tasks on this list – such as "hire a calligrapher to do a really neat version of the family tree I made with my cousin Vitaliano in Lucca in 1993" -- don't ever get urgent enough to make it onto a more timely list where they might possibly get my attention.

The above lists cover only me and my domestic, social, and financial chores. My business has its own set of lists including deadline schedules, detailed assignment checklists, and an office supplies inventory.

Then there are the Special Events lists:

- my child's vaccination timetable alert
- my annual All-Girl Oscar Party & Potluck invite list, and
- the 100 best Rock'n'Roll 45s of All Time list that I compiled with my best friend Maddy in 1989 to properly stock the jukebox we had rented for my husband's 50th birthday party.

You get the idea. Some people do scuba diving. Some do community theater. I do lists.

Look at my simple This Weekend To Do list. Revealed is a veritable rainbow of the roles I have been called upon to play in this life:

1. take bi-annual pix of Sofi [adoring mother]
2. wrap six birthday gifts [adoring mother of a five year old socialite]
3. call Bob B. re: architectural walking tour of the village [responsible member of the village master plan committee]
4. call Lois G. re: next month's Cafeteria Helpers' Schedule [responsible member of the PTA]
5. order the "Clint Eastwood Rules" tee shirt for my husband's birthday next week [adoring wife with a sense of humor]
6. call Ma

It's a window on my very soul. But then maybe you don't want to see my very soul.

My favorite lists are the purely entertaining ones. I have, for example, a list of the books I've most enjoyed reading over the years. I keep this one in case anyone ever asks. I was, in fact, once interviewed for a Sunday supplement featurette in the Boston Herald about very minor local celebrities. We were asked what three books we would take to a desert island. My list would have come in handy then.

I also have a list of my 100 favorite comedy movies of all time. I made it in response to the Best 20th Century Films list put out by the American Film Institute last year, which did not include nearly enough comedies to my way of thinking.

I have a list of all the songs I am prepared to sing in a public place plus the key in which I sing each one.

I have annotated clothes packing lists from past vacations including one for a week in New Orleans in June (tip: go for the nearly naked) and one for two weeks in Northern Italy in November (tip: never again bother with a jogging outfit).

I have an exhaustive toiletry list I made years ago when women wore white gloves and carried small, hard shell vanity cases onto airplanes. It has become a treasured keepsake of a vanished world in which women on the move carried shower caps and sanitary napkin belts.

I have a list on the frig for my husband: re-glue the wallpaper in the bathroom, attach the baseboard molding in the TV room, reinforce the cast iron pot holder over the kitchen table – real guy things. My Pop was a handyman who could do everything and the list my mother left for him taped to the frig made sure he did.

My own husband needs two people to steady the ladder while he changes a light bulb. So I recently changed the title on the frig list from "Daddy: To Do" to "Carpenter: To Do" – in the hope-springs-eternal that I'll ever find a fabulous, fast-working, neat and clean, $10 per hour carpenter who's available for a week in March.

I enjoy most whatever list I am working on at the moment. It gives me a sense of calm and collection in the face of cosmic entropy to sit at my desk and classify, collate, and triage my life's activities into small manageable chunks. It gives me indescribable pleasure to cross a completed task off a list.

For seven straight years I had "refinish Grandma's Singer sewing machine" on my annual Master List. The day I was able to cross that one off is right up there on my list of Joyful Life Passages with the birth of my first child.

February 2001

THE GOOD LIFE

NO WINTER HOLIDAY IN Mexico this year, caballeros. Nope. We've gone and done the sensible thing instead and put down our airfare on a brand new fire engine red emergency backup generator. We even upgraded to the model with the electric starter so that those of us with impaired upper body strength can rope that buckaroo in a snowstorm. Of course, it meant throwing in the cost of a week's lodging at my favorite hibiscus-covered posada in Veracruz.

And Christmas? None of that tasteless consumer over-indulgence in gift buying for our family this year. We did Christmas in July and bought ourselves a beautiful stainless steel indirect-fired water heater. This baby not only has the lowest pressure drop in the industry but it qualifies as a capital improvement with substantial tax benefits.

The child whined but I assured her that a nice three foot evergreen tree covered with the lights left over from Daddy's let's-make-an-outdoor-disco project would be all we needed for the happiest of holidays – that and lots of dark rum. (Four-year-olds can be so whiney.)

I thought I could make it up a bit to the child with a day trip to Manhattan and tickets to Radio City Music Hall. But that pesky leak in the basement turned out to be from a crack in the downstairs commode. The cost of replacing this essential domestic item exactly equaled two tickets to see the Rockettes.

Then there was my plan to throw an end-of-the-millenium New Year's Eve blowout for the neighbors. In fact, I had already concocted a fabulous continental buffet menu, booked a jazz quartet, and ordered two cases of very expensive French champagne. But when I went to pick up my car last month at the body shop (in a fit of anal retention I'd had one barely rusted fender replaced), Sandy told me that I needed two front tires. Sure enough, they were worn down to the metal.

When I retrieved the car at Mavis I was told that the brake shoes and ball joints were in life-threatening condition. And when I went to collect my now life-affirming vehicle at the shop I was handed the sad news that the right front axle and timing belt were about to go. If I dared to face winter with the car in this condition my mechanic refused to have it on his conscience.

Two days after I picked up a car that, I was assured, would run longer than Strom Thurmond, that slime bucket of steel and glass stopped dead in the middle of Pitcher Lane. It was the radiator. After getting my VISA bill for $1,387.63 I called the liquor store and told them to cancel all but two bottles of the French champagne. I figured my husband and I would each need one of our own.

But I'm not complaining. Our New Year promises to begin with a bang. My cousin Claire who lives in Northern Italy just sent me an e-mail announcing that, sometime during the first week of January, she, her husband, and their three-year old triplets (yes, dear, she said triplets) would be stopping by for a visit on their way home from a trip to Hawaii. "If that's okay with you?" Okay?? Three tots at the tail end of a 24-day vacation during which they will have endured eleven time zone changes. Why not!

I felt obliged to mention to Cousin Claire that they will be traveling during the peak of Y2K whimsy and that we often get heaps of snow in January. But my cousin does not seem the least bit perturbed. Why should I? Besides, no matter what happens, I know that we've got a generator to keep the furnace running, plenty of hot water, a working flush toilet, and a bionic car.

Who needs Mexico in the dead of winter, anyway?

November 1999

START THE NEW MILLENIUM RIGHT

THANK GOD, WE MADE it! If you are reading this newspaper then civilization as we know it did not come to an end at the stroke of midnight January 1, 2000 and the lights are still on.

This, of course, may prove to be a mixed blessing. Some of us were secretly hoping that the slate would be wiped clean and we'd have another shot at evolution. Maybe the second time around we'd evolve into truly intelligent creatures who do not believe that the high point of aesthetic achievement is the Taj Mahal in Las Vegas.

But it appears that we are stuck with civilization as we know it and each other.

Still, I think we should take this opportunity to start fresh on as many fronts as we can. And I am here to help you decide what to save and cherish, and what to toss in the garbage.

Have courage. This will not be easy.

Let's start with the bathroom. It is time to chuck those prescription drugs from 1987. They will not come back into style. And the pull-up diapers. I know you want to save them for your grandchildren, but since your own daughter is only 4 ½ it's pretty clear that the technology will have improved immensely by the time the grandkiddies come along. In fact, with all this genetic engineering, the children of the future will probably be born already toilet trained.

You can also dispose of the expensive bath salts that your sister gave you for Christmas two years ago. As long as persons under voting age are living in the same house, you should not expect to have time to take a leisurely bath.

You can, however, hang onto the Sally Hansen facial hair crème bleach. Now that you've reached a "certain age", shaving, plucking, bleaching, and home hair-coloring will occupy what little free time you do have before the school bus rolls up at 3:30pm – and that goes equally for guys and gals.

On to the bedroom... The Sonny & Cher poster and the mirror over the bed have got to go. It's also time to get rid of those ratty old red silk bed sheets. I don't care if you are sentimentally attached. The whole lot are bad feng shui, which explains why your bedmate has a perpetual PMS headache and/or chronic colonic dysfunction. If you want your 20th century relationship to survive into the 21st century you will do as I say and go directly to the nearest Bed'n'Bath for something in a deep plum percale.

Now the office is especially difficult. You never know when the economy will once again demand full charge manual bookkeepers. But since it probably won't be in your lifetime, I suggest that you let go of the heavy stock double entry charge sheets – they are strictly museum pieces at this point, although no museum wants them either. Make a box for the local library and throw in your 1972 edition of the Statistical Abstracts of the United States, high school world atlas, collection of everything ever written by Carlos Castaneda, and that eight year old Writer's Market – none of those magazines are in business anymore. If the library doesn't want them, which is likely the case, then make a trip to the recycling center. Don't forget to include all the software that was ever written on floppy diskettes plus their manuals. No one, not even the illiterate peasants of Turkmenistan, wants to see that stuff.

You can keep your old dictionaries but only if you are a professional writer or a Scrabble grand master. Give up your college course notebooks – the Periodic Table and the animal and plant phyla can, by now, I assume, be found on the Internet.

Save the fountain pens. Those, I promise, will be worth something one day.

If you have managed to survive this far, the kitchen will be a snap. Anything green that is not a vegetable or mint jelly goes. Any cleaning agent that was opened in the 20th century goes. Any paper plates not sealed in their original packaging go. If you cannot remember the last time you used the bottled steak sauce – toss it.

Keep the family photo albums, your vinyl records, Grandmother's pearls, and your collection of everything ever written by Mark Twain. Keep them together on the ground floor near a window in case of a fire so you can throw them out to safety.

Other than these few treasures get rid of everything else you don't use regularly.

Start the New Millenium with a clean, uncluttered living space and you will achieve peace, prosperity, and a lower cholesterol count. You will also be a better person than I am.

January 2000

A PENNY SAVED

IN 1987 AMERICAN AIRLINES reportedly saved $440,000 by eliminating one olive from each salad served in first class. Think of it! $440,000 by getting rid of one lousy olive. It gets me wondering about what simple economies in my own life might be turned into a pile of ready cash.

Take toilet paper. My husband insists on buying 2-ply toilet paper. (I confess that I never realized that there even were different "plies" until I met him.) Using my slide rule I figure that 2-ply costs 60% more than 1-ply on a per sheet basis. We could potentially save an average of 4 cents per swipe (given a conservative five sheet usage formula) which amounts to... calculating, calculating, calculating.... $2,628 per decade! Simply by switching to the single-ply alternative.

But, would we not use twice as much toilet paper to make up for the flimsiness of the single sheet? In which case we'd end up spending 24% more on toilet paper in the long run. Besides, any man who knows the difference between plies will surely settle for nothing less than maximum cush. Oh, well.

There are always the cherries in the pineapple upside-down cake. My mother taught me to put a whole plump red cherry into the center of each pineapple slice that lies in that caramel bath of brown sugar and melted butter at the bottom of the pan. But wouldn't half a cherry do just as well? Who would know?

Actually, now that I think of it, I did try the half cherry method once when I was low on maraschinos. Those little bits were buried in the sugary mix and all the birthday boy could see were slices of forlorn yellow pineapple. No, no, no. There can be no economizing here.

Pencils! I could demand that every pencil in this house be used to within an inch of its life. I read somewhere that a large and very rich corporation had a stern policy about pencils: you could not get a new one until you turned in the old one and that had to be used down to the very nub. That's it!

But we don't have regular pencils around here since I was introduced to the elegance of the disposable mechanical pencil. Of course, we could jettison the disposable model and return to the old ways, but then what would I do with the ten cases of mechanical pencils I bought on sale at the Price Club?

Wait a minute. I just spent $8 on a single bar of Caswell-Massey Savon Creme de Beaute. (Mama's secret little treat.) Why, for that kind of money I can make my own soap.

I go to the library and check out a book on soap making. Let's see here, I need olive oil, coconut oil, lye, and five pounds of Crisco, some aromatherapy scents to stir into the recipe, and a little pinch of color stuff. The book suggests that I also purchase a Bureau of Weights and Standards certified scale, an French enamel kettle, a laboratory-quality thermometer, and a pair of safety glasses. Don't forget a gallon of vinegar in case the lye, which can dissolve skin and eyeballs, splashes.

As I tally my shopping list and the time it would take to make my own soap, I have a sudden flash of deja vu -- me, college student, dorm kitchen, fabricating my own candles. I see slabs of droopy red wax that cost me the equivalent of a semester's worth of Friday night pizza and that, collectively, have the illuminating power of a five watt flashlight. Truth is, I'm no Martha Stewart.

The candles, though, remind me of a friend who once bragged that she saved a tidy sum by filling all the light fixtures in her house with 40 watt bulbs. I try it, but find that, given my declining vision, 75 watts is about as low as I can go without getting a migraine. Too bad.

There must be some little luxury lurking around this house whose sudden absence no one would notice. But I already stopped buying books in favor of the library. Ninety percent of my child's wardrobe consists of hand-me-downs and gifts from Grandma. I've learned how to recycle paper towel rolls, thread spools, and greeting cards into toys for tots. Every fourth dinner is leftovers. What to do?

It's a pity I never put olives in the salad.

October 1998

THE OLYMPICS

I DON'T KNOW HOW you plan to spend this February, but I'm going to be glued to my TV screen to catch every thrilling moment of the 2002 Winter Olympic games in Utah. Nothing makes my heart pound like the interminable ski jump competitions, the compulsory figure skating routines, or those goofy luge runs.

But, despite the addition every year of yet another obscure event (what, exactly, is "curling"?), I think the organizing committee is missing the boat. If those guys really wanted over-the-top TV ratings they'd add what I call "domestic events" to the program.

I mean, who wouldn't tune in to watch moms from 75 countries compete in events where they have to:

- Change an infant's poopy diapers on a full-to-capacity 747, during meal service

- Walk through a Steuben Glass showroom with a six-year-old boy whose Ritalin medication has been withheld for five days

- Dress for the snow a three-year-old child who refuses to pee until the last article of clothing has been buckled

- Field projectile vomiting in a 4-star restaurant

- Breast feed a teething baby in a crowded hotel elevator during a Shriners' Convention, without being detected

- Order at a Burger King drive-thru window for an entire ice hockey team of 9-year-old boys after they just won the pennant

- Feed strained beets to a tot while wearing a white cashmere business suit

- Shop Toys'R'Us with three children -- ages two, four, and six -- who have just had a lunch of jelly beans, Gatorade, and Rice Crispy treats

Scoring would be based on Speed, Form, Artistic Expression, and use of the fewest number of expletives.

I also see a few special events like a weight lifting competition where the moms have to pull a sleeping 90-pound third grader out of the car and carry him up two flights of stairs without, of course, waking him. Or a Triathlon where the moms have to feed, wash, and dress a tot for pre-school in a room full of new Christmas toys. And, naturally, a full-course Marathon: 10 errands in 10 locations that require -- at each location -- taking the kid out of a car seat, putting her in a stroller, completing the chore, and returning the child to the car seat (bonus points if Child is suffering from diarrhea).

If the Olympic Committee wants to play up to the changing demographics of parenthood, they might also restrict several events to First Time Professional Moms over 40. For example, how about having these ladies take a conference call with the Senior VP of Microsoft while doing CPR on a 9-month old crawler who's just discovered electric sockets.

The possibilities are endless and the potential audience is off the charts. I mean, what Mother wouldn't stop ironing to watch 37 of her Sisters vie to see who can baby proof an automobile body shop the fastest?

But until that happy day, I will be content to watch hung-over, body-pierced teenagers jumping, twisting, and flipping down a 400-foot-long curved ramp while listening to Snoop Dogg on a pair of concealed head-hones. They call it "half-pipe snow-boarding" but—hey, it's basically hung-over, body-pierced teenagers doing what they do. Only they get medals for it.

February 2002

KEEP THE RED SOCKS AWAY FROM THE YELLOW TOWELS

I'M READING A NOVEL that takes place in 12th century England, and I can't help noticing that life for children was a lot less comfortable under the reign of Henry I. Housing was typically one room with a mud floor where the pigs lay down with their owners on a bed of straw. Food was coarse bread and weak ale with a chunk of beef jerky thrown in on the high holy days. And everybody worked. If a tot couldn't manage in the fields she could at least help feed the livestock and pick the rat droppings out of the straw. No wonder that most people dropped dead before they were 37.

By the time we get to my childhood a couple of decades later life had already evolved to a level of comfort that was positively royal by Charlemagne's standards. I slept in a bed, could eat a banana whenever I wanted to, and used an electric vacuum cleaner to pick the rat droppings out of the straw. Though I had far more time than a serf's daughter to fool around, I still had chores to do.

At age nine, for instance, it was my job to polish the copper bottoms of my mother's pots, darn everyone's socks, iron Pop's dress shirts, dry the dishes, and do my own laundry. I complained, of course, but I got quite good at these tasks.

When my daughter turned nine and I decided it was time that she did more around the house than keep the guinea pig's food dish full, I realized that many of the skills I learned as a girl have become obsolete. Nobody polishes copper-bottomed pots anymore since it's more fashionable for them to look like someone actually uses them. Nobody darns socks since a Guatemalan peasant can now whack out a new pair for 11 cents. Nobody in this family has owned a garment that needs ironing since wrinkled linen came into style. And the electric dishwasher rinses, washes, and dries quite nicely, thank you.

That leaves the laundry. It takes me all day Saturday to do the laundry and I liked the idea of freeing up extra hours so I can devote more time to scraping mold off the shower tiles. But I did have reservations about turning this job over to a child. I foresaw the whites turned pink, the blacks scarred with bleach, and the lingerie shredded, the wool crushed into felt, and the elastic on the underwear melted and bonded to my lace camisole.

There would have to be rules. Always wash in cold water (just in case), never use chlorine bleach (just in case), and line-dry the panties (in all cases). But I realized that the most difficult thing to teach a child (or a husband) about the laundry process is How to Sort the Clothes.

In her book "Home Comforts: The Art & Science of Keeping House", the guru of housekeeping Cheryl Mendelson devotes three entire chapters to doing the laundry and six pages alone to sorting the dirty bits.

We pretty much agree, Cheryl and I, on how to batch up soiled laundry: make a pile each, I told the child, of the dark darks, the white whites, and the in-between colors. In addition, I tried to explain that coarse materials must not be washed with soft fabrics since they scratch and pill delicate surfaces -- but kept it simple with, "don't wash your sequin-studded denim pants with the pink spandex halter Uncle Jim bought you last Christmas or you'll be sorry."

I also warned her that dark fabrics can sometimes "bleed", but the very idea sent my daughter's eyeballs rolling into the back of her head.

So we stuck to the "always check the pockets for Kleenex" lesson. Sooner or later she would open the washing machine to find – oh, the horror – all of her pants and sweatshirts covered with tiny flecks of white tissue. It happens to the most heedful among us. But I drilled her on the pocket search protocol anyway.

Occasionally, on a Saturday morning I sit with my girl on the floor and watch her sort and search among the piles of dirty clothes. I re-assign as needed, explaining why the red socks should go in with the black shorts rather than the yellow towels, and why the nylon pajamas are better off with the delicate underwear even though they are an "in-between" color. In this way, as through time immemorial, Mother passes on to Child the secrets of domestic order. And all is well.

November 2005

PLAN B

SO, I'M WATCHING ONE of those TV news-magazine shows and there's a doctor looking ever so official and grim discussing the avian bird flu. Lyme disease, West Nile virus, E. coli, attack alligators in Ft. Lauderdale. As if we didn't have enough things to worry about. The doc is telling us that the usual disaster kit of water, batteries, portable radio, and M-16 assault rifle will not be enough if the bird flu jumps the border.

We'd better get hopping, he warns, and fill the basement with a month's supply of food just in case half the truckers in the country get the plague and the food chain goes bust. That's a merry thought. No more strawberries from California and neighbors battling over the last case of frijoles at the IGA.

A trained scout, I start to make a grocery list. Tuna fish, spaghetti, rice, condensed milk, peanut butter, marshmallows – the usual camping staples. My husband wants to know why I put 12 cans of artichoke hearts and a case of Jack Daniels on the weekly shopping list. I do my best impersonation of the grim doc.

"Don't be a fool," scolds my husband. "We've got a better chance of being downwind of the fallout when the terrorists hit the Indian Point nuclear power plant."

"Well, that's a comfort."

"Forget about stockpiling macaroni and cheese," he says. "We'll be outta here."

I recall my friend Maddy's flight from New Orleans last August. She took enough dental floss and clean underwear for three days, and found herself a refugee in north Florida for three months.

"Maybe we should think about what to bring if we have to evacuate to Manitoba."

We excuse the child from the dinner table, so that she won't ask uncomfortable questions, and start to make an Emergency Evacuation List.

First come the obvious get-away essentials: passports, credit cards, a Swiss army knife, and a beginner's guide to the Canadian healthcare system. Then there are the kits: sewing kit, first aid kit, toiletry kit, picnic martini kit.

And always there are the irreplaceable keepsakes. An evacuation, as my pals on the Gulf Coast discovered, is like a fire. When you run out the front door you don't know which of the stuff you've left behind, if anything, will survive. My husband and I do a quick scan of the house and try to figure out what to save. Do we bring the video tape of my husband's bar mitzvah? My Elvis 45s?? The tin clamshell tableau of Our Lady of Fatima that was blessed by Saint Pope John Paul???

The photos present an agonizing dilemma. I have 26 picture albums plus six boxes of the unsorted photos taken since my daughter was born in 1995, since no on-call mother has time to paste pix into books. "Can we take two cars?" I ask.

Working up a real steam of paranoia, I suggest that we bring along my mother's jewelry and my father-in-law's coin collection in case the financial system of the known world collapses and we have to barter for a night in a Motel 6. My husband thinks we should cash in our child's college fund U.S. Savings Bond and buy South African gold Krugerrands.

I wonder out loud if the Very Important Documents in our safe deposit box at the bank will survive the radiation fallout. "If they don't," reassures my husband, "there won't be anything left to document anyway."

Finally, I add food to the Evac List, just in case half the truckers in the country are downwind of the Indian Point nuclear power plant and the food chain goes bust. If we're hunkered down in our basement hiding from the avian flu it's best to have sensible supplies like rice and beans. But if we're on the move it's best, as every parent knows, to stock up on road food. So, to the weekly grocery list, I add two dozen bags of Twizzlers, a case of Cape Cod potato chips, a 12-pack of root beer, a party container of Gold Fish, and all the family-size Kit Kat bars the market has in stock.

Now all I have to do is box our Emergency Evac stuff and hope that the kids don't find the Kit Kats before we have to put Plan B into operation.

June 2006

GARDEN PARTY

WE'RE IN THE DEPTHS of the Dog Days and if your butterfly bush hasn't sprouted those feathery purple tufts by now you can fuhgeddaboutit. I've tried growing a butterfly three times. The first one died one brutal January morning. The second drowned in a May Day flood. And the third one looked so scrawny next to the house that I exiled it this spring to a bed at the rear of the property. Prove yourself or die!

Plants can break your heart. I came to this knowledge late in life. As a horticulturally blessed Californian, all I ever had to do was push a bit of green whatnot into the soil and watch it gush forth avocadoes or lemons or camellias or whatever I happened to fancy. Next to my writing cottage in Oakland I fancied wisteria and yellow climbing roses entwined in a lovers' embrace over a whitewashed arbor. On my stone patio in San Francisco I fancied red hibiscus and white gardenias. In my garden in Berkeley I grew tomatoes by the bushel.

I always grew tomatoes. When I left home to go to college, Pop dug up a tomato plant from his own garden and put it in a bucket for me to keep on the seventh floor balcony of my dorm building. My grandfather once told me that "you're never really home until you plant a tomato in the ground."

I guess I'm not yet entirely at home in the Northeast, even though I've lived through 23 winters, because I've failed to grow tomatoes that are worth eating. While my sister in San Diego sits in the middle of her tomato patch with a salt shaker and gorges, I am shamed into buying "vine-ripened" Best Boys at Adam's.

I finally gave up on growing tomatoes when the Cornell Cooperative declared that the soil around my house is contaminated with lead.

That, however, didn't stop me from trying a bed of perennials. Now I could've followed the example of my more sensible neighbors and stuck to evergreen shrubs with a tasteful border of hostas. But I longed for the glorious patches of color that the ladies on my block are able coax out of the earth each spring, and whispered to my private self, "we can do that!"

First I had to "amend" a patch of real estate that God Herself had abandoned. I ordered truckloads of topsoil, mulch, and compost, and hired a fullback to break up the solid block of clay that encases my house foundation. After the beds had been properly elevated and certified for drainage [all the plants in Armitage's Encyclopedia of Garden Perennials insist on "good drainage"], I grabbed my American Express card and headed down to the nursery.

Regardless of what all the books say about when, where, and how to plant, nursery owners are endlessly optimistic and supportive of experimentation. Full sun required? Give it a try in partial shade! Best to plant in early spring? I put things in the ground all through the heat of the summer! Deer resistant? Never had that problem!

Now I'm not suggesting that these good folks Lie. But, frankly, they can replace their mistakes at wholesale. The rest of us – and here I've done a random survey of friends and neighbors who share my weakness for delphinium – spend several hundred dollars a year in hopes of getting something, anything to survive.

Unlike weeds that grow out of rock face or in the Arctic tundra, perennials are like pure bred race horses. Each plant, for example, has its own special requirements for sunlight: "the elegant Ractagino senzalatte demands a blast of full sun from 7am to noon, unless you want bushier results in which case cut down the lilac that blocks southern exposure; and make sure that the cultivar enjoys afternoon light, filtered – ideally through a Japanese maple – from noon to the cocktail hour" when, presumably, we're all too snockered to give a damn.

There are also plant-specific directions for soil pH, moisture, mulching, fertilizing, and pruning. And if you insist on filling your beds with cuttings from your sister-in-law (and thereby saving thousands of dollars) be forewarned that they may carry all sorts of nasty diseases. Like a Typhoid Mary, one free geranium may doom your entire garden.

Call me morbid, but I keep an obituary of those plants that fail each season.

2002. A yellow rose, two bleeding hearts, three azaleas, a patch of lamb's ear, and a dozen delphiniums.

2003. two foxgloves, a half dozen dianthus, one butterfly bush, a flat of creeping phlox, and nine delphiniums.

2004. three Japanese andromeda, one butterfly bush, a passel of catmint, a stretch of vinca, and six delphiniums.

2005. one weigela, two dwarf lilacs, five veronicas, and four delphiniums.

For my last hurrah I've put in three Rose of Sharon this year. (No delphinium.) And I've sworn off day lilies and sunflowers, savagely decapitated year after year by gangs of deer.

What is thriving in my garden are those boring old hostas that were there when I moved in. There are, I've discovered, dozens of varieties to mix and match and have so made my peace with them. I stroll down the block stopping to admire my neighbors' lush blooming plots, my envy all worn out.

I know what you're thinking. That kid from out West, where the livin' is easy, just doesn't have the cojones to stand up to the Real Challenges of gardening. And, you know... you're right.

August 2006

EMPOWERMENT OVERLOAD

WHEN MY MECHANIC ADVISED me to put a no-name brand battery that he sells into my car, he said, "don't take my word for it, go on the web and compare batteries." I did. Next thing you know I'm up to my saddlebags in data on reserve capacity ratings and cold-cranking amps.

When I received a small inheritance in January, a pal gave me a list of mutual funds and instructed me to track these portfolios for a couple of months before investing my modest legacy. So I dutifully scour the business pages, stalk the market, and decode the fund financials.

After I was diagnosed with an annoying "condition" last fall, I spent hours tracking down info on the Internet, scanning medical texts, seeking out alternative health shamans, and interviewing friends of friends with the same malaise.

Honoring the mantra of the self-help industry, I am just taking responsibility for my own healthcare, road safety, and financial wellbeing.

But I'm exhausted. Enough already. What ever happened to division of labor? You remember division of labor. Even when Dick and Jane lived in a cave they figured out that it was, gosh, so much more efficient for one of them to vacuum and the other to dust. As life became more complex, people became more specialized, and so instead of each household taking care of every need, we invented Butchers, Bakers, Blacksmiths, and Certified Public Accountants.

Here we've reached the summit of complexity as a civilization and suddenly there's this reversal of social organization: do it yourself! It's become a cult in modern society. Whether it's remodeling the kitchen, preparing French charcuterie, or diagnosing your thyroid condition. Isn't that what we have carpenters, chefs, and endocrinologists for?

I barely have enough time to pursue the specialty for which I have been trained and with which I allegedly earn a living. I want to be able to go to my mechanic and say, "put in a new battery, Jimmy, and check the tires while you're at it." I really don't want to know about cold cranking amps, or the long term trajectory of mutual funds, or radioiodine ablation.

Yet I fear that I must. If I don't watch out for my own best interests, I tell myself as I stare at the ceiling at 3a.m., who will?

What began as a sensible take-charge attitude has become a self-inflicted wound my friend Lenny calls "empowerment overload." How did this happen?

Part of it is a vain but irresistible impulse to control our own destiny. Nobody cares about what becomes of me as much as I do – not the stockbroker who squandered my little nest egg on a sure thing or the gardener who sprayed poison on my herb patch.

Part of it is the explosion of information on the Internet. If the latest reports on the toxicity of root canal filling cements are available on the web, how can I, in good conscience, not look them up before seeing the endodontist?

Part of it is marketing. My newest doctor, after charging me $295 for an initial handshake, peddles his latest book where he tells me, right there on page 294, "empower yourself to take charge of your own recovery"! This piece of information costs me an additional $23.95.

We assume ultimate responsibility over matters trivial – because we can – and over matters major – because our life and those of our loved ones depend on it.

And so we do our own bookkeeping on the computer, cater our own affairs, handle our own divorce paperwork, and research the epidemiology of Lyme disease.

Ma used to say, "don't learn how to do too much or everybody will expect you to do it all." Smart woman. That was why I categorically refused to learn how to type in high school, preferring to take Advanced Placement courses in Chemistry and Physics. How was I to know that civilization would regress and that we're all now expected to type.... everything.

March 2004

6.
MARRIAGE, KIDS, PETS: THE WHOLE CATASTROPHE

THAT TELLTALE GLOW? -- NOTHIN' BUT A RASH0: Pregnancy -- if you picked up your archetypal vision from toilet tissue ads, Vermeer paintings, and the movies, you're in for a shock, sister. Page 139

THE FULL LOTUS. I'm beginning to wonder if the very essence of Motherhood is incompatible with the very essence of Enlightenment. Page 142

A DOG'S LIFE. Why am I so against getting a dog? Truth is that whenever I've lived with a man it was already like living with a dog. Think about it.... A man sheds and expects you to pick up after him; leaves the toilet seat wet; chews with his mouth open and drips food on his coat; growls whenever a stranger ogles his female; and -- when he likes you -- jumps up on your lap and drools all over your face. Page 144

A DOG'S LIFE PART TWO: THE SURRENDER. I underestimated the tenacity of my husband and daughter, who re-armed the troops in their Great Get-a-Dog Campaign. Page 147

MY DOMESTIC POLICY: Our Household Rules are modeled after the U.S. Marine Corps Code of Conduct. Page 149

BRAVE NEW WORLD: It's 2040 and The Spiritually Evolved & Intentionally Childless have taken over the world. Page 152

HOME SWEET WORK. One of modern life's dirty little secrets is that home is work and work is home. Page 155

LIKE A HORSE AND CARRIAGE. Marriage may not be champagne and roses; it may not be a guaranteed lifelong date for New Year's Eve; it may no longer be the bedrock of civilization. But it does have its small, essential compensations and so deserves to be available to anyone cockeyed enough to want it. Page 158

MAKING DO WITH PUBLIC SCHOOL. Be prepared to give up rug hooking and flamenco dancing. Page 161

TEENS AND THE SEVEN DEADLY SINS. My adorable baby whose universe has revolved around me, the Beloved Mother for most of her existence, just turned 13 and officially became a teenager. Page 163

THAT TELLTALE GLOW?
NOTHIN BUT A RASH

ACCORDING TO MY CALCULATIONS, Jeanne Crain is at least four months pregnant when Cary Grant marries her in the 1951 film *People Will Talk*. Slim, perky, and energetic as a pompom girl, Jeanne reveals her delicate condition in the denouement when, sitting at a concert, she pats her tummy and acknowledges what we presume to be a tiny kick. Everyone smiles. Dissolve.

Then we have Arnold Schwarzenegger who tosses his cookies exactly once after receiving news of his historic conception in *Junior*, then eases into a permanent "glow" phase where his skin softens and he eats everything in sight.

And how can we ever forget Demi Moore in her swollen state of bliss on the cover of Vanity Fair?

Pregnancy. Frankly, I picked up my archetypal notions of Woman's most feminine nine months from toilette tissue ads, Vermeer paintings, and, above all, the movies. See soft focus Madonna in diaphanous gown, powdery scent. A beautiful thing.

The reality, however, was a cruel shock. Forget "morning" sickness. I was nauseous every waking moment for the first three months. Luckily I slept a lot -- ten hours a night plus a pre-prandial snooze. I passed water every 20 minutes which pre-empted any plans to perform jury duty; my champagne-glass breasts jumped two cup sizes in six weeks (so long French-cut lace brassiere, hello Nurse Ratchet beige bombers in stretch cotton); and I turned a malarial green at the mere thought of grilled lamb chops while craving shredded wheat.

Fortunately, the nausea and weird food aversions passed and my husband could finally make a pot of coffee without my throwing up on his sleeve. But just as I turned that corner, the heartburn and back aches began. Mention BBQ ribs or Chinese take-out and a searing pain shot from my stomach to my esophagus. I don't care what Irene Dunne ate, you can forget ice cream and pickles. And I couldn't drive a car for longer than ten minutes before back spasms forced me to the side of the road. No more auto trips to Long Island to have lunch with my sister-in-law at the Bombay Pavilion.

When I first discovered I was with child my obstetrician gave me a copy of the current bible of pregnancy called What To Expect While You're Expecting. This book is a revelation. It outlines potential "side effects" of the Grand Adventure month-by-month, and it reads like the symptomatology of a plague patient in intensive care: fading eyesight, bleeding gums, excessive saliva (excessive saliva??!), varicose veins, acne, headaches, bloating, cramps, indigestion, constipation, flatulence, and dizziness, backaches, nosebleeds, hemorrhoids, anemia, carpal tunnel syndrome, rectal bleeding, swelling of feet and ankles, elevated blood pressure, breathlessness, skin blotch, red palms, itchiness, frequent urination (of course, we knew that), increased facial hairiness (great), and clumsiness -- as in, you drop your keys down the heater grate a lot.

Now I know where they got the cliché "barefoot and pregnant". After the third month none of my shoes fit anymore. And as for that telltale "glow", it's nothing but a rash.

The Book also cites emotional disturbances common to moms-to-be including irrationality, irritability, weepiness, fear, misgivings, depression, trouble concentrating, and forgetfulness (which explains why, when you drop your keys down the heater grate you immediately forget where they went). And, if you aren't irrational already, it adds a ponderous list of Don'ts.

Besides the familiar ones -- no pina coladas, Lucky Strikes, or crack cocaine -- there are some rather esoteric prohibitions such as: don't point your toes (could lead to cramping in the calves), avoid depilatories (just when you really need them), and make sure your partner doesn't blow any air into your vagina during oral sex (as if you don't have enough to worry about).

Now I don't mean to be a bad sport about this. I tried to *get* pregnant for many years, so few women could possibly appreciate the miracle more than I do. However, it might have been sisterly for those who have gone before to alert us novices to some of the ruder surprises. I mean, women share their experiences and complaints about other female functions in extravagant detail. Who doesn't know every vicissitude of menstruation, menopause, and mastectomy before the first onset of PMS? But there is an uncanny conspiracy of silence around pregnancy.

Oddly enough, once I became pregnant every female I know suddenly came forward with her personal tale of Nine Months in Purgatory. My own mother confessed to spending the better part of my gestation with her head over a toilette bowl. My husband's sister suffered the scourge of unbearable itching over 97% of her body. And a woman I met at the fish counter told me her hands became so arthritic that she couldn't dial 911.

So I puzzled, why did Arnold's skin soften while my ankles swelled up to the size of my thighs? And if the experience is not a non-stop Glow why does it have such great PR?

Then -- an epiphany! -- it hit me: menstruation and menopause are conditions that happen to females whether we want them to or not, so our daughters might as well know what's on the way.

But in these chemically enlightened, take charge times, pregnancy is still (political goons notwithstanding) pretty much a matter of free choice. Thus our social shepherds have to make it sound attractive, desirable, and the high point of femininity. Not even dear ole mom, aching for those grandchildren, will grant full disclosure. How many women would think twice if they knew about the rectal bleeding and excessive saliva?

Surely, if a thoughtful prospect had interviewed *me* at eight months pregnant with 14 new symptoms, she would have paused. My body, already pushed, pulled, twisted, stretched, pressured, displaced, gouged, and contorted to its anatomical limits, had discovered a couple of afflictions that weren't even in The Book!

Yet I must admit that at a certain point --somewhere between the gestational diabetes and the chronic sciatica -- I surrendered to my indelicate condition. In fact, like the Yogi who gives thanks for his bed of nails, I began to welcome each new test of my mettle.

I met a woman in my birthing class who claimed to have had not a single discomforting ailment in her seven months of pregnancy. Not one day of morning sickness. Not a single arthritic cramp. Not a varicose in her veins. She even looked like Jeanne Crain. My husband offered to beat her up. But I just turned up the heating pad on my back, adjusted my truss, took a swallow of Mylanta, checked my blood sugar, and leaned on my cane. "Poor dear," I sighed with the moral authority of a combat veteran. "She just isn't enjoying the Total Experience."

August 1998

My Philosophy of Life, plus a few handy tips

THE FULL LOTUS

ECKHART TOLLE SAYS THAT only when your attention is fully and intensely "in the Now" can you feel your True Being and achieve Enlightenment.

Eckhart should know. He's a certified enlightened guy who writes books about how to get there yourself. And he's made enough money with this gig so that he can live anywhere he pleases, though why he chose Vancouver over Oaxaca is puzzling.

Feeling emphatically unenlightened myself lately, I read an excerpt from Mr. Tolle's book THE POWER OF NOW for some tips. He starts off by talking about the little Voice inside your head -- aka "worry" -- that is formed by past experiences and is always imagining the worst possible outcome. For instance, if every blind date you've ever had was a disaster and if you have a blind date for this Saturday night, then the Voice will convince you that your sister-in-law's chiropractor (with whom you have the date) is a drooling dwarf with chronic flatulence. Mucking up the Present like this with judgments from the Past is, says Eckhart, the cause of untold misery.

The antidote is to assume the Lotus position and count the pores on your left calf -- thus, clearing your mind of all that annoying blather. Makes sense.

But, as I'm reading, I begin to wonder about the diaper bag. As a certified mother, I depend on my past experiences to help avoid future calamities. The embodiment of this modus vivendi is, as all certified mothers know, the diaper bag. For example, I know from past experience that as soon as the child is buckled in her car seat, she will require a snack. This is not a possibility; this is a given. I also know that as soon as we are ten minutes from home, preferably on the New York State Thruway, the child will have to make pee-pee. Shortly thereafter she will demand a toy and a beverage.

Thus the diaper bag must contain, not only diapers, but food, drink, entertainment, and one -- make that two -- changes of clothing. Even when the child is beyond diapers, my ability to anticipate all her needs and fill the diaper bag (now known as the "backpack") with the right stuff, is the keystone of every successful family undertaking.

And yet this ability to imagine contingencies and plan ahead condemns me, says Eckhart, to untold misery. I am constantly NOT living in the Now. And I'm beginning to wonder if the very essence of Motherhood is incompatible with the very essence of Enlightenment.

Listen to this: When "intensely conscious of the present moment...." says Eckhart, "you...create a gap of no-mind in which you are highly alert and aware but not thinking." Now the condition of being "highly alert and aware but not thinking" describes exactly the "no-mind" state of a three-year-old boy.

In order for HIM to be "intensely conscious of the present moment," his MOTHER must continuously search her cerebral data bank for past causes and consequences, and ask, "what's the likelihood that Teddy's next stunt will put him in the Emergency Room?" As he plays with his older cousin's Lego toys, she must mentally review the Heimlich Maneuver. And in public places, she must scour her memory for pictures of children on milk cartons and size up the kidnapper-potential of every stranger.

Mother must maintain a state of consciousness that furiously zigzags between past, present, and future. No mental hammock rest for her.

I personally would love to live in the Now -- to do the Sun Salutation at dawn, then sit with my legs crossed and meditate on the ebb and flow of my breath until the cocktail hour. But, frankly, the best I can do these days to stay focused on the present is to count the pores on my child's calf while checking her for deer ticks.

I know that Eckhart Tolle calls Enlightenment "the end of suffering." But wasn't it Phyllis Diller, a certified mother of five, who said that the end of suffering is when the children leave home and the dog dies?

Nita Micossi thinks that meditation, like canning pickles, is great and plans to do both when time permits.

August 2002

A DOG'S LIFE

EVER SINCE THE GUINEA pig died my husband has been leaning on me to get a dog. I knew I was in trouble when he insisted on selling the guinea pig's cage. "Won't need that old thing," he said. "It's time to move up!"

Then he brought home a half dozen library books about dogs including WE'RE HAVING A PUPPY! – a sensible and humorous introduction to the species; PAWS TO CONSIDER – an honest appraisal of breeds that tells the truth about shedding and all-night howling; and THE COMPLETE DOG BOOK – a tome that promotes the beauty and nobility of even the ugliest mutt.

My husband sat with our daughter, oohing and aahing over beagles, terriers, and bluetick coonhounds while I lost sleep replaying the comments of friends upon hearing the news of our impending blessed event.

"They bring in fleas, ticks, and dead rodents," warned Ada, a horse person but emphatically not a dog person.

"They pee on your upholstery and spray the hardwood floors," said Brother Jim, an unsentimental dog owner who knows my limitations. "And you'll never get that smell out."

"They shed hair and eat feces," added Carol. Gee, I'm glad you told me that.

Even the dog books -- the honest ones -- tell readers who want a dog to say good-bye to:

- Sleeping in on weekends
- Food without hair
- A dry toilet seat
- Spontaneous getaways
- White clothing
- Unbroken breakables

- Clean cars, and
- Walking barefoot

I don't even want to contemplate why I couldn't go barefoot in my own house anymore.

And what about the $2000 sleeper couch we wanted to buy so my sister-in-law won't have to camp out on the back lawn when she comes to visit? "How would you feel the first time the pooch pooped on your new $2000 sofa?" I taunted my husband.

"How will you feel about taking a puppy to your office everyday for six months until he's housebroken?" I threatened.

"What about my allergies to cats, dogs, and farm animals?" I wept.

But all he said was, "The kid needs a dog."

That's what my father said to my mother after my sister and I had left home and our younger brother was the lone child in the house. My brother frolicked with the mongrel he picked out at the pound. My father photographed Kodak moments of my brother and the dog frolicking. My mother feed, bathed, and brushed the animal, brought him to the vet, and mopped up his hair balls and excrement.

My husband is scheduling appointments with breeders. My daughter is telling all her cousins that she is going to get a dog. Yet still I refuse to endorse this project.

Why? Why am I so adamant about living with a canine? Aren't dogs cute and lovable and loyal?

The truth is that I've always felt that whenever I've lived with a man it was already like living with a dog.

Think about it. A man sheds and expects you to pick up after him. A man must be fed and groomed and commanded to do something – or he will just hang out reading the newspaper and do nothing at all. A man leaves the toilet seat wet.

He chews with his mouth open and drips food on his coat. He growls whenever a stranger ogles his female. He needs to be petted daily and stroked behind the ears. And when a man likes you he jumps up on your lap and drools all over your face.

Every man I have ever lived with had to be trained: when and where to eat, to not bark and disturb the neighbors, to heel when a girlfriend of mine he dislikes (or excessively likes) walks in the door. And I use essentially the same motivators as any good dog trainer: praise, food, and play.

Men are also prone to many of the same physical ailments as dogs. As one of the books points out, potential owners should beware of:

- Potbelly
- Bald patches
- Skin rashes
- Yellow teeth,
- Snarling, and
- Discharge from the eyes, nose, or ears

That's pretty much the same list I gave to my cousin when she was out scouting for her third husband.

Not only do human males resemble canines in many ways, but human females often make the same mistakes with men as people in general make with dogs. For example, perusing PAWS TO CONSIDER, I see the warning: "don't fall in love with a picture in a book." Alas, I'm sure I am not the only girl who has fallen for a scoundrel with a pretty face, to my everlasting regret.

And look at this: "You will know you are out of control when you leave messages on the answering machine for your dog and think the dog actually understands those messages." It took ten years of marriage before I abandoned all hope that my husband would read, let alone follow any messages I left on the refrigerator. And I know that the odds of a girlfriend getting a phone message from me are about the same whether I leave it with her husband or with her cocker spaniel.

Now I think dogs are okay. And I've had fond relations with two or three over the years. But do I really need to repeat a life experience I've already had more times than I care to recall? Besides I already have a man in the house.

September 2003

A DOG'S LIFE
PART TWO: THE SURRENDER

SEVERAL YEARS AGO I made what I thought to be an airtight case against bringing a dog into my life. As you may recall, I've found that living with a man was pretty much already like living with a dog.

Think about it. A man sheds and expects you to pick up after him. A man must be fed and groomed and commanded to do something, or he will just hang out and do nothing at all. A man leaves the toilet seat wet. He chews with his mouth open and drips food on his coat. He growls whenever a stranger ogles his female. He needs to be petted daily and stroked behind the ears. And when a man likes you he jumps up on your lap and drools all over your face.

So, I concluded, why do I need to repeat a life experience I've already had?

But I underestimated the tenacity of my husband and daughter, who re-armed the troops in their Great Get-a-Dog Campaign. They hijacked dinner conversations with debates over possible dog names. They chatted up every dog owner who passed our front porch about the plusses and minuses of their breed. They even recruited a formerly trusted friend, who dared to present my child last Hanukkah with a full-color coffee table picture book of pooches in various poses of adorability. I retaliated by giving the traitor's son a plastic replica of an Uzi submachine gun, but the damage to my cause had already been done.

Morale low, I launched one last desperate propaganda campaign. I sneaked copies of my brother's vet bills into my husband's checkbook; I carpet bombed the household with pamphlets on Diseases Transmitted by Canines; I deployed fake poop from the joke store onto the hallway runner.

But, in the end, I, like Napoleon, was defeated by the elements. The turning point in the war came after a snow storm in February. My girl, an only child, was on the front lawn building an ice castle by herself. She pleaded with me to join her, which I dutifully did for about five minutes before getting frostbite and an attack of sciatica. "If I had a dog," she whimpered as I deserted the field, "I wouldn't have to play all by myself."

That did it. Years of domestic combat resolved with one final twist of the guilt dagger into my poor mother's heart. If I wasn't willing to frolic in the ice and snow with my only child, didn't I at least owe her a companion? Oh, foolish weak woman.

It was, however, a conditional surrender. I made both father and daughter sign an armistice with provisions exempting me from walking, feeding, bathing, and grooming the critter, plus a clause stating that, under no circumstances am I ever in this life to mop up urine, feces, vomit, or any other bodily excretion from the animal. Furthermore, it is not allowed on the second floor of the house at any time and – the ultimate deal breaker – "if Mama's allergies are unbearable, the dog must go." My only contact with said dog need be expressions of affection at a time and place of my own choosing.

Shortly after the document-signing ceremony, my husband and I spent an afternoon sizing up a litter of fluffy white puppies from a Havanese breeder in Woodstock. As a gesture of good will to the vanquished, I was allowed to name the pup.

What's it like living with Gracie? Give me a few more months and I'll give you a progress report.

September 2007

MY DOMESTIC POLICY

THE WORLD IS DIVIDED into those households where the kids run things and those where the adults run things. We definitely fall into the latter group.

My own mother did not negotiate. "You can do it the way YOU want to do it," she would say, "when you have your own house." I did not get my very own house and family until I was on the brink of candidacy for AARP membership. By then I had seen the pitiful results of others' parenting errors and felt obliged to install in my household an oligarchy open only to family members who had voted in at least five presidential elections.

What this means is that there are certain places in our house where children are allowed to frolic and certain places where children may enter, perform their toilette, and leave and still other places where the slightest evidence that anyone under the age of 18 has even disturbed the dust results in a punishment to the full and merciless extent of the law.

This also means that I can have a living room where an antique glass lamp sits fearlessly next to the piano and where artwork hangs on the walls as low as a toddler's nose.

In our house, children and adults try to accommodate one another's irreconcilable differences using mature guidelines. For instance, if a proposed activity involves paint and/or glitter it (1) is confined to the kitchen, (2) requires a washable smock, and (3) should be undertaken the day before, not the day after Daddy has mopped the floor. If these simple rules are followed, everyone can cheerfully co-exist without screaming recriminations and threats of military school.

Limits apply also to bodily functions. It is not cute to make pee-pee in the bathtub. Potato chips and Milk Duds do not a healthy breakfast make. And a strictly enforced bedtime is not a fascist plot.

This philosophy is based on two assumptions. The first is that children, however cuddly and amusing, are feral creatures who will come to a sad and early end if allowed to do whatever they want. The second is that rights and duties should be in balance. Thus, since parents are required to mop up vomit during flu season, fight with the phone company over mis-billed calls to Easter Island, and kill garter snakes in the basement, it seems only fair that parents should also have a clean and quiet refuge and some uninterrupted time each week to enjoy the New York Times Sunday Book Section and listen to a Dave Brubeck CD.

Now in contrast to this sensible approach, I have friends and acquaintances who subscribe to the philosophy of the Child-Centered household where the kiddies run things.

You know who these people are before you even walk in the front door. The porch is littered with decapitated Barbies, fossilized Play-Doh, and tricycle parts.

Inside the house every room is a playground for the wee ones. Their plastic debris is equally welcome in the dining room, in Mama's office, and between the covers of the parental bed. In fact, the bed in that space designated as the "master bedroom" in most Model Homes, is usually -- in the Child-Centered household -- renamed the Family Bed with all rights and privileges communally attendant thereof.

In such a household, three year olds are encouraged to decorate the living room walls with Barney-inspired murals. Six-year-olds are invited to experiment with chocolate, honey, and Wesson oil in the kitchen or wherever the spirit moves. And ten year olds can be found at 11:30pm on a school night in front of the Soft Porn Channel eating Fruit Loops swimming in Coca Cola and memorizing all the dirty words.

Dare not make a disparaging comment to the adoring parents. You will be dismissed as an uptight, repressed, small-minded, humorless harpy who has been sucked dry of all life-affirming values by the nuns and the military-industrial complex.

Now in their defense, I must say that these parents are often -- not always, but often – more relaxed and easy-going than I myself am.

If their cat walks freely on the kitchen counter and the iguana nests in the basket of clean laundry, what difference does it make in the grand scheme of things?

If their tots go barefoot in January it is because the slippers are somewhere in the mudroom, but who knows exactly where, and, anyway, so what?

And if their children use Mama's leather-bound edition of Plutarch's Lives as home plate, well, a book is, after all, only a book and, when a child's wholesome pursuit of physical pleasure is at stake, who cares about such trifles?

Well, frankly, not I.

Unless, of course *their* children come to my house.

December 2000

BRAVE NEW WORLD

SEPTEMBER 2040. I AM very old now and further attempts to elude the Stability Patrol are becoming increasingly futile. They will surely track me down in a matter of weeks and send me to the Recycling Spa and Wafer Factory. Therefore I have little time left and nothing to lose in setting down my account of how the Hatcheries came into being.

Most citizens today totally accept the concept of the creation of human replacements by, what people in my day would call, artificial means – in test tubes and incubators -- and the rearing of these replacements in nurseries by robots.

The concept of family has vanished and the notion of natural mothers and fathers has become an obscenity. The brave new world of Aldous Huxley that we read about so many years ago in school came to pass with nary a whimper of dissent.

But I would like to believe that some day people will come to their senses and an opposition movement will arise to make a revolution against this silly business. Perhaps my little history will give these sturdy souls ammunition in the struggle…

The roots of this new world were in the demographic changes of the late 20th century. The statisticians found that people were marrying much later and having fewer children, and that growing numbers were deciding to remain childless altogether.

By then the technology to breed outside the human body was near practical realization. But a more frightening development occurred that would make this possibility acceptable to the public. I speak of the emergence in the early months of the 21st century of the Anti-Children Movement.

At first it made the population control folks happy enough. And the politicians began to fawn over this growing constituency with their vast discretionary income.

But then The Spiritually Evolved and Intentionally Childless (as they began to call themselves) started getting churlish. They ranted about the smell of dirty diapers on public transportation. They whined about whiffle balls careening over their backyard fences. They protested against childcare centers next to the corporate cafeteria and what they saw as a disgusting trend in "revealing" pregnancy fashions.

A watershed event was the publication of a cover story in the old New York Times magazine entitled "Your Kids Are Their Problem". In this heartfelt attempt to give ink to the gripes of yet one more unhappy minority, the militantly childfree came roaring out of the closet and cut loose with tales of how "crib lizards", "anklebiters", "sprogs" and "spawn of the devil" were infesting art museums and despoiling Caribbean beachfront resorts. "They are Everywhere!" shrieked one 31 year old vasectomized software consultant. Anti-children letters to the editor ran 25to1.

A festering prejudice was suddenly out in the open. Overnight, it became acceptable to slam toddlers, their parents, and diaper-changing foldout tables in movie theater toilettes. Radio talk show callers blamed global warming on Pamper build-up in landfills. And crosses were burned on the front lawns of homes with swing sets and tree houses.

Changes in public policy soon followed. Las Vegas reverted to its pre-Disney days and passed a law that barred entry to anyone too young to smoke, drink, gamble, and drive a motorcycle. Funding programs for high school marching bands were scrapped. Children's menus disappeared from diners.

People who did want children restricted themselves to a singleton so as not to enrage the neighbors. Some even disguised the child in adult clothing and claimed she was an aunt with a pituitary condition.

It was only a matter of time before the school system rewrote the biology textbooks and excised all mention of sexual reproduction. Marriage was redefined by law as "a license to register for flatware at Bloomingdale's". And compulsory donation of ones gametes to the National Bank for Sensible Reproduction became a high school graduation requirement.

By the time the last group of boys and girls to be born in a "natural way" was of breeding age it had been thoroughly brainwashed into believing that traditional baby making was an abomination.

And so, within the space of less than two generations we became transformed into a society run by people who loathe kids. With no reason to be role models to the young and impressionable, our new leaders swiftly became sulky, demanding, impatient, self-indulgent – dare I say -- childish?

Personally I do not have to endure this regime much longer – they also loathe old people who smell of dirty diapers on public transportation. But I do wish that the civilized adults among us would rise up soon and slap some sense into these brats.

September 2000

HOME SWEET WORK

AFTER 25 YEARS OF freelancing out of my home office where I can wear PJs at the computer, control the thermostat, and nibble out of the frig at will, I signed up for a fulltime-at-the-office job. This past semester I have been an out-of-the-house Working Mother.... and I now understand why 83% of all Working Mothers are on daily medication.

In addition to the tasks of my 9-to-5 job, which have somehow metastasized into evenings and weekends, I've adapted to conditions we freelancers habitually flout. I've had to shave my legs and get my hair cut twice as often, find a competent dry cleaner, and hunt down books-on-tape can best defeat the tedium of a two-hour roundtrip commute. Homemaking has suffered since I'm no longer around to do the laundry, stir the stew, and monitor the plumber during my self-scheduled work breaks. And my husband and daughter have improved their chess game as Mama has disappeared on yet another Sunday morning to correct papers.

The only days I've had off since Labor Day have been Thanksgiving and Christmas, bent over the stove, and Yom Kippur, spent inside of a synagogue lamenting my sins.... as if I had time for sins, already.

Despite the discomfort of squeezing a 36 hour day into 24 hours, I love my out-of-the-house job. Teaching and counseling 49 men in a maximum security prison is thrilling. My students engage me daily in the sort of vigorous intellectual debates I haven't enjoyed since graduate school. They share with me religious, political, and social views from a unique and insightful perspective. They work hard and, unlike many of their privileged peers on conventional college campuses, are deeply committed to learning. Most of all, they appreciate me. They appreciate me!

I enjoy going to work. It's the coming home that's become the trial.

Evidently I am not alone. In her book, THE TIME BIND, eminent sociologist and my old teacher Arlie Hochschild documents what we already know about the typical working mom's "time famines" and obsession with balancing work and family. But the pearl in Arlie's book is her revelation of the working parents' dirty little secret: that, for a lot of us, work is home and home is work.

Think about it. "Work" suggests something unpleasant and involuntary. It's a chore, it's a drag, it's a relentless time clock and a bottomless pit of unmet expectations.

Then there is "home" – a safe haven where you can kick back, be yourself, relax and laugh with people who care about you and applaud your efforts.

I don't know about you but, when I walk in the door at night there are no slippers and martini. I'm greeted by a sulking child, a fatigued spouse, and two dozen phone and e-mail messages that demand an immediate response. As I slip off the pantyhose I reschedule a dental appointment, write a bus note to the child's teacher, and renew a stack of library books on-line, while the child at my elbow insists that I attend to her recitation of Gunga Din.

After an hour or so of this feel-good romp, I retire to the kitchen and cook dinner. Dinner – the one leisurely half hour in our family's evening schedule, unless, of course, I am serving anything other than hot dogs or mac'n'cheese – is followed by the child's bath-and-bed routine. During this hour and a half which should, by all accounts, renew our kindred intimacy, the child spews forth the venom that she has repressed all day to achieve her perfect social presentation to the rest of the world while I do my best impersonation of the Wicked Witch of the West.

After the kiss and tuck, I'm back to my desk to prep the next day's lecture. As I roll into bed a few hours later my husband asks if I remembered to program the music for his company's holiday party the next afternoon. I growl, get up, and do the chore. A good wife would do no less.

There is little in this routine that is safe, relaxing, or amusing.

At work, on the other hand, I'm around interesting, respectful, and grateful individuals with whom I've been known to swap playful repartee. And I work in a prison.

Linda Avery, one of the people interviewed by Dr. Hochschild, sings a similar tune. "I usually come to work early just to get away from the house... (When I arrive) people are there waiting. We sit. We chit-chat for five or ten minutes. There's laughing, joking, fun. My coworkers aren't putting me down for any reason." In contrast, petty demands and quarrels await her daily homecoming. Linda feels best about herself at work where her help is prized rather than torpedoed by a cranky teenager.

Apparently this perverse reversal of the emotional magnetic poles beneath home and workplace, while new to me, is no surprise to my husband. "Oh yeah, a lot of men have always felt that way," he yawns. Well, an increasing number of working mothers are now in on it too.

How did this happen? High divorce rates have taken the security and safety out of home life (Linda has changed relationships more often than she has changed jobs). Paid work offers women challenge, positive feedback, and self-esteem while "homemaker" ranks below "migrant fruit picker" on society's status inventory. And the industrial engineering of time has spilled out of the workplace and into the home, where "quality time" with kin echoes an appointment at the office.

Pacifying a nine-year-old's prepubescent temper tantrum while a grease fire is consuming the stove top and a squirrel is loose in the laundry room... I often feel that home is becoming more work than fun. But not until I took a job outside of the house did I understand that work can be downright homey.

January 2005

LIKE A HORSE AND CARRIAGE

WE ALL KNEW THAT the 21st century would bring unimaginable changes. But who thought that old standbys like the Big Mac and marriage would be among the early casualties? I'll let the FDA sort out the toxic beef thing. But -- in the current debate over what is marriage? and is it as socially relevant as bowling? -- I feel obliged to say a few words.

Straight off, I admit that most of the traditional reasons for getting married are no longer persuasive. Procreation? You can now do it with a test tube and a board certified reproductive endocrinologist. Property distribution? Along with keeping their own names, a growing number of young working brides are maintaining their own American Express cards and unnumbered Swiss bank accounts. Emotional support? Isn't that what your girlfriends are for? Sex? About the only people around who aren't having sex with each other are married couples.

And we all know that marriage and family long ago surrendered their religious, educational, economic, and play functions to churches, schools, office complexes, and video arcades. Still, from somebody who's been there a few times and back, I must say that having a committed mate in the house most of the time has some very positive benefits. From the point of view of the wife – which is the only point of view I can offer on this subject – let me just say that marriage provides me with:

- Someone to go downstairs with a baseball bat while I call 911
- Someone to keep my wineglass full while I chop garlic for the spaghetti sauce
- Someone to clean the garlic press
- Someone to warm my sub-zero feet in January with his hot back and fanny
- Someone to blame for living in a place where January lasts three months

- Someone to shout at and with during Miss America Talent Finals, presidential primary debates, and Hollywood Square reruns
- Someone to pick up the kid when I have a three hour cut-and-color with Lorraine
- Someone to provide in-laws so I don't have to spend the holidays with my sister in California who refuses to fly
- Someone to go outside in the middle of a snowstorm at midnight and turn on the backup generator
- Someone to shovel the path to the car to drive to the service station and buy gas for the backup generator when it runs dry at 6:30am
- Someone to bring the car around to the front door of the restaurant when I'm wearing sling back high heels in the rain
- Someone to feed, wash, and nag the child while I spend a long weekend in New York City with my old college pal
- Someone to scratch my back, a little bit lower and to the right
- Someone to assure me that the claims adjuster with whom I had a screaming match over a medical bill on the phone is the psychopathic jerk and not I
- Someone to confirm my diagnosis that the child's latest tantrum is her problem and not mine
- Someone to deal with my computer's capricious behavior (even though he knows little more than I do about technology) because he appreciates the fact that I cannot emotionally handle confrontation.... not with a sibling, not with a neighbor, not with someone who is trying to cheat me, and emphatically not with a computer.
- Someone to provide me with a lifelong renovation project
- Someone to say he loves me in spite of my cranky temper and relentless expectations
- Someone to point out the obvious flaws.

Marriage may not be champagne and roses; it may not be a guaranteed lifelong date for New Year's Eve; it may no longer be the bedrock of civilization. But it does have its small, essential compensations.

And, for that, it deserves to survive and be available to anyone cockeyed enough to want it.

Nita Micossi wishes her husband, who is a good sport and has no sense of humor whatsoever, a very happy birthday.

January 2004

MAKING DO WITH PUBLIC SCHOOL

A FEW MONTHS AGO I was at a barbecue talking with a woman whose kids go to a private school that doesn't believe in television, reading at an early age, or Harry Potter. (When we parents of school age children meet at a party, the talk inevitably turns to school, even though I'd rather discuss the humor in Franz Kafka or the privatization of Social Security.)

This mother was passionate about the school -- at $8000 a year per child she'd better be passionate -- and informed me that the reason the school requires parents to toss out the TV and forbids children to see the Harry Potter movie is that the neural synapses of young children are too delicate to sort through and process the onslaught of images careening through the popular media. Phew!

So what do they teach the children? Sewing, knitting, and juggling. On cue, the woman summoned her nine-year-old son who gave an outstanding demonstration of his juggling talent. Everyone at the party was dazzled. I was ashamed. My daughter can barely throw a horseshoe. And not only do I let her read books and listen to the radio, I took her to see the Harry Potter movie at the mall.

As if I weren't feeling bad enough, a friend who home schools her two girls informed me that she's teaching her eight-year-old "world philosophy." They started with the Greeks, were currently somewhere between Hobbes and Locke, and intended to end up with Wittgenstein. I couldn't decipher Wittgenstein in col-lege. And my poor kindt is still struggling with fractions and the value of coins.

I confess that the public school where I do send my child has a rather dull by-the-book curriculum -- no rug hooking or Aristotle in sight. It has a lousy student-teacher ratio compared with the private schools and can't touch home schooling with its Holy Grail of education: a private tutor.

My daughter is going to have a hard time getting into Harvard or Princeton. The Ivies love eccentric geniuses who can deconstruct the complete essays of Francis Bacon while crocheting an afghan.

But I'm too cheap to send my kid to a private school that's a two hour roundtrip commute from home and costs one third of my annual income, and too self-absorbed to surrender my life to teaching a seven year old long division on the kitchen table.

So I try to compensate with some one-on-one attention and enrichment programs of my own. For instance, I'm exposing my daughter to the great movie and stage musicals. She can mimic the different tap dancing styles of Shirley Temple, Fred Astaire and Bo Jangles. She can sing the entire score of Rogers and Hammerstein's South Pacific. And she can deconstruct the film career of Leslie Caron.

Her father takes her to 4-H meetings where she is learning about the anatomical characteristics and grooming needs of the cavia porcellus.

And she has become pen pals with her six-year-old cousins in Italy who will expand her knowledge of world geography, Romance languages, and Prada accessories.

I also spend some time each day playing Scrabble or Chinese checkers with the child and listening to her read from the collected works of Shel Silverstein. With strained resources, our family must rely on the currency of imagination, the village library, and the public school.

Public school. It has its shortcomings. But it's free, it's a short bus ride away, and, most of all, it ensures that my daughter has friends next door, around the corner, and within biking distance. She is growing up as part of a community that's growing up with her. And that counts for something.

Twenty years ago Nita Micossi was a professor of Child Development at the University, but she gave it up when she found that experts with theories about children's neural synapses can't beat the instincts of on-the-job parents.

September 2002

TEENS AND THE SEVEN DEADLY SINS

WELL IT HAS HAPPENED. My adorable baby whose universe has revolved around me, the Beloved Mother for most of her existence, just turned 13 and officially became a teenager.

Of course, she's been ramping up to this stage for years.

At age seven, according to Catholic doctrine, children are capable of distinguishing between right and wrong. The priests say that an eight-year-old can technically commit a mortal sin, a capital offense. The premeditated malice required to make it truly mortal, however, isn't fully developed, except in those rare precocious cases, until the kid is 13.

Children have six years to perfect the arts of manipulation and deceit, so that by age 13, in most cultures throughout human history, they are considered sufficiently skilled to become part of the adult community where they can enjoy adult rights [primarily procreation] and fulfill adult duties [primarily procreation].

Yes, turning 13 is a momentous leap forward in the social dance, corresponding to vast physical and mental changes. Even our society, which criminalizes many of the behaviors that come naturally to a 13-year-old, acknowledges it.

Jews, for example, mark the passage into adulthood with the Bar or Bat Mitzvah where the young person is forced to sing off-key in a foreign language in front of elderly relatives who show their appreciation by writing large checks. Christians note the transition with a Confirmation ceremony in which the newly minted adult gets a slap across the face while singing a boot camp ditty {"An army of youth flying the banner of truth, we're fighting for Christ, the Lord."] Secular teens generally get a new cell phone and a lame promise from Dad that she's entitled to a car only if she gets straight A's for the next three years.

Since my daughter is the youngest in her crowd, I've had ample opportunity to observe her teen friends for almost a year. And I've concluded that, along with menstruation and credit card debt, 13-years-olds share another adult trait: they are capable and culpable of the Seven Deadly Sins.

You know the Seven Deadly Sins: Lust, Gluttony, Greed, Sloth, Wrath, Envy, and Pride.

Lust – obsessive desires of a sexual nature -- is obvious. Human beings are at their randiest as soon as the pituitary gland flips the switch on those juicy teen hormones. In some cultures lust is channeled into early marriage and sanctioned baby-making. In ours, we wink at teen sex-drugs-and-rock'n'roll excesses so long as she gets a sensible job and life insurance by the time she's eligible to vote.

Gluttony or over-consumption to the point of waste can hardly be called a sin in a society where over-consumption to the point of waste is an act of patriotism. From the cradle, our kids are taught to consume what they don't need with money their parents don't have. By the time they're teens, little wonder that the brats hang out at the Mall and engage in competitive shopping.

Which brings us to Greed. As every parent knows, no matter how many times you say "yes" to a teen's numbing demands, the minute you say "no", you are a hideous stingy monster. Kids want more than they'll ever have and they use their manipulative skills [see above] to squeeze ever more out of a parent -- also known as The Cash Register. Don't even suggest gainful employment as a path to acquisition.

Hence Sloth, my personal favorite. The father and I frequently urge our now-young-woman to leverage her considerable talents – babysitting [certified], animal husbandry [all species], calligraphy [in two different alphabets] – to earn enough money to pay for her AAA battery habit. This is met with a contemptuous sneer. And if she won't work for money [why bother when she lives with a Cash Register?], forget about her "doing chores around the house for the common good" despite gentle training from toddlerhood. A simple request to "dry the dishes" requires from six to twelve increasingly shrill nags before the now-young-woman abandons her FreeCell computer game. And her efforts are so shoddy that the chore has to be redone by The Parent. The kid definitely has a black belt in passive–aggressive behavior.

What about Wrath or Anger? Ask my daughter and she'll tell you that I am the angry one. True, true. All that futile nagging. But the core emotion of the teenager – often expressed as random contrariness or the high-pitched whine -- is anger: at ones parents, at ones teachers, at the best friend who betrays, at the boy who ignores, at the whole damn world. These rebels don't need a cause.

And then there is Envy. Envy is the desire for what others have – their qualities, talents, position, or whatever. Like gluttony, envy is part of our cultural Zeitgeist. Few teens can escape the longing, however unspoken, to be Hannah Montana. I give them a pass on this one.

Finally, we have Pride, the original and, according to the people who make up these lists, most Deadly of the Deadly Sins. Except for the strutting biker, the prom queen, or the class valedictorian, however, few teens that I've known truly believe in themselves, let alone stoke that excessive belief in their own superiority that we call pride. Insecurity and self-doubt seem to be the defining qualities of a teenager. And frankly, I wouldn't mind if my child had a bit more pride in herself and her extraordinary qualities. If she did, she might be less prone to the other six sins.

Nita Micossi spent her adolescence in an all-girls school with the nuns.
Enough said.

August 2008

7.
HOORAY FOR THE HOLIDAYS!

HOW I LEARNED TO STOP WHINING AND SURVIVE CHRISTMAS COMMERCIALISM. When the campaign revs up in early autumn for the iPod, ultimate terrain traction battery-operated jeep, purebred Lhasa Apso puppy, American Express card, or whatever the kid is pushing this year, just say "No." Page 167

XMAS ON THE WEB. You can take a tour of Virtual Finland, reputed home of the Claus clan; check out a slide presentation of competitive Christmas home light shows in Central Texas; or find out who put the "X" in Xmas. Page 170

BLESS US ALL. Contemplating my blessings on Thanksgiving Day I'm grateful for water pressure, four-wheel drive, garlic, elastic waist bands, daylight savings time, and Buddy Holly's music. Page 173

IN DEFENSE OF FRUITCAKE. It's a frigid and snowy December night.... Go to the freezer, remove the fruitcake and cut paper thin slices that look like tiny stained glass windows when held up to the refrigerator light. Brew yourself a nice cup of tea to go with this singular sensation and cozy up with a murder mystery....Trust me. Page 175

THANKS IN THE GALILEE. All afternoon curious kibbutzniks wandered into the kitchen to offer advice on the pies, sample my stuffing, and fight with David, who democratically denied all a peek at the turkeys for fear that drafts would dry them out. Page 177

HOLIDAY GREETINGS: We've made it through another twelve months without being hit, while in a moving vehicle, by a deer. Page 179

CHRISTMAS SCHNOOK: A college-educated intellectual is sucked into the holiday hysteria by Tickle Me Elmo. Page 181

THE PARTY OF THE MILLENIUM: "Oy vay!" cried the Blessed Virgin Mary. "Only ten months left and we don't even have a plan for J.C.'s 2000th birthday." Page 184

HOORAY FOR THE HOLIDAYS. There's no better way to fight the gloom outside than to fill up the inside with the twinkle of a dozen beeswax candles and the slightly mad laughter of an overfed crew tucking into the dessert wine and hot chestnuts. Page 187

HOW I LEARNED TO STOP WHINING & SURVIVE CHRISTMAS COMMERCIALISM

YES, THE DEPARTMENT STORES hang the holly swag in September. Yes, TV kid shows shill for Macy's. Yes, Christmas is commercial. But it's been so during the lifetime of everyone within the sound of my voice. So stop complaining. Go with the flow. And swallow as little water as possible.

You can get through the holidays without dropping from combat fatigue at the Mall in December and facing Chapter Eleven in January. Just listen up.

First, learn to say "No" to the kids. Repeat after me: No... No... Not on your life, not in this millennium, not even over my dead body... Practice that in front of the bathroom mirror every morning for five minutes starting in July. And when the campaign revs up in early autumn for the iPod, ultimate terrain traction battery-operated jeep, purebred Lhasa Apso puppy, American Express card, or whatever the kid is pushing this year, just say No.

Do not succumb to that old canard "everybody else has one." Are you so old that you've forgotten that ploy? Nobody has one, until, of course, the day after Christmas, when every kid is on the new cell phone with-text-messaging-and-zoom-camera bragging to her pals about how she conned her brain-damaged parents again this year.

I know that it's not easy to shut up a twelve year old who is committed, down to the very core of his being, to getting a new drum set. But you must be firm. (Whenever you weaken, consider the long term consequences of capitulation.) Tell him that a drum set is out of the question but that you'll be happy to pass along to Santa his wish for a new metronome. When the child then falls to the floor, does an Oscar-winning performance of an epileptic seizure, and moans pitifully, "but everybody has one", you withdraw the idea of the metronome and suggest coal as a more apt measure of the child's behavior. It's surprising how well the old "coal" gambit still works even among children who have never seen a lump of coal in their lives.

Second, forget TV and peer group pressure, and take responsibility for your family consumption habits. I'm puzzled to see parents loading multiple carts at Wal-Mart with luxury electronics and big-ticket toys before Christmas, only to wail with self-pity when the Visa bill arrives on January 15th. Don't they know that, starting with the birth of their first child, they themselves set the family standard for gift giving and receiving. And when their eight year old threatens to enlist in the Navy if she doesn't see everything on her ten-page Wish List under the tree, her parents have only themselves to blame.

I prefer to take a lesson from none other than the pious Mrs. John D. Rockefeller, who once remarked to a neighbor, "I am so glad my son has told me what he wants for Christmas, so now it can be denied him." The Rockefellers held sacrifice to be the foundation of moral character and, though wealthy enough to buy a bicycle factory, insisted that their children share one tricycle.

I'm not quite so harsh, but I have mastered fiscal restraint during December, when this family celebrates both Christmas and Chanukah. My daughter knows that Mr. Claus delivers one and only one gift to each child, plus a generously endowed stocking, heavy on chocolate, citrus fruit, and small games suitable for travel. In addition, she receives modest gifts for each of the eight nights of Chanukah. It's amazing the treasures you can find out there for under $5 if you remember that kids have ample imagination to transform the simple into the remarkable. Think: a dollar store journal and pen; a ball of yarn and a crochet hook; a spool of fishing line and a bag of beads; a bucket of chalk; a map of China.

Third, go for the quantity discount. Least you think I'm off the hook with an only child, there are a dozen nieces, nephews, and assorted small friends that I buy for. Take a tip and pick out a modest one-size-fits-all gift and purchase in bulk. One year it was snow caps, another it was sea monkey kits.

The holiday shopping task for this mother is unpressured, and no threat to my year-end mortgage payment. In fact, by refusing to get suckered into stalking the season's hot item (I learned my lesson with Tickle-Me-Elmo in 1996), I actually enjoy wandering around the stores during December, singing along with Brenda Lee, sampling the smoked sausage at the Hickory Farms booth, and chatting up Santa's elves during their break.

Repeal the Christmas morning potlatch and your children may accuse you of being cruel and unusual. But you will know, in your heart, that you are offering them the greater gifts of simplicity and imagination. And you will find yourself on December 25th with less stress and more money on the debit card that you ever thought possible. Stand firm and God bless.

December 2006

XMAS ON THE WEB

WHEN YOU TYPE "CHRISTMAS" into a Google search you get 18,500,000 results.

There are, of course, tens of thousands of web sites ready to sell you boxes of hand-dipped chocolates, exotic fruit baskets, and naughty lingerie. There are almost as many who will suggest unusual gifts for the guy on your list who already has everything. A day of Formula One race car driving, perhaps? Or a Sponge Bob inflatable chair?

But Christmas is more than retail. There are countless sites on the Internet devoted to the cultural effluvia that has, over the centuries, attached to this holiday like barnacles on the belly of a mine-sweeper.

For instance, you can download over 10,000 recipes for eggnog, every verse to every shopping mall carol ever recorded (including the sacrilegious ones), directions for a tabletop salt-and-flour crèche set, instructions on how to make a festive tree out of $1 bills, and a dozen seasons worth of Top Ten Santa Jokes from the David Letterman show.

You can take a tour of "Virtual Finland", reputed home of the Claus clan, and hear the Sibelius High School Chamber Choir deliver a musical greeting. (www.virtual.finland.fi)

Or you can check out a slide presentation of over-the-top competitive Christmas home light shows in Central Texas. (www.io.com)

You will further find every holiday symbol and tradition parsed and analyzed by scores of self-anointed Xmas scholars. Starting with the word "Xmas", which I have always felt was a slightly disreputable 20th century corruption. But no! I was informed by any number of holiday myth slayers that "Xristos" is actually the Greek word for "Christ" and that Christians have been using Xmas as an insider's shorthand for centuries.

Just as this profane symbol has a sacred root, so too many holiday customs popular among Christians have a pagan lineage. Like kissing your sweetie under the mistletoe, a plant whose association with romance goes back to the Druids who believed that it had magical fertility powers.

And didn't you always wonder about those tiny glass fruit and vegetable ornaments that Grandma put on her tree and which fetch a bundle on Ebay? A little-known German tradition calls for a pickle to be the last item hung on the tree. (I guess you have to be German to get it.) A soggy gherkin was eventually replaced by a pickle-shaped glass ornament and, on Christmas morning, the first child to spot it got a special present. (You'll have to ask Grandma about the acorn and cabbage-shaped ornaments.)

On the subject of food, there are rumors among the faithful that those red-and-white striped candy canes represent the "J" in Jesus. Truth is, according to Elesha Coffman of the online Christian History newsletter, that a 17th century choirmaster at the Cologne Cathedral gave out sugar-candy sticks curved like shepherds' staffs to fidgety kids during the Living Nativity pageant. And the custom caught on.

One could fritter away an entire afternoon nibbling at this smorgasbord of holiday trivia. I know I did.

But the really juicy stuff on the Net is found on those sites that urge us to rethink Christmas altogether.

Take the Christmas Resistance Movement at www.xmasresistance.org. "You know that holiday shopping is offensive and wasteful," shouts the group's homepage Manifesto. "You know Christmas 'wish lists' and 'gift exchanges' degrade the concept of giving." The Resistance – which nails our guilt and ambivalence over spending what we don't have to buy what we don't need -- calls for a boycott of all Christmas shopping, cards, decorations, and "every variety of Christmas crap". "Refuse to support the Holiday Industry!...(and show) love for friends and family by giving our time and care, not by purchasing consumer goods!" The idea seems to be catching on since the Movement offers links to over a dozen similarly minded sites including one in French.

Then there's the fervent plea of Baptist Pastor Greg Wilson to "Keep Christ Out of Xmas!" The holiday, argues Pastor Wilson, has nothing at all to do with Christ. December 25th in the Roman world, was the feast of the Sun God Mithras, a Persian deity adopted by the Romans in the 1st century B.C. The Roman Catholic Church freely admits that it took the holiday from paganism and adapted it for its own purposes. And many Protestant immigrants to America considered Christmas a pagan blasphemy up to the late 19th century, when Macy's rewrote the script. "Christmas is a thoroughly pagan holiday," scolds Wilson, "in its origin, in its trappings, and in all its traditions."

But my favorite iconoclastic web site is "No Christmas Puppies, Please!" by dog lover Ruth Ginzberg. Even though "the loyal, loving, uncorrupted, hauntingly simple innocence of a puppy.... is the perfect symbol of the true spirit of Christmas," says Ginzberg, "a living puppy should not be thought of in the same category as a Christmas toy." She laments the fate of the newly-weaned, easily-frightened pup who is thrown into the chaos of Christmas morning, just one more novelty among a dozen toys that will be broken, traded, or forgotten by Valentine's Day. Right on, Ruth!

Christmas. It doesn't take 18,500,000 web hits to remind us that it's a potlatch, a birthday party, a religious commemoration, a theatrical extravaganza, a sentimental journey, a pleasant fiction, a bawdy fraud.... it's whatever you want it to be. This year, let's hope it's peaceful

December 2004

BLESS US ALL

THANKSGIVING DAY. EVERYONE IS seated around the table that is sagging under the weight of enough food to feed a Roman legion. Even though we've all been snacking since noon on chips, dips, and a block of cheddar cheese the size of a footlocker, the aroma of roast turkey, mashed potatoes, yam casserole, and string beans sautéed in garlic butter is irresistible. Time to eat.

But no.... wait .... after the obligatory grace, Aunt Rose suggests that we all take turns declaring what we are most thankful for. So around the table we go, each one mumbling a meager thanks for "health," "family," and, in the case of the child, "my new guinea pig."

This year I decided to think about my blessings well in advance so that I won't be caught up short in front of the cranberry sauce.

So, here 'tis, some of the things that I'm truly grateful for:

WATER PRESSURE. Every morning, as hot needles of shower water revive me, I think of Katharine Hepburn. Hepburn, legend has it, never bought or rented an apartment before she had first ditched the real estate agent, stripped down, and taken a shower in the prospective bathroom. If the water pressure didn't cut it, the lady – who took three or four showers a day – didn't sign. I totally understand.

BUDDY HOLLY'S MUSIC. How could I have ever crossed the continent in a VW van in 1970, kept the faith with my aerobics workout while on the kibbutz in 1982, or packed up the detritus of my mother's 83 years on the planet last year, without it?

FOUR WHEEL DRIVE. The first car I bought when I moved to the Northeast was a 1974 Dodge Dart 4-door sedan. It was a big bulky brown and black two-tone, with old-fashioned bench seats front and back. It was the car of choice for taxi drivers back then. And I loved my old thing. But it didn't love that ice patch on Route 17 outside of Boston one January morning on my way to work. The Dodge and I skidded into a Pontiac that had skidded on the same patch seconds before. I walked away from the accident, but the Dodge's drive shaft did not. Ever since, I have bought only vehicles with four wheel drive, and I high-five St. Christopher whenever I have go out in a snow storm to pick up the pizza.

GARLIC. I believe that when the physicists eventually crack open the smallest particle of matter they will find within the true trinity of Nature: olive oil, lemon, and garlic.

EMIL VON BEHRING. I was five months pregnant when my husband and I took that last fling to Puerto Rico in 1995. The puddle jumper to the island of Vieques resembled a sardine can. The airplane had no interior aisles and the exterior metal doors on one side peeled back to allow passengers to crawl into one of six pairs of seats lined up one behind the other. In managing this maneuver in my bloated condition, I snagged my right thigh on a rusty nail. I dashed to the San Juan hospital where I and my unborn child were rescued from a fate worse than death (usually followed by death) due to the swift intervention of a manic intern wielding a syringe of tetanus vaccine. I shall be forever in debt to Emil von Behring, the German bacteriologist who prepared the first tetanus antitoxin serum in 1890.

DAYLIGHT SAVINGS TIME. Why can't we make it year round?

ELASTIC WAIST BANDS. Especially at the Thanksgiving dinner table.

MIKIE'S LEMON SQUARES.

....When my kith and kin are sharing their thanksgivings around the table I shall be meditating upon these gifts for which I'm grateful every year. But when it's my turn to give thanks aloud for this year's greatest blessing, I'll say only, THE RED SOX.

November 2004

IN DEFENSE OF FRUITCAKE

NO HOLIDAY SEASON IS complete without a cheap shot at fruitcake. A few years ago on the front page of THE WALL STREET JOURNAL, a reporter sneered, "Nobody really eats the stuff." And good old boy Garrison Keillor, on that otherwise tolerant Saturday-night radio entertainment show, once challenged us all to "do the honorable thing! and eat your fair share to save the state of Nebraska" – which had been chosen as the national dumpsite of unwanted fruitcakes.

Back off, Garrison. You've never tasted my Ma's homemade fruitcakes. They arrive from California just before Thanksgiving with a cautionary note to let them age a few weeks more. Foolish woman.

Every holiday season when I cut into that first little cake, savoring the aroma of brandy and the silky gloss of maraschino cherries, I recall those years I watched my mother unwrap her liquor-soaked wreaths. She made the fruitcakes then, as now, in early autumn to ensure a good two months for aging.

Swaddled in cheesecloth, then bundled in terry towels, the fruitcakes were placed in the bottom drawer of the mahogany sideboard. Even before we could read, she taped a sign on those fragrant mummies: "No tasting until Thanksgiving."

I remember the lost experiments before Ma perfected the ratios, when the holiday cakes molded in their cheesecloth sacs. Too much brandy? Not enough air? She wept and vowed to never again invest her love and money.

The economics of the fruitcake, you see, are not incidental. You need eight cups of the candied fruit stuff and each cup costs two, three bucks. Pecans from Georgia run $7 a pound. And a fifth of decent brandy can set a cook back a week's worth of car fare.

But despite the costly disasters, my mother continued to figure those fruitcakes into the Christmas budget every year until she came up with a foolproof combination of ingredients and optimal aging conditions.

Hers are the best, of course, but that doesn't help you. When shopping around for a fruitcake the operative word is "fruit", so you should look for one with just enough mortar to hold the whole thing together. Years ago my mother-in-law Pauline Finley introduced me to a delectable version made at the Collin Street Bakery in Corsicana, Texas. The Collin Street cake is 80% fruits and nuts. Good enough for the King of Belgium who orders them by the case. Pity the King never got to taste my mother's.

Ma stopped making the traditional round fruitcakes when we all moved away from home, since small loaves are easier to send through the mail and easier to store in the freezer.

The freezer? Ah, now comes the secret!

It's a cold, snowy night in December. Due to a happy coincidence of events you're all alone in the house. Go to the freezer, remove the fruitcake from its ziploc bag, and cut paper thin slices that look like tiny stained glass windows when held up to the refrigerator light. Brew yourself a nice cup of tea to go along with this singular sensation and cozy up with a murder mystery.

Say you'd rather fight the hoards at Filene's the day after Christmas than face a plate of the dread fruitcake? Trust me on this one.

December 2003

GIVING THANKS IN THE GALILEE

It was early October and nights in the Galilee were still warm and dry when I began thinking about turkeys and Thanksgiving.

There were 40 of us Americans on the kibbutz and we'd clearly need two very large or three medium-sized birds. My friend David was assistant to the supplies manager in the kitchen who knew a farmer near Nazareth who raised fowl and would sell us what we needed. The manager also agreed to special order mushrooms and squash, raisins, yams, and sweet cream for us. But we had to find the nuts and cranberries for ourselves.

The nuts were no problem. I had an appointment to cut Stephen's hair on Wednesday. He usually paid me in olive oil, a dear commodity he procured during his monthly visits to Haifa. This time I'd ask him for two pounds of walnuts instead.

The cranberries were more difficult. David had heard that a kibbutz in the far north raised them, but I was skeptical. Israel went to a lot of trouble to drain the swamps in which cranberries thrive.

What about canned berries? I once found a jar of Skippy peanut butter in a dusty market in a small village in the interior of a Greek island off the Turkish coast. Who knows what unusual bounty had washed up on the local Mediterranean shores? David volunteered to scour the grocery stores of Haifa.

I had no trouble recruiting a cooking crew. The lure was a holiday afternoon in the kitchen peeling vegetables and playing with dough while enveloped by the fragrance of roasting turkey.

And what a kitchen! The kibbutz fed 1,200 people three times a day. Stripped bare, that kitchen could have easily held a Bedouin wedding party or the 108th Congress. But it was never empty.

There were rows of stainless steel vats used to simmer sauces and boil rice, each mounted on two thick legs bolted to the concrete floor. And each vat could be tilted on its side to spill its load into an oversized colander. There were a half-dozen huge rectangular frying pans, 2'x 3' and 10" deep, that could be filled with oil by pumping like a milkmaid from a large oil drum on a dolly. The ovens were stacked in tiers of three. And instead of refrigerators, there were two refrigerated rooms – one for butter and cheese, one for meat and salads.

One wall of the kitchen was lined with sinks where young volunteers from Holland and Denmark scrubbed the pots and pans that couldn't go through the immense conveyor belt dishwasher that occupied a room all its own.

Giant size in every way, the kibbutz kitchen was still homey. It was the cherished turf of two dozen elderly Polish women and their commandant, a tall, bald man named Moishe who had served in the celebrated Polish cavalry unit that attacked Nazi tanks on horseback in World War II.

After lunch on Thanksgiving day, Moishe and his crew reluctantly surrendered their stools at the wide tables set between rows of sinks and ovens, and I put my people to work. Some of them chopped potatoes into steel bowls that sat on dollies for easy wheeling to pots of boiling water. Others minced mountains of garlic and parsley and scallions for the stuffing. Some rolled pastry dough into thin sheets for pumpkin pies and apple turnovers. Others made sure the rest of us had a steady supply of clean bowls, sharp knives, and hot coffee.

I mothered a great crackling pan of fried mushrooms, buttered croutons, celery, onions, raisins, and nuts. David – who'd kept an all-night vigil with the turkeys, cooking them by the slow roast method – slumped in a chair nearby, and we dickered over the ratio of sage to thyme.

All afternoon curious kibbutzniks wandered into the kitchen to offer advice on the pies, sample my stuffing, and fight with David, who democratically denied all a peek at the turkeys for fear that drafts would dry them out.

By 4pm the white potatoes were mashed in a quart of cream, the gravy was bubbling in a vat, and every oven was full. We scrubbed the sinks so that the regular dinner cooks could begin the evening meal for the community. As they reheated dumplings from lunch, we carried our golden birds off to the music room where another team had set a long table with flowers and candles and baskets of peaches, pears, and dates picked from the kibbutz orchards.

We said a prayer in English and one in Hebrew, and wished blessings on our families who were just greeting the day on the other side of the world. We raised our wine glasses and David deftly slipped a carving knife into our Thanksgiving turkey. Nobody missed the cranberries.

November 2003

HOLIDAY GREETINGS

DEAR FRIENDS,

IT'S TIME to admit that the days of my writing individual notes on the back of each and every one of my Christmas cards are over. I know that for the past few years I've been making excuses as to why I was writing the Dread Collective Holiday Letter. I truly believed that it was a temporary lapse and that, as soon as I got my affairs in order and my days neatly scheduled into color-coded slots, I'd be able to give each one of you the tender time and attention you deserve.

But, clearly, that fantasy is one more casualty on my long slide down from the summit of perfection. Blame it on Motherhood. Blame it on The Job. Blame it on those 24 boxes of files from the storage bin in Oakland that, after being shipped East two years ago, are still sitting unopened in my dining room. Blame it on the whole mess. I know I do.

Still I cannot complain. Though the child is losing her teeth, Mr. Wonderful is losing his hair, and I'm losing my grip on my Weight Watchers' daily points range, we've made it through another year having dodged the bullet of ill health and worse. Yes, we're all in fine fettle. And counting our blessings.

We're thankful, for instance, for not having been hit while in a moving vehicle by a deer in the past twelve months. Thankful that we made it through another winter without the old furnace exploding and the pipes freezing. Thankful that we are spared earthquakes.

I feel blessed that the leak in my office roof over the summer only destroyed volumes "F" through "Q" of my encyclopedia, sparing vital entries on Afghanistan, Ebola, and Lee Radziwill. I thank the Lord I lost only $800 on that multi-level schmatte-selling pyramid scheme last May. And I deeply appreciate the generosity of the Fates in letting our rental house tenants burn only a hole in the bedroom floor, when they could just as easily have burned down the whole house.

Of course, I do fret about what computer guys call MTBF or the "mean time between failures." Since major catastrophes are strung out on a continuum of probability, the longer you go without one, the closer you are to having one. Which is why I am grateful for the relatively benign distresses of the past 12 months.

Like losing my job in January. I like to think of it as being ahead of the recession curve. I also like to think that Ultimate Justice does prevail and that I will be in on the first wave of recovery. There is, in fact, cause for optimism. Just last week I got a part time temporary job teaching in the Federal Penitentiary for Women in Danbury, Connecticut. Given the 3-hour commute and the 9 hours a week spent correcting papers, it turns out to be a minimum wage gig. But, hey, I earn 60 cents more per hour than do my students and, unlike them, I can sneak out to the Mall whenever I want.

Yes. Minor annoyances relieve pressure on the tectonic plates of life so that you don't have major eruptions. And everything is relative.... Which just about sums up my year: in the grand scheme of things, it's been pretty darn okay.

Hope your year has been okay too and that you and yours are all well.

Merry Christmas, Happy Hanukkah, & a Peaceful New Year!

December 2001

CHRISTMAS SCHNOOK

IT ALL STARTED A year ago September. I was scribbling down some ideas I had for Baby's First Christmas: a wooden rocking horse -- an heirloom from F.A.O. Schwarz, a toy for the ages; a profusely illustrated copy of Alice in Wonderland -- to keep us both entertained; and a little piano -- so my daughter can learn to play like Fats Waller and fulfill my life's ambition.

These essentials, I figured, plus a few stocking stuffers were enough to keep up my end of Santa's business.

Until I saw the doll on TV.

I don't watch daytime television or the kind of program that advertises toys. But one morning at the gym, after I was 40 minutes into the Stairmaster and at my most vulnerable, there it was on the overhead set: a ragged orange creature that giggled and shook when you squeezed its tummy. I had to have one! I turned up the volume on my walkman in time to catch the name of this adorable thing: Tickle Me Elmo.

I didn't get to my holiday shopping til the day after Thanksgiving. But with such a puny list, I reckoned, we could surely make this a one-day, hassle-free family outing. I called Toys'R'Us just to make sure that they had what I wanted. We could wrap this up before lunch.

To my surprise, however, the clerk at Toys'R'Us said that the store was "out of" Elmo and had been for weeks. Odd, I thought and rang up K-Mart. "We've got a waiting list," said the manager, "but I doubt we'll get enough product in before Christmas to accommodate everyone." A waiting list? Caldor's was also out of stock and invited me in to pick up a rain check. I was getting a bit unnerved. It's just a dumb doll. If it's on TV somebody's got to be selling it.

I had to call four more stores til I finally got a woman at KayBees who confided that there were "still a few left, if you hurry." Good sense told me that it was probably some kind of marketing scam going on here -- you know, create the illusion of scarcity and suckers will rush to pay anything. Still I was getting restless, so I corralled the family and told my husband to drive -- fast -- to the Mall.

While he parked the car I dashed in, found the store, found the aisle, and was walking swiftly but lady-like in the direction of the Sesame Street Display when a man in a New York Rangers jacket raised a box above his head and shouted "is this what you're looking for?" "Why, yes," I said with relief. It was pre-mature. "Aha!" he laughed. "It's the last one and it's mine!" His little pip-squeak of a wife peered out from behind that expanse of jacket and gloated that they had been to 13 stores that week alone. I guess they expected me to raise my arms and holler "touch down!" But I didn't. I slinked off to find my husband and child, puzzled. How was it that everyone else had suddenly decided to buy the same silly doll I'd picked out two months earlier?

A few days later when the newscasters were reporting on the first weekend of Christmas shopping, I heard the news I had been subconsciously dreading: Tickle Me Elmo was the phenom of the season, the Cabbage Patch of the decade, the marketing sensation that was bumping Tyco's stock up to dizzying heights. And I was smack dab in the middle of the suck zone.

I felt like a complete schnook. You see, I invariably make life choices that are obscure and marginal. I avoid the popular out of a well-founded conviction that mass appeal tastes like cardboard. Point to a crowd and I flee in the opposite direction. Yet here I was wanting, seeking, dare I say needing the same object as 89% of the American buying public. I was deeply ashamed.

But not so ashamed that I was willing to give up the hunt. I called up my sister-in-law in Queens, my brother in Chicago, and my mother in San Francisco and told them to be on the look-out. I asked a friend who used to work on the maintenance crew at K-Mart to see if he had a pal on the inside who could snag me a doll if any came in. I went to Caldor's and got that raincheck.

I did not, however, realize just how pitifully hopeless my quest had already become until, one day, back on the stairmaster at the gym, watching the Rosie O'Donnell show, I learned the sickening truth. Rosie herself is something of a phenom and everybody who watches daytime TV watches her show. One day weeks before she had evidently done an unsolicited promo of the doll and single-handedly incited this unseemly demand. Stock from coast to coast sold out over night. And Tyco, the manufacturer, was so grateful that they sent Rosie a truckload of Tickle Me Elmos.

The woman was immediately inundated with pleas from mothers all over the country whose children were sick, homeless, depressed, dying (pick one) and who would surely recover if they could only get one of Rosie's dolls. (Okay, the thought did cross my mind.)

O'Donnell was not only a Tyco flak but now a sister of mercy spilling her cornucopia into the laps of tots with pushy mothers and any celebrity guest who hinted that her grandson would grow up to be a philanthropist if only there was a Tickle Me Elmo under the Christmas tree.

I was getting sour on the subject.

But I kept the faith. I e-mailed my family agents daily for progress reports, I scoured out-of-the-way toy shops, and I bonded with the shipping manager at Caldor's. He left hopeful updates on my phone machine right up until December 24th when we both knew that we'd been fooling ourselves all along. There was to be no Elmo under our tree.

My mother sent a purple Sesame Street creature with horns that honk when you grab its nose. Baby loved it and didn't notice that anything was missing. She never watches TV.

Me? I was a good sport. I cooked the turkey, spiked the eggnog, led the caroling, and wondered to myself it Rosie O'Donnell's son had broken his Tickle Me Elmo yet.

December 1998

THE PARTY OF THE MILLENNIUM

"OY VAY!" CRIED THE Blessed Virgin Mary, "Only ten months left and we don't even have a plan for J.C.'s 2000th birthday." The Heavenly Hosts were in the middle of Bach's Magnificat when the BVM burst into afternoon choir practice.

"Now, now, Mama," cooed the Father Almighty, that honey baritone camouflaging His pique at the interruption, "don't you worry yourself."

"Don't worry?!" shrieked the BVM. "It's not just the Boy's birthday, You know. People have been planning these end-of-the-millennium parties since 1989. All the nice spots have been booked for years. And we'll never find a good caterer at this late date."

"I'm certain that I can locate a few cooperative souls to help Us out," said His Beneficence while signaling the Cherubim to work on their four-part harmony. "Just tell Me what you'd like to do."

"I'm glad You should ask," replied the BVM, calmed by His unusually receptive mood. "I say we pull out the stops. Open the wallet. Throw an Affair that people will be talking about for centuries!"

"Can you be more specific?" He asked.

"Well, just look at these articles. There's some very good ideas in here," said the BVM shoving a folder of newspaper clippings at The Divine Majesty. "It seems that that annoying post-WW-two 'baby boomer' crowd -- as they like to call themselves -- started turning 50 a few years ago and they've been trying to outdo each other in throwing the most outrageous, extravagant, meshuggeneh birthday parties ever."

"Fifty? What's all the fuss?" He wondered.

"Well, that's what I say," said the BVM, "but that gang always had more chutzpah than talent. Full of themselves. Still, they have good ideas when it comes to making a party. Just look at this: it says here that, to celebrate his 50th birthday 'New York stock broker Irving Blecher rented Madison Square Garden for the night and hired the Knicks and the Celtics to play an exhibition game for 12,000 of his closest friends.' Now there's an event to remember!"

"Are you suggesting that We invite all of J.C.'s friends? Wouldn't that be rather crowded?" asked His Exalted Holiness.

"We could keep it down to those people who attend services regularly," answered the BVM. "Or we could have it very exclusive -- say the Pope, the Dalai Lama, some Reconstructionist rabbis -- and go for something lavish but tasteful. Here's an item from the Society Page about one Selma Fuchs, a dentist from Detroit: 'Last Friday Dr. Fuchs flew her pals to Paris on La Concorde for a tres magnifique weekend that began with brunch at the Eiffel Tower and concluded with an all-night saturnalia at the Follies Bergere. Bravo, Selma!'."

"What's a saturnalia?" asked The Creator.

"Some kind of a pagan ritual... before Your time," said the BVM. "The point is, the woman spared no expense."

"I'm not suggesting that We economize...."

"Good. Listen to this one. Dave Kowalski, a computer mogul from San Jose, observed his 50th birthday for an Entire Week. According to The Chronicle, 'Mr. Kowalski and his entourage of 100 intimate friends checked into the Fairmont Hotel on Monday, June 1st. They kicked off what Mr. Kowalski called his "gangsta fantasy" with a helicopter buzz of the Golden Gate at sunset, followed the next day by a hot air balloon picnic over Alcatraz Island, and a catered affair at Bay Meadows race track on Wednesday...' And so on.... Is that not one classy guy?!" exclaimed the BVM who was on a roll.

"Don't you think J.C. would prefer something simpler?" interjected The Eternal One without any impact whatsoever on her momentum.

"I'm thinking of a trim-the-tree brunch on December 25th -- where He can get all His presents. We start the week with something private and informal -- just the saints, the apostles, a few prophets perhaps -- since Christmas is, after all, a family day," declared the BVM. "Then on the 26th something really different but elegant. Maybe a black tie ice skating party. Do You think You could freeze the South Seas just this once? It's such a pretty setting. And then on the 27th how about a come-as-your-favorite-biblical-character costume ball. I see an oasis in the Sahara desert, a fabulous tent, Harry Connick Jr...."

"I really think J.C. would be happier to stay at home with Us. A few balloons, some noise makers, a nice sheet cake. We could get the Heavenly Hosts to sing a fugue version of Happy Birthday."

"Some noise makers? Are You nuts?!" A few eyebrows shot up in the Seraphim section, but the BVM raved on. "This is Your Only Begotten Son, the Lamb of God, the original Jewish Prince -- and You want to honor His big day with a lousy sheet cake!"

"So make it a double layer cheese cake from the Carnegie Deli," He replied.

"But the Boy is going to turn 2000!" moaned the BVM.

"Exactly," replied The Father of Us All. "At a certain age, don't you think that all this birthday business is just a bit... unseemly?"

Obviously, The All-Knowing One did not have the heart to inform His Son's mother (caught up as she is in millennium fever) that the Lad will only be 1999 in December. So we won't either.... By the way, Nita Micossi plans to celebrate her 50th birthday (should she ever decide to have one) in bed with a box of Dove bars, a bottle of Dom Perignon, and a good book.

March 1999

HOORAY FOR THE HOLIDAYS!

WHILE I WAS PICKING up the turkey at Northwind Farm this Monday morning before Thanksgiving, my husband was trolling the aisles at Adams for Greek olive tapenade and chopped walnuts. Suzanne is bringing the garlic mashed potatoes; Ada is in charge of all the green stuff; and Aunt Dolly, who hasn't seen the inside of a kitchen since 1972, has been asked to contribute a bottle of vodka for the late morning Bloody Marys and a box of after dinner mints for the postprandial Scrabble game. The menu is tacked onto the frig, the good tablecloth is airing on the line, and my mother-in-law's silver plate is out from under the bed.

So begins the six week season we fondly call The Holidays. It's our collective antidote to the cold and darkness that attack this part of the world in early November and keep us locked in a pitiless grasp until March. As soon as the last leaf falls we leap into action. We brew a glorious pot of stew, string up as many lights as we can get our hands on, and plan a party.

The first one, of course, is Thanksgiving Day itself. I hate to go to someone else's place on Thanksgiving. It's not just that I like to cook for three days and set a table with my mother's cut crystal serving bowls. It's that there's no better way to stave off the growing gloom outside than to fill up the inside with the aroma of nutmeg and butternut squash soup, the twinkle of two dozen cream colored candles, and the slightly mad laughter of an overfed crew tucking into the dessert wine and hot chestnuts.

We scold ourselves for going to excess with creature comforts during this holiday season. But, if we are to endure the heartless months that follow, we need to do it. Like bears before hibernation, we gorge knowing that a long lean stretch lies ahead. And that's okay.

This afternoon I'd planned to make the cranberry salad for Thursday but ended up instead pruning a dead heap of irises I'd overlooked in October. A glance at the long term weather forecast revealed that, unless we get one of those freak spells, this might well be one of the last days the temperature will break 50 degrees for many months. The flip side of sealing the windows, filling the kindling box, and otherwise making the inside of the home toasty and inviting for winter, is tidying up the outside bits and securing them as best we can against the cruel cold. So I harvested the last of the sage and oregano from my herb patch, spread a bag of mulch over the dormant tulips, stashed the garden tools in the shed, and coiled up the hoses in the basement.

Performing these quiet duties I felt an aching tenderness towards the small plot of land and all the living things upon it entrusted to my care. Like a mother putting a child to bed, I handed over their fate to the gods of winter sleep and darkness, and prayed for happy dreams.

And then it was 4:30 and night fell with a damp chill. I locked the shed, went inside to my kitchen, and turned the flame on under the kettle. While sipping my hot tea I thrilled over a new recipe for braised venison. It was winter outside and The Holidays here inside. And my Mediterranean soul was cheered.

Here's Auntie Nita's method for roasting chestnuts: 1) soak the chestnuts overnight (or longer) in a bucket of water in the frig; 2) cut an "X" on the rounded topside of the nut with a sharp hunting knife (attend that you do not slice yourself); 3) roast the nuts on a cookie sheet for a half hour or so in a 450 degree oven – or in a basket over the open hearth, if you're blessed with one; 4) enjoy the hot chestnuts with a nice glass of whatever holiday tipple your fancy.

December 2005

8.
WHO THE HELL IS RUNNING THIS JOINT, ANYWAY?

FEAR ITSELF. Madam was afraid. Very afraid. And ready to get her husband's hunting rifle from the back of the closet, if he'd had a hunting rifle. Page 191

KARL VS. KARL. "The ideas of the ruling class are, in every epoch, the ruling ideas" – is one of the few things that the Karls -- Rove and Marx -- agree on. Page 193

FRATERNITE, YANKEE STYLE. Got a problem? We've got a solution based on our country's tried and true formula of Independence, Individualism, and Self-Interest! Page 196

TAX CUT SWINDLE. While my income bracket gets a tax cut of about $1090 this year, my fuel oil is up $525, local property taxes have increased by $278, and my health insurance premiums were jacked up by $320….. A tax cut in my pocket? Think again, Cousin. Page 198

RONALD MCDONALD MADE ME DO IT. Thanks to our ever vigilant Congress, if you eat the French fries, you now take the rap for the cellulite on your thighs. And don't go looking for a lawyer, darlin', to save your full figure fanny. Page 201

THEY BUSTED CHONG. Tommy Chong, age 65, father of six, Bel-Air property tax payer, and Internet entrepreneur thought that the Federales would be too occupied chasing down Islamic terrorists, Columbian drug lords, and Enron executives to fuss with the likes of him. Wrong. Page 203

DEMOCRATS ON PARADE. After gazing into Howard Dean's cornflower blue eyes and shaking his hand [firm and dry], this reporter promises to bird-dog every presidential candidate who comes to our area and report on the quality of his or her handshake. Page 205

POLLS SCHMOLLS. In the most shrewdly calculated marketing campaign of all time, GW has terrified the bejezus out of the American public. So we cancel the vacation to Disneyworld, we stockpile potassium iodide pills, and we tell the pollsters that we want to keep George Bush in office, even though we know better. Page 207

WAR FROM THIS PERCH: My experience with one black-and-white war and one psychedelic war didn't prepare me for this you-are-there mini-series in literal living color. Page 210

My Philosophy of Life, plus a few handy tips

A NUKE IS A NUKE: "Mini-nuke" -- don't let that cute petit fours name fool you. Page 213

THE SOUL OF THE NEW REGIME: learning to live with homeland terrorism. Page 216

THE EASY STREET BLUES: The agony of being super-rich -- why doesn't W feel *their* pain? Page 219

WRITE ME IN & ADD (1) tsp SALT: It's about time that this country was run by a short Italian woman who can really cook. Page 221

IRAQ & THE FAT FLUSH DIET: Flush out political enemies and your metabolism slips into a coma. Page 223

FEAR ITSELF

THUS MORNING'S TOPIC OF conversation on the radio, boys and girls, is civility.

Civility: 1. the state of being civilized; 2. courteous behavior; politeness; good breeding.

Naturally the conversation jumps immediately to incivility. There is nearly unanimous agreement among the callers and radio hosts that we're a less thoughtful, less courteous, and just less nice society than we were when whoever is speaking was a kid.

Witness: more people are indulging in more outlandish displays of road rage than ever before; cell phone assaults in the Mall are on the rise; and preteens spew obscenities over the Internet at people they've never even met. Do you need more proof? Incivility is everywhere.

But I'm not so sure that we're in a morally defensible position to brag about the Good Ole Days of civility when folks RSVP'd to party invitations and automatically gave up their bus seats to pregnant women. As I recall, the same genteel ladies of the mid-20th century who were punctilious about bringing the new neighbors a basket of home-baked cookies might also cheerfully supply the matches for a cross-burning when a family of the "wrong" color or religion moved in next door.

Civility is as fragile as a Spode teacup and as rare as a pink diamond in any era or locale.

Incivility, on the other hand, is ubiquitous and highly adaptable to new circumstances. Remember the Boom Box? I believe came with instructions on how to create mayhem in public places.

But more disturbing than its stupendous capacity to adapt, is incivility's genetic link to barbarity. Aren't screaming threats to another driver on the thruway just the first step on an emotional journey that ends in vehicular homicide?

Rudolph Giuliani was onto something when he declared zero tolerance in New York City for squeegee vigilantes and subway graffitistas. To permit these small offenders against courtesy and civil propriety, reasoned Rudy, was to invite criminals, the real deal, into our community.

But my attention wanders. Back to the radio.... A listener calls in to explain why we are uncivil in the first place.

"Fear," he declares, pausing for dramatic effect. "Lack of civility is an expression of anger and anger is rooted in fear."

This is making sense to me. And it explains equally well the etiology of savagery, incivility's distant cousin. Aren't the monstrosities humans perpetrate on one another – think Shiites and Sunnis, Hutus and Tutsis, Republicans and Democrats – raw expressions of anger driven on by blind fear?

The root of all bad action, be it sidewalk rudeness or planetary evil, is, if I may paraphrase and extrapolate, fear itself.

Why then do we fear?

The radio is a font of inspiration for me this morning.... An immigrant woman comes on to tell a terrifying tale of being ambushed in her home on her first Halloween in this country. Packs of masked hooligans of all sizes swarmed around her front porch, punching the door and chanting unintelligible curses. Madam was afraid. Very afraid. And ready to get her husband's hunting rifle from the back of the closet, if he'd had a hunting rifle. On the brink of bad behavior or perhaps felonious behavior, the woman was pushed to the brink by fear. And her fear was born of ignorance. A short explanation of this playful pastime would have instantly lowered her blood pressure.

Aha! On every level we fear what we do not know and that fear propels us into misdeeds. Whether it's that boorish boy on the school bus who persistently taunts the little girls, or the 14-year-old kid who wants to blow up as many Jews as he can, fear is at the bottom of it all. And the only antidote to fear that I know of is knowledge.

The people who have been running this country for the past six years know it too, which is why they work so hard to keep us in the dark. "Keep 'em ignorant and you'll keep 'em afraid and they'll be angry enough to commit, or let us commit, any sins we concoct in their name."

The elections are over. But the campaign of deception and fear mongering is not. So stay alert, be aware, and the next time one of our so-called leaders conjures up boogiemen that are meant to frighten us, go to the library and read a book that teaches you something you don't know about the enemy.

Nita Micossi recommends THE PLACES IN BETWEEN, Rory Stewart's account of walking across Afghanistan by himself in 2002.

November 2006

KARL VS. KARL

SUMMER'S OVER, THE INSURANCE hawks are descending on New Orleans, and Mr. Karl Rove may or may not be having his hot pastrami and coleslaw delivered to the Oval Office every day.

His boss is in a predicament over the Rove matter. (If you've been shipwrecked off Tierra del Fuego for the past four months you might not know that Karl is alleged to have blown the cover of a C.I.A. spy to a reporter.... a behavior some consider treasonous.) When asked if he intended to fire anyone found to be involved in the C.I.A. leak scandal, George W put his hand on his heart and keened, "If someone committed a crime, they will no longer work in my administration." The chances, however, of Brother Karl having to fall on his sword for W are about as likely as Tom DeLay lobbying to double the minimum wage. But if Rove decides it's a politically astute move, I assure you that it will be a rubber blade.

In the meantime, life in Washington goes on, which is to say that Karl Rove is calling the ideological shots on Supreme Court nominees, gay marriage, and the optimal amount of Russian dressing on pastrami.

To take my mind off all these shenanigans, I have been reading Saul Padover's intimate biography of that other Karl -- the great philosopher and humanist himself -- Marx.

As I travel with Padover through the early childhood, university days, and romantic heartaches of young Karli (yes, he did have a doting mother), I can't help but wonder how the ideologue of our times, Karl Rove, would interpret the thoughts of the man whose ideas have been co-opted and exploited by any number of other ideologues.

Let us listen in as Karl the Rove adapts, for his own purposes, the wisdom of his namesake....

MARX: "Anyone who knows anything of history knows that great social changes are impossible without feminine upheaval. Social progress can be measured exactly by the social position of the fair sex."

ROVE: Social progress can be measured exactly by how many female evangelists are willing to go on the air and tell Larry King that homosexuals are Satan's spawn.

MARX: "Catch a man a fish, and you can sell it to him. Teach a man to fish, and you ruin a wonderful business opportunity."

ROVE: Drill for oil in the Arctic National Wildlife Refuge and you can sell it to the Koreans. Tell the American public that you're drilling for oil in the Arctic National Wildlife Refuge to sell to the Koreans and you ruin a wonderful midterm election talking point.

MARX: "Experience praises as the most happy, the one who made the most people happy."

ROVE: Experience praises as the most happy, the one who made the most multi-national conglomerate campaign contributors happy.

MARX: "Democracy is the road to socialism."

ROVE: Democracy is the road to "Law & Order" re-runs in every household in the Hindu Kush.

MARX: "The development of civilization and industry in general has always shown itself... active in the destruction of forests."

ROVE: The development of civilization and industry in general has always shown itself active in the expansion of dessert flora and fauna for the recreational pleasure of all its citizens.

MARX: "The oppressed are allowed once every few years to decide which particular representatives of the oppressing class are to represent and repress them."

ROVE: As it should be.

MARX: "The production of too many useful things results in too many useless people."

ROVE: It is impossible to produce too many useful things since the Liberty and Prosperity that flow from Democracy entitle, yea compel, all citizens to buy as much crap as they can possibly stuff into their three-car garages.

MARX: "The rich will do anything for the poor but get off their backs."

ROVE: If one diversifies the family portfolio wisely and hires a Wharton graduate to do the tax returns there is no reason for anyone to be poor.

MARX: "The writer may very well serve a movement of history as its mouthpiece, but he cannot of course create it."

ROVE: A cunning political operator, however, can.

MARX: "For the bureaucrat, the world is a mere object to be manipulated by him."

ROVE: "For the bureaucrat, the world is a mere object to be manipulated by him."

MARX: "The ideas of the ruling class are in every epoch the ruling ideas."

ROVE: Damn straight.

September 2005

FRATERNITE, YANKEE STYLE

CAN YOU BEAT THIS?! Prime Minister Jean-Pierre Raffarin of Paris, France is asking his countrymen and women to give up one of their cherished national holidays and go back to work. Why? To raise an estimated $2 billion a year to improve health care for the elderly. The idea comes after a heat wave last summer that killed 11,000 Frenchmen and women, most of them old and living in isolation.

The plan, supported by 71 percent of Frenchmen and women, is, says the Prime Minister "a true appeal to national brotherhood."

Wouldn't you know it? These are the same guys who came up with generous healthcare and pension benefits plus free education through college for all citizens. And now they are considering working one entire day each year just to make sure that crotchety old Aunt Fifi can live out her August days in air-conditioned comfort.

Those Frenchmen and women are just trying to show us up once again with all that Liberte, Egalite, and Fraternite business.

Me, I'll put Yankee-Can-Do up against their crackpot communalism any day. Got a problem? We've got a solution based on our country's tried and true formula of Independence, Individualism, and Self-Interest!

1. Problem: vehicle pollution. The French Solution: force everybody out of their SUVs and snow-mobiles "for the good of clean air." The U.S. solution: excuse SUV manufacturers from complying with clean-air emissions standards, keep gasoline prices artificially low, and let weekend warriors drive their ATVs through Yosemite because, gosh darnit, they've earned it.

2. Problem: the high cost of prescription drugs. The French solution: put restrictions on drug company profits and subsidize drug costs for low income families. The U.S. solution: give grandma a choice between hamburger helper or her heart pills. It's a free country.

3. Problem: gun violence. The French solution: make guns illegal. The U.S. solution: make it possible for every 15 year old in the country to get a gun along with his driver's permit license so that he will have a fighting chance when the school bully is having a bad day.

4. Problem: terrorism. The French solution: go to the United Nations and get global consensus and cooperation. The U.S. solution: go to war after bullying poor nations who need American economic largesse to be our allies.

5. Problem: poverty. The French solution: "acquis sociaux" – a package of social benefits that are the birthright of every citizen and a safety net for the vulnerable. The U.S. solution: let 'em eat cake (a solution, I should point out, stolen from a famous French lady). Yes, poverty. We've got it, no question about it. But we don't waste our time trying to "help out the helpless" (cf. "communism"). We believe that there is a Divine Plan and that the salvation of each and every individual is in his or her own hands. True blue Americans don't believe in handouts (at least for the poor).

The idea that people would give up their wages from a day's worth of labor in order to fund a program for the "less fortunate" is repugnant to the American sensibility. Liberty? Depends on how regular John Ashcroft is these days. Equality? We've got the best that money can buy. Fraternity? Be your brother's keeper and he will never learn how to fish, or something to that effect. Those Frenchies need a new slogan.

February 2004

TAX CUT SWINDLE

HERE WE GO AGAIN. The Republicans are tootin' their horns about Tax Cuts. You got 'em and, if you give us four more years, you'll get more! Who can resist?

Well, Cousin, let's cool down for a minute and walk through this one.

The end game of the GOP plan is the elimination of Progressive Taxation. You remember Progressive Taxation. It means that the higher your income, the higher your tax rate. You either love it or hate it. The more money you make the less you like it. I don't make a heck of a lot of money and, so, I do like it.

Now there are all those smarmy liberal reasons for supporting Progressive Taxation, like "rich folk can pay lots of taxes and still have piles of money left over to pay their country club dues."

But I prefer the reasons laid out by retired corporate management consultant and weblogger Chuck Kelly. Since the Reagan Days, Chuck reminds us, conservative politicians have manipulated the prime rate, forced Americans to compete with the most underpaid workers in the world, and passed all kinds of anti-worker legislation, such as the recent law that dumps overtime pay for up to 6 million U.S. employees. As a result, corporations have gotten more profitable and the rich have gotten richer. Waaay richer.

Who got all those conservative politicians elected? Why, the rich folk who benefit most from their policies. "It's only fair," says Chuck, "that those who caused these conditions.... and benefited from them, pay their fair share...." What's a fair share?

Back between 1942 and 1962 the tax rate for our richest brethren was from 88% to 91%. If you were one of the 400 wealthiest taxpayers in 2000 who made, on average, $174 million, you, Mr. Rich CEO, would have been able to keep -- under this scenario -- only about $20 million. You'd just have to manage somehow.

Between 1962 and 1982 that high end tax rate dropped to 70%. So now you'd get to keep over $52 million. Can you cope?

No? Well, in 2003 you'll be happy to know that the highest tax rate dropped to 35%. So whether you earn $322,000 or $322 gazillion you pay 35% tops. So, Wealthiest Taxpayer, your take home is now $113 million. Per year.

But those 400 Richest Folk actually paid out only about 22% of their income in federal taxes in 2000 (they know loop holes you and I can only dream about). And that's before the latest GOP tax cuts.

Doesn't seem quite right. Especially if you're the school teacher who makes $39,000 and watches 25% go straight off the top to the IRS.

So.... since the Reagan Days the Progressive Tax initiated by Roosevelt has been gutted despite the efforts of all those socialists over in Massachusetts. But, opponents of Progressive Taxation aren't yet satisfied. They won't be happy till we've got a "flat tax" – that is, where you and me and Bill Gates pay the same percentage. In the meantime they holler that "the rich are still carrying more than their fair share!"

Not so fast, Rush. According to an August 2004 report from the non-partisan Congressional Budget Office the top 1% of Americans with annual incomes averaging $1.2 million – Bush's beloved "haves and have mores" -- not only got one third of the latest tax cuts but they saw their share of the total tax burden FALL.

On the other hand, families in the middle with incomes ranging from $51,500 to around $75,600 saw their share of federal tax payments INCREASE.

How can this be? While everybody is paying less taxes, the rich are paying EVEN LESS taxes. The Federal revenue pie got smaller but the middle class' slice of it got larger.

Which – besides being a raw deal for millions of Americans, including this one – doesn't make economic sense.

Listen to this from the Congressional Budget Office:

"In general, analysts believe that the taxpayers who are MORE LIKELY TO CONSUME rather than save a temporary tax cut are those with LOWER INCOME. It follows from that premise that a temporary cut in personal taxes most likely to PRODUCE ECONOMIC STIMULUS would be one that put more resources IN THE HANDS OF LOWER-INCOME TAXPAYERS."

What did Bush do? "I convinced the Congress to cut the taxes on the people," said George, "because I felt.... (that) if people had more of their own money .... the economy (would) get moving."

Unfortunately he didn't put enough of it in the right hands. While the top 1% of households enjoys an average tax cut of $78,460, the middle income group gets on average a $1,090 tax cut.

Whoopee! $1,090! I can buy a real nice kayak or a wide screen TV. I can take my husband out for a fancy dinner once a month for the next year or I can send my daughter to that spiffy sleep away camp for a week.

But, wait. I just did this month's bookkeeping and here's the news....

* In 2003 fuel oil cost me $1.249 a gallon; this year my fuel oil is costing me $1.599. My pre-payment in August on 1500 gallons is up $525.

* I'm paying $277.50 more in local school and property taxes this year than I did last.

* And my health insurance premiums went up $320 over the past 12 months.

A tax cut in my pocket?? It's a swindle, Cousin.

September 2004

RONALD MCDONALD MADE ME DO IT

IT'S OFFICIAL. YOU EAR the fries, you take the rap for the cellulite on your thighs.

The House of Representatives just passed the Personal Responsibility in Food Consumption Act which says that you can't sue a restaurant for making you fat. This measure, aka "the cheeseburger bill", is the latest in a long line of legislation drafted by Republicans, challenged by trial lawyers, and aimed at providing legal immunity for specific industries over the nasty consequences of their products. Gun manufacturers and dealers, for example, tried to get such immunity, as did the tobacco industry, vaccine producers, and the makers of a gasoline additive that pollutes the water supply.

However, these guys failed. You can still hold RJ Reynolds responsible for hooking your granddaddy on Camels when he was 15. And if your child goes into anaphylactic shock after getting a measles shot, you've got a case.

But if you never met a French fry you didn't like and you balloon up to a size 24 as a result – well, darlin', don't go looking for a lawyer to save your big fat fanny.

Now, this is a tricky one. Unless you are a mechanic or a pediatrician, gas additives and vaccines are not common household items. But Food is pretty much in our lives on a regular basis and generally found in the typical American kitchen. In fact, most people would agree that without Food we would all starve to death.

So Mother Nature made us Homo Ravenous -- ready to eat anytime, anyplace Food appears. This was smart because in the old days Food appeared rarely and unpredictably, so it would not do to have creatures who needed cocktails and cheese canapes to invigorate/provoke the appetite. Thus, as a primal survival mechanism, we are biologically programmed to pounce at the sight of a ballpark dog slathered with mustard or when we catch a whiff of a hot knish.

And therein lies the problem. Food supplies are no longer rare or unpredictable. In fact, on any given day in any given Mall or on any City street there can be found an excess of Food.

Remember the last time you walked down an avenue in New York City? Pouring out of restaurants, diners, cafes, and street carts are the irresistible aromas of pizza, falafel, burgers, ribs, donuts, souvlaki, fried rice, beef tacos, chicken empanadas, curry roti, roasted chestnuts, cheese blintzes, and candied cashews. You are defenseless. Your primal programming switches into overdrive no matter how deep you are into Atkins, Fergie, or kelp.

Walk past the Food Court at the Mall – strategically placed between Sears and the multiplex so there is no way to avoid it – and it's the same ruthless attack on your senses. Pass the Chinese Wok and you salivate. Pass the Pizza Hut and your stomach growls. Pass the Vegan Bazaar and….. well, that's not really Food, is it?

Even I, a virtual model of disciplined self-control, cannot drive past a Burger King without longing for a fried fish sandwich with extra lettuce and a small (the best I can do at restraint) fries. How often do I surrender to the impulse to detour my car via the drive-in window? Less than the national average. More than I care to admit in a family newspaper.

So over the years those French fries have added up and, when I look in the mirror, I have no one to blame but myself. Representative F. James Sensenbrenner, Jr., Republican of Wisconsin, chairman of the House Judiciary Committee said, "Look in the mirror, because you're the one to blame." There it is.

But am I truly to blame? Am I not the helpless pawn of a Food Industry committed to creating a nation of high fat, high salt, high sugar addicts? Aren't those ten unsightly pounds distributed around my mid-region simply the profits of a greedy Fast Food Mafia made manifest?

And shouldn't they have to pay for their exploitation of the most basic and irremediable of human instincts?

Evidently not.

Our nature has not caught up with changes in our nurture. So what to do? I suggest that before you venture out into any public place where Food is being peddled that you avoid visual contact with the temptations and that you stuff your nose with Vicks VapoRub.

April 2004

THEY BUSTED CHONG

IT'S BEEN A ROUGH year for the Bush people, what with Osama Bin Laden and Senator Robert Byrd still on the loose and dozens of sleeper terrorist cells lurking in Dunkin Donuts shops across the nation waiting for the call to bomb Krispie Kremes. We won the war in Iraq but the cleanup operation is priced out at more than it would cost to send every 18 year old in this country to college next year. The economy is forcing a lot of working folks to dig into their cookie jar savings and rethink their voter registration. And gas is up 40 cents at the pumps.

So I'm sure everyone in the West Wing was uncorking the 20-year-old scotch last fall when U.S. District Judge Arthur J. Schwab struck a blow for freedom and democracy and sentenced Thomas B. Kin Chong to nine months in prison for selling bongs on the Internet.

You remember Tommy Chong who, along with fellow miscreant Cheech Marin, has been corrupting our youth for the past 30 years with his drug-besotted antics on stage, screen, and vinyl. Who could forget those two crazy-eyed rascals sharing a joint the size of a Havana Supremo while driving a tie-dyed van made entirely of marijuana?

After several hit movies, comedy records that went gold, and a shelf full of Grammies, Chong took his ill-gotten gains and bought a home in Bel-Air, California, got married, and raised six kids. Not bad for a Chinese-Scotch-Irish Canadian who grew up in a town called Dog Patch on the outskirts of Calgary where his father, a truck driver, supported the family on $50 a week.

But Tommy Chong just could not leave well enough alone. Thinking that America is still a free country, at least where unfettered capitalism is concerned, Chong bought himself an Internet domain name, hired 25 glass blowers, and began to sell rather expensive art piece marijuana pipes and bongs online. (A bong, for those readers who are Republicans or not of a certain age, is a fancy long stemmed pipe used to deliver cannabis – or, if you prefer, tobacco -- into the body's blood stream.)

I guess Chong thought that the Federales would be too occupied chasing down Islamic terrorists, Columbian drug lords, and Enron executives to fuss with the likes of him.

Wrong.

With time on their hands, the U.S. War-on-Drugsters cooked up "Operation Pipe Dreams". And in one sweeping raid last winter they rounded up 55 distributors of drug "paraphernalia" (a six-syllable word meaning pipes, clips, rolling papers, and sundry items used mostly by college kids and criminal defense attorneys of a certain age).

Along with owners of small Head Shops across the country (if you've gotten this far in the article I can only assume that you know what a Head Shop is), Chong got busted.

He disappointed fans by showing up at court in a herring bone suit and tie and no pony tail. And he asked the judge if he might not use his celebrity to counsel youngsters in an anti-drug community service program. But Judge Schwab would have none of these shenanigans. He seized Chong's glass inventory and over $100,000 in cash receipts, made him pay a fine of $20,000, and sent him off to the federal pokey for nine months.

And so on this frosty February morning while you and I and Osama are enjoying our freedom, Tommy Chong, aged 65 and father of six, is doing time in the Taft Correctional Institution in Taft, California. We can all rest easier tonight.

February 2004

DEMOCRATS ON PARADE, PART 1

THE EDITOR OF THIS fine publication sent me a press release last week announcing that presidential hopeful Howard Dean was coming to Hudson. A possible column here? he asked.

Since the editor of this fine publication has never before volunteered a column idea I had to wonder out loud: "are you a Democrat or do you simply want me to poke fun at the Democrats?"

Neither, he assured me. "I was just thinking that you rarely get the chance to get personal with a politician who is licensed to perform a rectal probe. Besides they're going to have free snacks at the event."

Like every journalist, I live for free snacks. So I wiped the spaghetti sauce off my press badge and dragged the family up to the Waterfront Park in Hudson on Saturday afternoon.

About 500 of the curious, the committed, and the party core showed up, plus a couple dozen reporters. It's fun to be a reporter at these events. You get to park in the closest lot. The organizers have your name on a special list. You wear a badge that says "press." And folks don't think it's weird when you walk right up and ask them to state their opinions.

Once I was in Tel Aviv during a huge Peace Now rally without my press credentials. So I nudged my way to the press pen, pulled out an expired International Youth Hostel card, covered everything with my thumb but my name and photo, pushed it into the face of the security guard, and, over the roar of the crowd, shouted "Spokane Sun-Times." Being a reporter requires moxie as well as a badge.

So I dusted off my moxie and dove into the crowd in search of Opinions.

"Why Dean?" I asked.

"John Kerry let me down by supporting the war," said Ellen from South Egremont, Massachusetts of her home state senator.

"Even Republicans I know have turned against Bush on the war," added her daughter Andrea.

Even Republicans? I gasped, although I failed to see any Republicans-for-Dean signs in the crowd. Everybody else, however, seemed to be standing up for the Governor: Saratoga for Dean, Syracuse for Dean, Central New Yorkers for Dean, Berkshire Grandmas for Dean, Independents for Dean, Folkies for Dean, Bardies for Dean, Family Docs for Dean, and Gays for Dean.

I spotted to two nice looking young men holding hands.

"Why Dean?"

"I like him on health, immigration, and gay rights," replied Joseph of Hudson. "But can he beat Bush?"

"Why Dean?"

"Because he can beat Bush!" declared Stacy of Philmont just as the skies cleared, the P.A. system went live, and the Governor appeared.

"Did you know that Dean was born and raised in New York?" whispered Gloria, an 80-something supporter from Kingston.

"Gee, no," I mumbled, momentarily distracted by the Governor's cornflower blue eyes.

"What a stud muffin!" chimed in her retirement home roommate Delores, reading my mind. I had to admit that Howard Dean looked a whole lot more handsome in person than he does in photos and he was far more relaxed than he appeared on the TV debates. He joked with the crowd, teased the vocal minority, and, after a 20 minute speech, schmoozed with his supporters.

As he worked the crowd, the Governor reminded me of our family doctor when I was growing up – patient and kind and a man who appeared to have all the time in the world to spend with you when, in fact, he did not.

He also reminded me of Bobby Kennedy, who was the last presidential candidate to visit Hudson. Governor Dean shares the populist views of Kennedy and the straight forward speaking style of Harry Truman.

He strikes me as honest and decent. He's an authentic feminist – supporting his wife's choice to tend to her medical patients rather than stump with him. He speaks for working and middle class people. He is no a creature of the oil industry. And his handshake is firm and dry.

Can he win? Ask Jimmy Carter.

By the way, the editor of this fine publication lied. There were no free snacks.

October 2003

POLLS SCHMOLLS

MY MOTHER ALWAYS TOLD me that popularity is not what life is all about. It does seem, however, to be what politics is all about.

Checking the latest Gallup poll I see that George II's approval rating among the American public is holding firm at 70%. But I am genuinely puzzled. I hang out with teachers, mechanics, carpenters, nurses, bookkeepers, and housewives -- a fair cross section of the public -- and I've yet to encounter one of the 7 out of 10 Americans who think this guy is doing a great job.

Looking over his record it's pretty clear who might have a hard time pulling the lever for George. 8.8 million Americans, for example, are out of work -- three million more than 2 1/2 years ago. 2.6 million jobs have disappeared altogether from the private sector and long term unemployment (longer than six months) is up 145% since he took office. George's response? A "job stimulus" philosophy based on cutting taxes to the wealthy and opposition to an extension of unemployment insurance which passed Congress last week in spite of the White House. So there are at least 8.8 million votes he can't count on.

The current administration also holds the record for mortgage foreclosures and private bankruptcies (over 1.5 million in 2002). And it has presided over one of the biggest drops in the history of the stock market (the NASDAQ lost 78% of its value and the S&P500 49% within 21 months of GWB taking office). There go the voters who have lost their homes, been forced into bankruptcy, or plowed their retirement savings into mutual funds.

And, even as the man drags us into what could be a perpetual state of war, he's cut healthcare benefits for war veterans. Can vets, in good conscience, vote for a guy who was suspended from the Air National Guard in 1972 and who thinks it's okay to cut burial benefits for Vietnam War amputees?

The Bush gang has further alienated voters who support the United Nations, the World Court, and the Constitution. Check it out: George has actively opposed (alone with Libya's Muammar Kaddafi) the International Criminal Court of Law, unilaterally attacked a sovereign nation in defiance of the U.N., and -- in the guise of the "Patriot Act" -- called for wiretaps and internet surveillance without judicial supervision, secret searches without a warrant, and FBI access to any of our financial and medical records.

Now you might think that traditional anti-big- government Republicans stand firm behind the man. But how can they when he has just created a brand new $380 billion-a-year Homeland Security bureaucracy?

And let's not forget those Texas Rangers fans. When George bought the baseball team in 1989, he traded Sammy Sosa to the White Sox. If I know my sports bar guys they still gotta be holding a grudge over that one.

Speaking of Texas. One of the man's first acts as governor was to cancel the auto pollution inspection program and gut other state anti-pollution laws. Today Houston has replaced Los Angeles as the smoggiest city in the nation. I figure that anybody in Houston who breathes has got to think twice about voting for GWB.

So who the heck is supporting this man? And -- given his track record of enthusiastically removing all restraints from the uber-rich class of his birth and dismantling the civil liberties of the rest of us -- how is he doing it?

Well, clearly Dubya, who has taken more vacation days than any other president (including, like the French he despises, the entire month of August), has got the vote of the hospitality industry. And with the creation of his secret shadow government, Ian Fleming fans everywhere have got to be swooning over this presidency. Bush can also count on votes from bankruptcy lawyers, snowmobilers, and Ken Lay.

But if you want to see a flag waving corps of true believers you must look to the military. In fact, that's the only place you can look since George tends to give speeches almost exclusively on military bases and aircraft carriers.

The 1,411,634 men and women in the military and their families, plus those happy-for-the-work Americans who labor in the defense industry have a true champion in George Bush. He has given them a reason to live, die, and kick butt as he zips up his flight suit, declares war on another crippled backwater, and raises the military spending budget to $380 billion for FY2004.

But added all together, I still didn't get a critical electoral mass. Then I realized I was looking at this all wrong.

Americans don't support George. They don't think his policies are in their best interests. In fact, many of us are terrified of his policies, domestic and foreign. And "terrified" -- as in "terrorist" -- is the operative word here. In the most shrewdly calculated marketing campaign of all time, Bush has terrified the bejezus out of the American public.

With a snap of his fingers and a nudge on the color-coded terror thermometer, the anxiety level of the nation is put on high alert. We cancel the vacation in New York City, we stockpile potassium iodide pills, and we tell the pollsters that we want to keep George Bush in office. Because that's what you do during times of mortal threat.

The polls are not measuring support for George. They are reflecting the level of fear he has created by leveraging off 9/11.

And what becomes of a society held together by fear?

Nita Micossi says, "don't believe me. Check the sources of the above info yourself": US Census Bureau, US Bureau of Labor Statistics, Mortgage Bankers Association of America, US Congress (house.gov), Business Week, The American Prospect, Canadian Broadcasting Corp., ABC News Online, Human Rights Watch, The Miami Herald, American Bankruptcy Institute, AFL-CIO, Whitehouse.gov, U.S. House of Representatives, Sierra Club, Environmental Protection Agency, Dept. of Defense, Environmental News Network.... to name just a few.

June 2003

My Philosophy of Life, plus a few handy tips

WAR FROM THIS PERCH

WAR. MY FIRST EXPERIENCE of war was in the 1950s. No, not Korea. Warner Brothers. As a small child I watched all the great war movies of the 1940s on Dialing for Dollars -- Mrs. Miniver, Casablanca, Thirty Seconds Over Tokyo, Since You Went Away, To Be or Not To Be.

It was, of course, in black and white. My experience of war. It was earnest and honorable. It was fought by a citizen army. Everyone had a boy in combat -- a son, a brother, a husband, a pal. And so it was supported with deep conviction and real sacrifice. Folks recycled tin, rolled bandages, and made baloney sandwiches for the USO canteen. It was patriotic to give up nylon stockings and long car trips.

No one, at least in the movies, questioned the righteousness of that war. Although I must confess that I was a bit uncomfortable to find that my people were on the wrong side of it. I knew that my Italian cousins would rather drink wine and play bocce than follow into battle a bad actor with a lousy fashion sense. (What Italian gentleman would ever wear brown, for goodness sake?) Hollywood seemed to agree since they often portrayed Italian soldiers as misguided lotharios who could be easily distracted from the war effort by an ample female fanny swaying down the street.

My Uncle John and Uncle Frankie were both shipped to the Italian front where they used their fluency in the language to capture a Pisan war bride and some Friuli real estate, respectively. In the movies and in my family's folklore Italy was not much of a threat.

The Germans were another matter. But even they seemed to play by a set of culturally comprehensible rules. The movies showed recruits from opposite sides laying down their weapons to sing Silent Night on Christmas. Prisoners of war were treated decently. And waiving a white flag really meant surrendering.

My second experience of war began in the mid-1960s. This one unfolded in a psychedelic riot of color and a rage of angry protest music. I lived it at the Oakland Army Induction Center, at the East Bay rail terminal where napalm shipments were being transferred, and at Fort Ord in Monterey. We studied the history of that war. We held teach-ins. We counseled pacifists. Under the guise of the Movement for a Democratic Military, I sat with recruits in the base canteen and talked about Vietnam. A lot of the soldiers, as young as I or younger, did not want to go. But there was a draft in those days and if you didn't have money or connections you went.

My cousin John was a bomber pilot. He never saw his victims and never used the word "honor". It was a dirty job and he did it.

And now we have this war. The experience is painted in neither black and white nor super-saturated Day-Glo markers, but in literal colors indistinguishable from the commercials that interrupt the frontline footage. With fighting in the background and an "embedded" journalist whispering a commentary in the foreground, the war action on our TV screens echoes that 1950s program "You Are There" where a "reporter" delivers a play-by-play at the Battle of Waterloo -- or today's so-called reality shows where a commentator pops in to give a status report on the survivors. The effect is frightfully authentic and oddly fictive at the same time. It does not, I find, make this combat seem more immediate and real, but more like a TV mini-series.

And even though Diane Sawyer is going to great lengths to give us those "up close and personal" stories from soldiers and their families like they do at the Olympics, the actors in this war seem strangely remote. In WWII everyone knew someone involved in the shooting war. In Vietnam everyone had a draft number and had to decide whether to fight or flee, and take the consequences in either case. In this war, I know no one personally in the field of combat and only two people who do know someone in Iraq. As the New York Times recently pointed out, our armed forces are essentially "a working class military (fighting) and (dying) for an affluent America."

We see that in the token involvement on the home front. We can stand with a sign for or against at the village crossroads every Saturday. We can send "audio greetings" to the troops or donate a phone calling card to a soldier so s/he can call home. Sending care packages is a security risk, but our money is good (and tax deductible) at the USO who will do it for us. As for "sacrifice", our leader urges us to tank up the SUV, go to the Mall, and buy.

Though we are genuinely anxious that the battle might be brought to Grand Central Station or L.A. International, most of us go about our business, reminded of war only when we turn on the radio or TV. If we don't have family or friend directly involved, our experience of this war has become a passive diversion, a choice of channels. Even our acts of conscience can be discharged with a mere click as we sign yet another online petition.

For most of us, is this war, I wonder, yet one more virtual experience in a pampered life of safe experiences? And when we get up from the couch will we realize that the bill -- compromised freedoms, gutted social programs, the enmity of half the planet -- has come due?

April 2003

A NUKE IS A NUKE

IT ALL STARTED WHEN Milo Klapp, a disgruntled mail sorter in the Department of Defense, leaked the Pentagon's top-secret Nuclear Posture Review to the Los Angeles Times. Sent to Congress in January 2002, the review proposed the shocking idea that the United States circumvent the 1970 Nuclear Non-Proliferation Treaty by slicing and dicing its big nuke bombs into petit bombettes.

"It's actually quite easy," explained retired General Jack "Pitbull" Rapier. "You take one of those fifteen kiloton puppies like we dropped on Hiroshima and break it up into three 5-kilotonners. Detonate one of those mini-nukes on a 30-foot-thick missile silo door and it'll vaporize the door and the missile on the other side."

"But why would we want to do that?" asked an incredulous Dan Rather.

"To get the terrorists, boy, the terrorists!"

This, remember, was only months after the 9/11 attacks on New York City and Washington. And all everyone wanted to do was get the terrorists.

Actually the terrorists never had missile silos. But, said the classified document, they did have labs buried deep underground that produced Anthrax, Ebola, and a few party drugs.

An earth-penetrating weapon with a nuclear warhead could go after targets deep inside mountains and under deserts. And only a nuke, said one official, could wipe out the terrorists' chemical and biological weapon kitchens.

Now during the Cold War, nuclear had been taboo. Scared though we all were, everybody believed that no one would be wacko enough to actually push the nuclear button. In fact, being scared was the whole idea.

Problem with these new mini-nukes was that the Pentagon guys soft-peddled the "nuclear" part. The American public was already cool with "daisy cutters" and had learned to love the smart bomb. So when the generals called mini-nukes just another "low-yield" weapon "with highly accurate delivery systems for deterrence" that avoided too much messy "collateral damage" -- generals talk like that -- most people went about their business. Frankly, I think it was the "mini" thing. Made them sound kind of cute.

Anyway, nuclear went from being unthinkable to being okay -- just one more useful tool in the war against terrorists and other nasty thugs. Unfortunately, some of these thugs already had a few little mini-nukes of their own.

Even though it was unpatriotic in those days to gripe about anything the military wanted, a few old Lefties from the original anti-nuke movement tried to make trouble. They bussed in 3,000 geriatrics from Fort Lauderdale for a Ban the Bomb wheelchair march on Donald Rumsfeld's office; they went on Larry King to take calls from concerned citizens about nuclear fallout and drooling mutants; they convinced Hollywood to re-release Dr. Strangelove.

A few people panicked, which was good for the backyard shelter and Spam businesses. But the general public yawned and the military held tough.

Then the Pentagon got intelligence that Osama had fled into Iraq and was attending a potluck hosted by Saddam at one of his underground bunkers. This was just what they'd been waiting for. They launched a mini-nuke into the bunker. Kim Jong-il of North Korea was really sore about this. As part of the original Axis of Evil he felt that he should have been invited to the potluck. Since he couldn't complain to Saddam, Kim sent a terrorist to blow up downtown Las Vegas with a micro-mini-nuke that he'd been saving for a special occasion.

The Pakistani Ambassador, who had a secret weakness for showgirls and the slots, perished in the tragedy. When the government in Islamabad found out that the North Korean terrorist had spent his junior year abroad at the Om Shanti Institute of Computers in West Bengal, it felt justified in lobbing one of its own mini-nukes over the border into India.

And so it went until two-thirds of the planet was rubble.

That was six years ago. Luckily, at the time I was visiting my brother who'd been posted with the Peace Corps to Easter Island. I tried to explain to the natives here about mini-nukes and terrorists and what had happened in the world outside. But they found the whole story preposterous, so I just let it drop.

Life here is safe so long as you don't eat the fish or wander outside when it rains, and the turnip crop is pretty darn good this year. But I do miss bagels and "The Simpsons."

April 2003

My Philosophy of Life, plus a few handy tips

THE SOUL OF THE NEW REGIME

IT WAS A STUNNING June day in 1982. I was walking in the Old City of Jerusalem with my friend Ellen and her mother Irma. Born and raised in the Bronx, Irma left the United States when she was in her mid-50s and immigrated to Israel under the Law of Return. She and her husband Howard owned an apartment in the Old City where Ellen and I were staying.

As we strolled and admired the haunting beauty of an ancient metropolis that is the center of the world for so many, a young couple approached us. The man thrust a camera into Ellen's hands and in a European-accented English asked if she would mind taking their picture.

As Ellen put the camera up to her eyes to oblige, Irma yanked it from her hands, threw it back at the startled tourists, and told us under her breath to walk quickly in the other direction. When we were out of earshot of the couple Irma told us in no uncertain terms that we were never NEVER to do that again.

Ellen and I were puzzled. "A bomb," shouted Irma impatiently. "They put them in bundles as small as a pack of cigarettes. That camera could be a bomb!"

This was not the first time that I'd encountered Israeli vigilance. Earlier that month before boarding an El Al flight from JFK to Tel Aviv I was ushered into a room with my baggage to undergo a search and interrogation by an Israeli soldier.

He gave my goods a quick once over but asked me countless questions about when, where, and how I packed my suitcases, what I planned to do in Israel, and if I'd been approached by any strangers at the airport. At one point he looked me straight in the eye and asked, "do you understand why I am asking you these questions?" I replied that I did, though, frankly I did not, exactly.

In fact, I thought the whole routine was a bit over the top and tried to joke with the soldier who was not much younger than me. But he was as self-possessed as a Marine drill sergeant and answered my flirtations with a cold stare.

At the other end of my journey, at a bus station in Tel Aviv, I experienced it again. I propped my two suitcases and portable typewriter against a pillar within view of the ticket window and went -- five feet away -- to stand in line. Within seconds two armed soldiers leading a German shepherd were upon me, asking in the same quiet, controlled voices as the soldier at JFK if those bags were mine. "You do not ever EVER leave your bags unattended. Someone could slip an explosive into one. Do you understand?" I was starting to.

I had never lived in or near a really dangerous place, unless you count mid-town Manhattan, and my first weeks in Israel introduced me to a world where terrorism shapes how people attend to the daily details. There were armed men on all the buses. There were searches at entrances to movie theaters and shopping centers. Uniformed soldiers were everywhere. And, I soon learned, all men over 18 who were not crippled or Orthodox were also soldiers.

In the kibbutz where I lived, a pal who picked pears with me in the orchards, would show up one morning in full battle gear carrying his weapon. He was on his way to do his yearly reserve duty. In 1982 that might mean a tour of combat in Lebanon.

Those of us who stayed home were protected by teams of armed kibbutzniks who guarded the perimeter of the commune each night -- while young people made their entertainment in a makeshift disco in one of the kibbutz's many subterranean bomb shelters.

In 1982 the Palestinian Intifada had not even begun. Yet Israel was always and everywhere on combat alert. And I quickly learned the rules.

I think about how we Americans might be forced to adjust to a routine circumscribed by terrorism. The worst of it is not the inconvenience at airports or e-mail surveillance or money for education diverted to ever more security.

The worst of it is what it does to people's minds and souls. How paranoia and perceptiveness get all tangled up. How the dehumanization of The Enemy leaks into simple interactions with people who look like the enemy. How the normal chronic anxiety of a parent is ratcheted up to, as Israeli author David Grossman calls it, "an unending state of military stress."

My family planned some months ago to spend the Columbus Day holiday in Washington, DC. I wrote my congressman for tickets to the

White House, to the Senate Gallery, for a special tour of the FBI. Now that happy anticipation has been transformed into an agonizing question: do I really want to take my small child to the very buildings that are on the top ten list of terrorists who haven't yet finished with us?

October 2003

THE EASY STREET BLUES

I WAS STUNNED NOT long ago to see a picture of an attractive woman dressed in black starring gloomily out at me from the pages of a fashionable magazine.

She wore $1500 alligator skin boots -- I know this because my cousin, who's married to an oil company executive, has an identical pair -- she had on three carat diamond stud earrings -- I know this because I've been shopping diamond stud earrings for seven years -- and she was slumped in a museum quality leather chair -- I know this because I hang out in museums. Despite the fancy gear, however, the woman was clearly depressed.

"Everyone thinks we lead this charmed life," said the quote next to her picture. "Great jobs, a wonderful house, private schools. They don't see the flip side." I flushed with embarrassment. I had no idea.

The text on the facing page -- which turned out to be an ad for U.S. Trust, an investment management firm that "only deals with the wealthy" -- went on to describe in shocking detail that flip side:

Each day this sad woman, and hundreds of super rich people just like her, has to slog through a zillion e-mails and voice messages. Florist, caterer, jeweler, and vet, personal trainer, art dealer, interior decorator, travel agent, landscape architect, plastic surgeon -- won't they ever just leave her alone??!

She stays awake nights terrified that her children might never need to work. She struggles to hang on to her sanity and her ideal weight.

And all the while she tries to cope with ever more possessions, more assets, more investments, more Tiffany flatware. "More to lose" -- the advertisement points out sagely. And, worst of all, nobody understands.

Five pages later in the same magazine the face of a kindly man with a meticulously trimmed white beard all but shouts "I understand!" Peter

White of the Citigroup Private Bank Family Advisory Practice has taken out an ad addressed to people who've inherited vast fortunes and assures them that being born into wealth need not be a burden.

He too refers to the stresses and strains of having a lot of money such as not having to work and figuring out an appropriate allowance for a child who already has a net worth greater than Luxembourg.

As I read these ads the scales fell from my eyes. All these years living on the economic margins, frantically transferring credit card debt to low interest rate accounts before the balance comes due, and eating lima beans..... why I've had it good!

I've never had to waste precious time with the cat masseuse discussing my Siamese's weekly rubdown and pedicure. I don't pace the floor at night fretting over which private school uniform will best enhance my daughter's sense of self worth. And I certainly don't have to spend one minute choosing an appropriate family philanthropy.

My life is easy. I stand at the top of the stairs every month, toss the bills into the air, and pay the ones that land on the highest step.

But in my devil-may-care universe I totally lost sight of the anguish suffered by the rich. As one of the ads asks "Who would believe all that money could be anything other than a blessing?" Certainly not I.

Now that I have been made aware of their plight, however, I intend to be more sensitive. When, for instance, my cousin (the one married to the oil company executive) complains bitterly about how hard it is to find a private jet pilot who's available 24-7, I will not slap her.

And the next time I see a layout in Town & Country of a beautiful young countess lounging by the pool next to her Tuscan villa, I will offer up a novena for her troubled soul.

But one thing does puzzle me. If having so much money is such a painful burden why is Mr. Bush giving so much more of it to the rich? Doesn't he understand the meanness of such largess? Somebody ought to take him aside and teach him a little compassion.

August 2001

WRITE ME IN & ADD (1)tsp SALT

THIRTY-SEVEN MORE SHOPPING days till the presidential election and there are still no truly appealing products on the market. We got the tall white guy from Tennessee and the tall white guy from Texas. That makes two TWGs with twangy accents, Ivy League educations, and memberships in clubs that won't ever suffer the likes of you and me.

So, in the interest of consumer choice, I hereby toss my beret into the ring and declare my candidacy for the highest public office in the land. It's about time that this country was run by a short Italian woman. Just close your eyes and imagine the fragrance of olive oil, garlic, and rosemary wafting from the White House kitchen. It gives me goose bumps.

Not that this is simply about culinary superiority – although I'll put my roasted fennel chicken and zucchini frittata up against George's chili any day of the week.

No, I've got an actual platform.

On the arts: Let's take the defense budget and give it to the National Endowment for the Arts. Put all those soldiers into tap dance classes and bombard our enemies with CDs of Funny Girl and West Side Story. Nobody would ever want to go to war in the middle of rehearsals.

On agriculture: I say a chicken in every pot and some pot in every chicken. How often does a society find, in a single product, the solution to clothing, shelter (they say hemp withstands a wind chill factor of minus 60), and the Friday Night blahs?

On education: Absolutely, positively yes! Everybody over the age of 18 should be required to study one dead language, one Gilbert & Sullivan libretto, and the biochemistry of photosynthesis. Conversations would be ever so much more interesting.

On technology: Here I must declare a conflict of interest since 70% of my taxable income is derived from pithy observations about the Internet Economy. Having said that, my position is as follows: Everybody should learn how to use computers and the Internet, but all discussion of computers and the Internet should be banned from public discourse. It is boring, it is tedious, it is banal. Better to discuss Anglo-Saxon epic poetry.

On the United Nations: This is an under-used opportunity for some absolutely world class potlucks. It's also a perfect forum for resolving conflicts: simply have Indonesia and East Timor stage a cook-off to decide who should rule whom and enforce the restaurant sanitation codes.

On the environment: Trees, trees, and more trees. I can't get enough of trees. It's a personal thing. But it is also an environmentally healthy thing so, sorry, lumberjacks, you are out of a job.

On lumberjacks: As compensation, you get all the dance solos in the touring company of Oklahoma.

On family values: Everybody should have a really nice family with as many children and adults as they want. Good food, shelter, and a musical instrument should be a guaranteed right of every child born in the U.S. of A.

As for my Vision for this great country of ours, I think I can best summarize it in a single word: Bicycles.

Let it be known that I am willing to meet with Mr. Gore and Mr. Bush any time, any place to debate my agenda and swap cheesecake recipes.

One more thing. My husband makes the best darn focaccia in the mid-Hudson Valley. Therefore, in his name – Bob - I hereby challenge Tipper Gore and Laura Bush to a 3-way baking contest. I think we all know the really important qualifications for The First Spouse.

October 2000

Nita Micossi

IRAQ AND THE FAT FLUSH DIET

MY FRIEND ADA WANTS me to go on the Fat Flush Diet with her. Designed to purge toxic fluid buildup and cleanse the accumulated fats in your poor over-worked liver, the Fat Flush Diet promises to restore your body's beneficial fat ratio and allow you to slip into a spandex tube dress -- in just two weeks!

Of course, for the duration, you have to give up fettuccini Alfredo, sourdough French bread with sweet butter, baked potatoes with sour cream, goat curry, Hershey bars, and vodka gimlets. The usual.

You do get to eat eight ounces of lean protein a day plus two eggs, and all the kale, collards, and turnips your little heart desires. And you get to dress up all that "purifying chlorophyll" with dry mustard, bay leaves, and parsley. Yum!

The regime? "On arising" you chug a "Long Life Cocktail" composed of a teaspoon of powdered psyllium husks, seven ounces of water, and a pony of unsweetened cranberry juice. "Before breakfast" you pour another eight ounces of water into your system, this time hot and with a dash of lemon. Before my first cup of coffee, I'd have to down a half a quart of water.

Of course, coffee is not allowed. But two scrambled eggs with dry mustard, bay leaves, and parsley are. Plus another eight ounce glass of that cran-water. And it's only 8a.m.

The rest of the day is laid out in a similar fashion with copious amounts of water, dull dinners of poached this and steamed that, and two compulsory tablespoons per day of organic high-lignan flaxseed oil. All in all there are eleven low calorie pit stops per day on the way to a total Fat Flush.

The cost? There's about $50 in required supplements and $25 for the book. But if I don't buy my mother a birthday present this year and cut my own hair for the next two months, I can balance the budget.

We can do this! I tell Ada. Heck, we can do anything for two weeks. But I have one concern: what if I perform flawlessly for two weeks and lose the weight. I know for sure I can't keep up this regime beyond that, so will I gain back all the weight and toxic fluids the minute I unwrap a Snickers bar? And will my metabolism strike back by going into its usual post-diet coma?

I have to wonder if the whole thing isn't ultimately self-destructive.

Which makes me think of Iraq.

George II has told us that we have to go into Baghdad and purge it of its toxic anti-American attitudes and accumulated weaponry. We put many of those nasty things into Iraq's body politic in the first place and it's up to us to flush them out.

The mission, however, is not for the faint of heart. Troupes abroad and patriots at home -- we will all have to suck it in and accept the deprivations of wartime. We can, for example, expect temporary oil shortages (is that diesel or flaxseed?), an embargo on our two-party system of government (haven't we been revving up for this since last September anyway?), and the preemption of Larry King's interview with Carol Channing (the fettuccini Alfredo of talk show guests) in favor of but another battle zone update by Donald Rumsfeld.

But, says George, with full commitment by the American people -- plus several trillion dollars pulled from the public schools' hot lunch program -- it shouldn't take long to flush out Saddam, put up a few hundred McDonald's franchises, and stuff all those Muslim girls into spandex tube dresses.

But then what? Just like the Fat Flush Diet I have to ask myself to look beyond the quick fix and consider the long-term consequences. Will we be able to sustain the effort in Iraq beyond Valentine's Day? If we can't, will whatever we do accomplish be for naught? And might the whole thing back fire?

Just as the Fat Flush Diet will probably annoy my metabolism so much that it will conspire to pack on the pounds, perhaps the Saddam Flush War will get Mr. Hussein so annoyed that he will load the cannons with the stuff of our greatest fears.

November 2002

9.
NEXT IN LINE

FATHER'S DAY.   Pop enlisted in the Marines to be a fighter pilot in the Pacific during WWII. But the fates had a different plan for us both. Page 226

IF IT'S BROKE, DON'T FIX IT.   Grandpa returned to his village in the Old Country where he flaunted his wealth till he alienated the natives; repaired something of theirs they didn't want repaired; and left in a huff when they weren't appreciative. He'd become a real American. Page 228

LUNCH WITH MOM.   Whosever name my high school pals and I picked out of the hat would be "the one."   I picked your father's name and we all had a good laugh about it because at the time he was carrying on with Thelma. Page 230

NEXT IN LINE.   When your last parent and witness dies, that floppy pre-self-conscious baby-You really no longer exists at all except in fuzzy black and white photographs. Page 232

HAPPY MOTHER'S DAY: Ma finds a new reason to live, plus all the fruit she can carry back to her room. Page 235

LA DOLCE VITA REDUX: A tot's golden memories of summer at the seashore are lodged in Mother's memory somewhere between hangover headaches and a near-fatal bout with ptomaine poisoning. Page 237

THE ORIGINAL DOMESTIC GODDESS.   In the case of my Ma we're talking about an icon of the 1950's – a professional mother who attacked her role with the vigor of a combat general. Page 240

THE LONG HOT SUMMER.   Despite the efforts of the eponymous restaurant franchise to trick Easterners into thinking that Fresno is Palm Springs with spurs, it is actually Cleveland without the waterfront. Page 242

EXTINCT SPECIES.   Once my mother-in-law passed 80, her conversation quickly deteriorated to a running complaint about how everything had changed and how everything she was familiar with was gone. Page 244

FATHER'S DAY

MY POP DIED IN 1974, the winter before his fifty-fourth birthday. It was one of those protracted and painful deaths, endured in a progression of noisy, colorless, foul-smelling hospital rooms. It was my father's worst nightmare of death. He had always wanted to go in a plane crash. He was not morbid. He was a pilot.

Pop left home after high school graduation in 1938 and made his way to Alaska where he became a bush pilot. He flew freight and mail for Star Airlines and, like most of the frontier flyboys, occasionally smuggled contraband pelts between the territory and Canada.

Besides flying, he learned how to build and repair airplane engines because, as he once explained to me, when your Ford Tri-Motor goes down on the tundra you'd better be able to fix it yourself.

Pop was passionate about flying and his diaries reveal a boyish romantic soaring above the Arctic Circle, over migrating herds of caribou, into the face of the Northern Lights. But the diaries also ache with loneliness for his sweetheart back home. So life was perfect when my mother agreed to marry my father and come to Anchorage. I would have been born there, if it hadn't been for Pearl Harbor.

When the war started Pop didn't wait for the draft, but enlisted in the Marine Corps on the promise that he would be a fighter pilot. He and my mother were sent to Coronado Island in San Diego where he joined a squadron of pilots being trained for combat in the Pacific Theater.

Weeks before Pop's unit was scheduled to be shipped out, his commanding officer discovered that Pvt. Leo Nello "Mike" Micossi was an experienced airplane mechanic. While they had plenty of men who wanted to be pilots, the Marines were desperately short of mechanics to keep the planes in the air. So Pop was promoted, grounded, and told that he would spend the war teaching other men how to fly and maintain their aircraft.

My mother told me many years later that after receiving this news, Pop came home and wept, as she had never seen him, in all the years of their marriage before or since, weep.

Ten days later Pop's unit shipped out of San Diego Bay.

Soon after, my father, devastated at being left behind to sit out the war in an airplane hangar, got word that his comrades' ship was attacked and sunk before it reached its destination in the Pacific. There were no survivors....

More than thirty years later Pop finally joined his Marine buddies. After his death my mother and brother took the box of his ashes to the small airfield at Half Moon Bay, on the coast south of San Francisco. There on the tarmac they met a pilot who was to fly them out over the Pacific Ocean to scatter the remains.

My brother, who is also a licensed aviator, handed the pilot the box of my father's ashes while he inspected the small craft appreciatively. The pilot turned white and nearly dropped the box that was labeled simply "Micossi."

"Micossi?" he finally murmured. "I once knew a Mike Micossi up in Alaska.... we flew for Star together before the war."

My mother nodded. The pilot went mute and dropped his head so she could not see the tears. Then the three of them climbed into the Cessna and flew out over the Pacific.

My Pop didn't get to die in combat or in a plane, as he had always wished. But I like to think that he would have been satisfied at this ending, so much more to his liking than in an antiseptic hospital room.

And on every Father's Day since, when I look at the photograph of that beautiful young man in the leather fly jacket and review his too brief life, I am reminded of life's extravagant ironies. The denial of one of my father's dearest dreams, saved him -- and me.

Alaska Airlines--1932: (Mac) McGee Airways, Anchorage AK. 1934: Merged with Star Air Service. 1937: Renamed Star Airlines. 1942: Became Alaska Star Airlines. 1944: Alaska Airlines, on acquisition of Livery Airways, Mirow Air Service, and Pollack Flying Service. 1946: Moved to Seattle WA. 1968: Absorbed Alaska-Coastal and Cordova Airlines. 1986: Acquired Jet America.
  • *First over-the-Pole commercial flights*

June 2005

My Philosophy of Life, plus a few handy tips

IF IT'S BROKE, DON'T FIX IT

MY MOTHER'S FATHER, VITANTONIO Giovanni Sapone, left the Italian village of Acquaviva delle Fonti, in the hilly province of Bari, nearly 100 years ago when he was 16 years old. Alone he sailed the Atlantic Ocean, navigated Ellis Island, and trained across the North American continent to hook up with his cousin Domenico who had already settled in the Great San Joaquin Valley of California.

Although he never lost his thick Vito Corleone accent, Grandpa learned a passable English and, being handsome, exuberant, and playful, he easily made friends in the Valley. He worked odd jobs for other Italian immigrants who'd arrived a decade ahead of him until he saved enough money to marry my grandmother and open a grocery store.

The business did well and his family thrived. His daughter, my mother, was the first generation to afford the luxury of marrying simply for love, and both of his sons became rich dentists.

In 1954 Grandpa decided to make a trip home to Acquaviva to see his cousins and parade his success. What's the point of doing well in America if you can't show off to the family left behind? Since Grandma was not a traveler, he sailed from New York to Naples alone, retracing the journey that he'd made a half century earlier as a teenager.

Grandpa lavished gifts from the States on his country cousins who weren't as thrilled to see him as he was to be seen. Barese men and women, you see, are proud and belligerent and they don't take well to being shown up by somebody who has the audacity to desert their grim struggle for the wealth and ease of America.

But Grandpa, besotted with his own good fortune, didn't seem to notice their resentment.

One day he decided to pay a visit to the village priest, a man he had assisted so many years before as an altar boy and who had made it clear that he didn't think Grandpa, always the clown, would ever amount to much.

When he arrived at the rectory and opened the screen door to knock, Grandpa noticed that it made a loud squeaky noise when opened and a deafening crash when it closed. The screen door hinges were ancient and rusty and the old-fashioned coil spring between the door and frame caused the door to slam.

No one was home in the rectory. And Grandpa had a brilliant idea. He went to the general store and got some tools and hardware to fix the screen door. He spent a long hot afternoon disassembling, reassembling, sanding, and testing the screen door and he installed a quiet pneumatic door closer so it shut smoothly and silently. Grandpa was proud of his work and certain that the old priest would reassess his opinion of him.

Later that night, however, as Grandpa was having supper at his Aunt Olympia's, the old priest came storming into the house.

"You fool!" screamed the priest. "How dare you touch my screen door without asking me!"

"But it was making such a terrible noise," explained Grandpa, startled.

"Of course it was making a terrible noise, you idiot! And that's just the way I like it. It tells me when anyone is coming into the house," raved the old man, "and gives me a chance to hide out if I don't want to be bothered. Now you've gone and spoiled a perfectly good system."

Instead of apologizing, Grandpa was furious at the ungrateful priest and his cousins who took the old man's side. "Stupid, ignorant peasants!" he muttered to himself, escaping his aunt's house. He returned to California and never again paid his Old World family a visit.

So there it was.... Grandpa went overseas; flaunted his wealth till he alienated the natives; took it upon himself to repair something of theirs that they did not want repaired; and then left in a huff when they weren't appreciative. Grandpa Sapone, I realized when Ma told me this story, had truly become an American.

May 2005

LUNCH WITH MOTHER

I HAD A LOT of promise. My high school counselor always said so. I was the smartest kid in my class and I enjoyed studying. I especially liked history and I think I would have made a good teacher. But girls didn't go to college in 1938 – at least first generation Italian-American girls didn't – so Mama and Papa sent me to Blake's Secretarial School where I learned typing, shorthand, and some bookkeeping.

It didn't take much effort to be at the top of my class and I won the California State Typing Championship during my second year at Blake's. After graduation I got a job at Leask's Department Store in the accounting office and was so good at everything they asked me to do that Mr. Leask wanted me to be his personal secretary.

But Papa needed me at the grocery store, especially after my brother John enlisted in the army, so I had to give up the job. I was still living at home, of course, and Papa gave me a little spending money but I sure missed that paycheck from Leask's. I was kind of hoping to save enough money to go to San Francisco. I'd stay with Uncle Bill until my cousin Lena and I could afford to get our own apartment and then we'd go to work for one of those big law firms. I thought that maybe I could go to night school and become a paralegal.

Instead I worked in Papa's store during the week and hung out with my friends at the beach on weekends. Sometimes on a Saturday night we'd go to the Cocoanut Grove Ballroom on the boardwalk. All the top bands played Santa Cruz on their way up the coast from L.A. to Seattle. Benny Goodman, Artie Shaw, Kay Kyser, Tommy Dorsey. I was a terrific dancer! Did you know that?

One night while my girlfriends and I were talking about men and marriage, Norma suggested that we write down the names of all the boys we knew on scraps of paper and put them in a hat. Whose ever name we picked would be "the one."

I picked your father's name and we all had a good laugh about it because at the time he was carrying on with Thelma.

We got married in May 1942 and went to live in Anchorage, Alaska where your father was flying the mail for Star Airlines. Anchorage was still a pretty wild frontier town in those days. You could occasionally see a moose strolling down M Street where we lived. And everyone kept a rifle in the house in case a bear showed up. Now and then your dad would let me ride on one of the mail runs with him up to Nome or Point Barrow. From the plane we could see herds of caribou stampeding across the frozen plains.

Although we loved Alaska and your father had a job that exempted him from the draft, he wanted more than anything to join the Marine Corps. So off we went to San Diego where he enlisted and spent the war training Marine pilots. I got a job with a military contractor. I did everything for them. I'm a great organizer, you know, and I coordinated all the factory operations and made sure that the incoming supplies and outgoing product moved on time. The more work they gave me the happier I was. And I was making good money. My boss said that the plant would fall apart if it weren't for me and I think he was right.

Every Friday night your father and I would go to the Coronado Hotel and dance to some of the same bands that had come to the Grove in Santa Cruz. Those were wonderful times!

After the war I didn't work anymore, at least not the kind of work where they appreciate you and pay you. Men like to come home to a clean, comfortable house filled with happy children. They haven't a clue. I worked from six in the morning until nine at night seven days a week. Cook, clean, do laundry, pay bills, nurse, chauffeur, and pick up all the litter that three children leave around – do you know how much I hate to pick up after other people? The best times were late at night when everybody was asleep and I could lie in bed and read.

I never really wanted kids, you know. It was your father's idea.

July 2004

NEXT IN LINE

WHEN BOTH OF YOUR parents are dead there is no longer a comfort zone between you and mortality. You look in the mirror, see not your mother but your grandmother, and realize that you are next in line.

Boundaries of the possible have been closing in for years, what with all sorts of pesky physical compromises and the steady erosion of erotic allure. You learn to cope with the trick back, the dry skin, the need for multiple eyeglass prescriptions. But the death of the last parent is still a nasty jolt. You weep for Mother. But at 83, in ill health, and with all spark of joie de vivre long extinguished, She would not have lamented the passing.

You weep, if truth be told, for yourself. There is no one left who remembers you as a baby. With all witnesses to your floppy pre-self-conscious form gone, that baby-You really no longer exists at all except in fuzzy black and white photographs.

Thus, when my brother, sister, and I assembled this past December in San Diego to fling Ma's powdery remains into the Pacific Ocean and dispose of her worldly goods, the most precious items to be divvied up were the photograph albums that she had meticulously kept for decades.

I flew out to California where my sister lives not far from Brookdale Manor, Ma's home for the last two years of her life. I planned to stay a full week so that we had plenty of time to do what had to be done. But Brother Jim was anxious to take care of business and rush back to hearth and wife in Raleigh, North Carolina.

And so it was that, on one frantic Monday morning while my siblings sorted through debris in the kitchen and the moving men filled boxes in the living room, I retired to Ma's bedroom to sort out the photo albums.

There are 21 books documenting our family saga -- from 1925, when Ma was four years old, to 1999, when my daughter and her last grandchild was four years old.

I wanted to linger over each book and every face, so many loved and gone, and revisit the Me that was fading into sepia-tinted memory. With all of these books assembled together in my mother's house, my history, though receding, felt safe and intact. But with my sister and brother living parsecs away I realized that once the library of our congress was broken up into pieces I might never see some of these faces again.

Time and a growling crew disrupted the spell. So I went to work and lined the books upright in chronological order and began to make three piles so that each of us would get every third picture album.

As the movers scooped up my brother's seven books, tossed them into a box, strapped them with packing tape, and hauled them out to a truck bound for Raleigh, I watched an irreplaceable record of my childhood depart.

Later that night I sat in my sister's guest room alone surrounded by my share of Ma's photographic legacy.

The really early pictures that cover the years before my birth form a fascinating diorama of a by-gone era filled with old cars, vintage clothing, homes and stores long ago torn down, orchards long ago paved over. Looking at them was like looking at a Ken Burns documentary in which all of the players have been dead for years, as indeed many have.

But the pictures I truly longed to see were those from the 1950s and 1960s when we were all children and living together with my parents as a family.

My sister, brother, and I each got one book that covered the 1950s and our earliest childhoods. The one in my keeping recorded my First Holy Communion (I look as if my new white shoes were too tight), Grandpa standing in front of his 1952 Buick (he looks like he just won the lottery), and the birth of my brother (my sister and I look like a pair of injuns up to no good circling his bassinet).

When I opened the book that promised a peek at the 1960s -- the years of my adolescence and flowering – I was dismayed to find that it wasn't a photo album at all, but a scrapbook from the year our family lived in Europe. It was full of matchbooks, menus, beer coasters, and other detritus, and it was identical to a scrapbook I'd made for myself that year. So I put the book in my sister's pile.

Due to a distribution mishap, I found myself with no photographs of my family life from 1955 to 1970. I was bereft. Without an image of me at 15 skipping in front of the Eiffel Tower, will That Me, I wondered, cease to remind This Me to keep my dancing shoes polished and my passport current?

Then I remembered the faces in Ma's first photo album. They are all gone and I am next in line. The days are dwindling down and I've got so much left to do. When the hell am I going to have time to lolly over picture albums anyway?

March 2004

HAPPY MOTHER'S DAY

THE SATURDAY AFTER THANKSGIVING last November my mother had a dizzy spell. Alone at home, she called her pal next door, and before you could say Metamucil, Ma was in the hospital for what turned out to be two weeks of poking and prodding, trying to find out: did she have a tiny stroke? Was her insulin off kilter? Was dementia setting in?

The fleet of docs enlisted to decipher Ma's condition finally concluded that whatever the heck caused her tumble, she could no longer live in her two-story home alone. She could no longer live alone. Period.

My brother saw her and declared that she would not survive to see her 81st birthday in February. My sister rearranged a room in her house at the other end of the state so that Ma would be comfortable until whatever was going to happen happened. I, who live on the other side of the continent from the rest of my family, suggested that removing my mother from her home and putting her in somebody else's house was not such a keen idea.

My mother is too independent and, like both of her daughters, too much of a control addict to go gentle into that good night especially if it descends upon her in the back bedroom of her son-in-law's house. But I didn't have an alternative so I cheered on my sister's good intentions and let the plan play itself out.

Ma fell into an inconsolable depression and spent a month at my sister's sun-soaked hacienda near San Diego sitting zombie like in front of the TV set from dawn to dusk with the drapes closed. She barely ate. She talked to no one.

Then one day she had a good cry. She had been summarily separated from the neighbor who was her one and only friend, the house she'd lived in for 25 years was being sold, and she'd never get to use the new kitchen towels she'd bought on sale the week before Thanksgiving.

My sister conceded. Ma needed some sort of "assisted living" situation where she could have her own apartment and be surrounded by her own stuff.

Brookdale, a well-appointed senior living complex ten minutes from my sister's, has a swimming pool and hot tub, library, game room, chapel, and gym. There's a beauty salon where a manicurist does Medicare-covered pedicures for the diabetic residents and a masseuse who comes in once a week to pummel those weary old bones. Meals are served three times a day in a vaulted dining room with white linen covered tables and a serving staff so pleasant and accommodating that my sister whispered, "They're tooo nice…. Do you think they eat the inmates?"

If the establishment looks like a spa, it feels like a cruise ship. Everyday a calendar is posted in the elevator announcing the day's diversions: a guided yoga meditation in the chapel with Miss Rajmani, a weenie-roast at the beach, a billiards tournament, a no-host cocktail party at the pool ("Jackets please, Gentlemen.")

Of course, the female to male ratio is four to one, which makes for some awkward pairings at the Sunday afternoon tea dances. And seating arrangements at meals can get tricky when everybody has a least one bad ear.

But the all-you-can-carry-to-your-room fruit bowl is free and, for the first time in her life, my mother has a very nice lady who comes in once a week to clean her house.

The proceeds from the sale of her home should support my mother at Brookdale for eight to ten years. By that time one of her n'er do well children will have married old money, so we're not worrying.

Neither is Ma. Every time I call her she's on her way out the door: Luella is meeting her downstairs for brunch; Mr. Shapiro promised to teach her a new Contract Bridge move; the van is leaving in 10 minutes for the Zoo. At 81, my mother -- unwillingly flung out of her familiar, comfortable old life -- is rediscovering that you need never outgrow the pleasure of new experiences and that there are always new experiences to be had.

May 2002

LA DOLCE VITA REDUX

SOON AFTER COUSIN CLAIRE birthed triplets in 1996 we began to plot a holiday for the following summer. How jolly it would be for her three wee ones and my tot to meet at the seaside, just as Claire and I had done as children.

Claire, who now lives in Florence, Italy, offered the family beach house in Follonica and said that her nanny would cheerfully join us for two weeks.

"Are you mad?" asked my mother. But I had already bought the tickets.

Settling into my airplane seat with a nearly-two-year-old child on my lap, I tried not to envy the woman across the aisle who was sipping a highball and zipping through a Times crossword puzzle. Instead, I silently blessed the pediatrician who had prescribed the tranquilizing effects of cough syrup for traveling children.

But Dimetapp Elixir had the opposite effect on La Sofia who spent the dark trans-Atlantic hours running up and down the aisles adjusting pillows and practicing her new favorite phrase, "weady for nigh nigh?" on all 274 Alitalia passengers. I didn't dare to eat or drink anything the entire flight, having lost confidence in my ability to negotiate an airplane toilette, a growing posse of irate flight mates, and a tot on speed.

When Claire rescued us at the airport in Pisa I was near collapse from sleep deprivation and dehydration. But one glimpse of the aquamarine Mediterranean instantly revived me and my sunlit fantasy.

So after lunch and a short nap -- girl, you can always sleep at the beach -- we took the four babies to the seaside.

But wait. You don't just take a toddler to the beach, or anywhere, for that matter. There was a nap-reviving bottle of juice, a diaper change, a rubdown with sunblock No. 45, and a to-the-death struggle into the bathing suit, into the terry cover-up, into the sandals, into the hat. Times four.

Then there was the Great Gathering of Essential Items: drinking water, diapers, wipes, Kleenex, towels, and snacks, dry clothes, beach toys, hair brush, Band-Aids, a camera, some change, the keys, a pen, my reading glasses, and.... a crossword puzzle.

It took three women one hour and fifteen minutes to get four tots out the front door, down two flights, and into their strollers.

I don't recall much of the afternoon except that we were back at home by 6:00 and immediately set up an operation that would have made General Patton glow.

Ground zero was a laundry sink off the kitchen. While Stefania the Nanny was bathing baby #1 in the sink, I chased babies #2, #3, and #4 around the apartment, and Claire put dinner on the stove. Baby #1, now cleansed, was handed off to her mother to be powdered, dressed, and deposited into one of four high chairs. Then Nanny snatched up dirty baby #2 for the bath. By the time #4 was in the sink and #3 was getting his fanny dusted, we had two children in chairs as I fed them a spoon at a time in rotation. By the time the last baby was in her high chair, the first was ready for dessert.

By 8 p.m. the babes were fed and in bed. By 8:10 Claire, Stefania, and I were snoring face down in our plates of cold ziti.

Every day we went to the beach for several hours in the morning and again in the afternoon. The rest of the time we spent getting the babies ready or hosing them down. During their naptime we women did the laundry and prepared a dinner to re-heat later.

And at the beach? At the beach! The babes frolicked in the sand with their shovels and buckets -- we kept them from burying one another. The babes crawled the length of the densely packed beach -- we kept them from being stomped on by nearsighted uncles. The babes splashed and giggled in the water -- we kept them from drowning.

We soon gave up on bathing suits and stripped the children naked. They rolled in the damp sand and rubbed it into their hair, into their mouths, into their little ears, and into cracks and crannies you don't even want to know about. We bought them ice cream that dribbled down their bare chests and bonded with sand caught in remote crevices.

Between tending to bodily intake and elimination, doing damage control, and averting near death events there was no rest, no relaxation, and certainly no crossword puzzle for the ever-vigilant Claire, Stefania, and me.

By the end of the day, our kiddies, soaked in a marinade of salt water and urine and encrusted with a paste of sand, sunblock, and sucrose, were unspeakably happy. We were demented.

I thought back to my girlhood summers in California. There I was, a small child standing in the ocean up to my knees and waving back at my mother and aunties sitting on the beach. I realized that my happy memories of summer at the seashore are probably lodged in my mother's memory somewhere between hangover headaches and a near-fatal bout with ptomaine poisoning.

As I watched my own radiant little girl standing in the sea up to her knees and waving back at me and Claire sitting on the beach, I wondered when, exactly, I had come to loathe sand.

July 2001

THE ORIGINAL DOMESTIC GODDESS

NOVEMBER 24th IS THE fourth anniversary of my mother's passing. In the Jewish tradition it's called the Yahrzeit and is marked by the lighting of a candle that burns for 24 hours. It's also a time to recall the repertoire of qualities that made that one person unique and irreplaceable.

In the case of my Ma we're talking about an icon of the 1950's – a professional mother who attacked her role with the vigor of a combat general. For example, though we lived diagonally across the street from school, 50 yards from the front door, she would, on seriously rainy days, stuff us into the car in the attached garage and drive us to a spot in the school yard where there was a canopy so we could get door to door without enduring a single drop of damp – that foul carrier of cold and fever. Whenever I was sick and had to stay home from school, Ma would rub me down with alcohol and spirit of wintergreen, swaddle me in a Vicks VapoRub poultice, tuck me into bed, and deliver a tray of warm oatmeal cookies and hot lemonade with honey. My mother had the finest costume box on the block, the best recipe for salt and flour maps, and a gift for transforming clotheslines and old blankets into a tent from the Arabian nights. When I was in fourth grade she sewed me a splendid angel robe for the Christmas pageant, and when I was in eleventh grade she typed my essays because I was too busy studying chemistry and physics to take a typing class.

Ma was, of course, a stupendo Italian cook and there was always a pot of spaghetti sauce made from homegrown tomatoes bubbling on the stove. When the enormous apricot tree in the backyard exploded with ripe fruit, every surface in the kitchen and dining room was covered with canning jars, pectin jelly, blocks of wax, and bowls of pitted apricots. Cobblers, pies, and tarts carried us through till Thanksgiving when Ma would unwrap the first of the fruitcakes she'd been marinating in brandy since September.

The Pope could drop by any old time for some of that fruitcake since Ma kept our house religiously clean and tidy. She passed on to me her secrets of how to unclog a drain pipe, remove candle wax from a linen tablecloth, and wash windows without streaking the glass. And she schooled me in all the domestic crafts including how to darn socks, blind stitch hems, iron men's French cuff dress shirts, and organize a family jaunt with the efficiency of a military supply officer. Take a night out to the drive-in movies (we lived in California and everyone with kids went to the drive-in). She'd make a nest of blankets and pillows in the back seat of the old Chevy for us kids, and put a couple of coolers on the floor filled with a picnic fit for Martha Stewart: fried chicken, popcorn, homemade brownies, lemonade, and hot chocolate. (It was always a double feature.)

Faced with truly complex projects, her talents soared. As President of the Mother's Club the year our parish built a new convent for the eight nuns who taught in the school, Ma supervised the complete furnishing of the convent. For months she commandeered a brigade of carpenters, painters, carpet layers, and appliance installers. And she guided the nuns on department store excursions to help those otherwise cloistered ladies select everything from bedsteads to potato peelers for their new home. This was around the time Jacqueline Kennedy was refurbishing the White House, and Jackie had nothing on my mother.

Simple task or elaborate venture, Ma saw her efforts as a legacy for the ages. For decades she'd assembled and labeled our family snapshots into what became several dozen thick oversized photo albums. Ten years ago she completely redid all of the old albums into fresh books, so that they'd last longer for me and my brother and sister and our children.

My mother's scope was narrow. She grew up in a time and in an immigrant culture that limited women to the home. Her two brothers were sent to medical school. She was sent to secretarial school. But she always did an extraordinary job within these confines. During her second year at Blake's Secretarial School she won the California State Typing Championship.

Old school and nobody's fool, my mother educated me to wear a hat and gloves on trips to the city, to make my own bed when I'm a houseguest, to write thank you notes promptly, and, whenever I have a problem, to go straight to the bank manager. She also taught me all the lyrics to all the songs that were popular between 1920 and 1950.

I could never talk with Ma about men, my ambitions, or feelings – hers or mine. But we did speak on the phone every week. The evening before she went to sleep for the last time we talked about yams. We both, it turned out, were baking yams for dinner that night. She was most comfortable with the simple, the basic, the domestic. And that's where she and I, together, made our mother-daughter connection.

November 2007

THE LONG HOT SUMMER

THIS HAS GOT TO be one of the hottest summers in years. The Dog Days began in June and are still wagging their collective hot-humid-and-hazy tail here into August, which is where they actually belong. Life's a drag for those of us without a pond in the backyard or membership in the Rec Park pool. And we're all bellyaching about having to sleep in A/C chill for weeks on end. Yep. It's hot.

But as I sit on the front porch with my feet in a bucket of ice water, my mind wanders back to those long hot days of summer in Fresno before there was residential air conditioning.

My mother was born into a vast extended family in Fresno, California. When I once mentioned that fact to a New Yorker she moaned, "Oh, Fresno.... how neat is that!" Despite the efforts of the eponymous restaurant franchise to trick Easterners into thinking that Fresno is Palm Springs with spurs, it is actually Cleveland without the waterfront. Out of respect for my great grandparents who settled there with eight children a century ago, I concede that Fresno once possessed appeal as a small farming community in the heart of California's Great Central Valley. I remember my Great Aunt Minnie, who worked in the fruit packing houses, sending us crates of raisins, dried apricots, and canned peaches every Christmas. Fresno was the place where succulent fruit grew and it's still the nation's largest producer of almonds, nectarines, and figs.

But, by the time I got to know it in the 1950s, it had already sprawled out for miles in every direction with single-story stucco bungalows and two-bedroom ranch homes. And even my Aunt Mary who had married the rich man could only keep cool by closing the thick drapes and living inside, from June to September, in twilight darkness.

I loved spending summer days with my cousins in Fresno, but the heat shaped every moment of the adventure, starting with our departure from the temperate climate of the San Francisco Bay Area where my family lived. For years I thought that all vacation car trips began in darkness before dawn. But, no, I discovered years later, we left our house at 5am to finish the five hour road trip before the thermometer at my Aunt Lena's on Olive Avenue in Fresno hit three digits.

We often did not succeed since our old Chevy almost always overheated at we crested the Pacheco Pass that spilled into the Valley. The good news was that Pop was a mechanic. The bad news was that the Pacheco is barren of trees and, while Pop nursed the car, the rest of us were stuck in the open sun already bearing down mercilessly at 10 in the morning. For that reason my mother usually picked up a bag of ice when we stopped in Gilroy for breakfast. As we sat by the side of the road looking as miserable as the Joads counting their last nickel, Ma had us kids take turns slipping ice cubes down her back.

We knew we were almost to Fresno when the funky juice stands in the shape of giant oranges and grapes started appearing by the side of the road.

Finally we arrived and, leaving my parents to unload the car, my brother, sister, and I dashed to the back yard with my cousins Laura and Nancy and turned the hose on full blast. Didn't even bother to change out of our shorts since we knew when we did they'd dry on the line in minutes.

One summer we were thrilled to find that Uncle Bud had bought Laura and Nancy a little wading pool. But the thrill was short lived when Pop, Uncle Bud, and a 6-pack commandeered the pool. Good thing we still had the hose.

I and my cousins – between five and fourteen of us on any given day – spent our time running around the back yard, spraying each other with water, and growing browner. Sunscreen hadn't been invented as far as we were concerned.

Those days in Fresno were hellishly hot – my cousins still complain today – but nights in Fresno were heaven. The darkness was a warm silk wrap and there were a billion billion stars in that wide Valley sky. Sometimes all the aunts and uncles would congregate at Aunt Lena's and sit outdoors at a long table under the arbor and play low-stakes poker. Sometimes we'd haul over to Uncle Eddie's to watch home movies on a screen he set up in the back yard. Almost always we'd go to a little creamery near Uncle Lou's and get enormous cones of fresh peach ice cream.

All the cousins slept together in the garage on cots covered only with sheets and we distracted ourselves from the heat, still oppressive indoors at 11pm, by telling stories and singing rounds. Yep, it was hot. But we kids didn't mind so much.

Thank God they came up with air conditioning by the time I grew up.

August 2005

My Philosophy of Life, plus a few handy tips

EXTINCT SPECIES

MOVIE PALACES WITH USHERETTES and balconies, the automat, telephones with heft, over-sized taxi cabs with jump seats, car bench seats, car wing windows, car running boards, chrome fins, elevator attendants, unlocked churches....

Once my mother-in-law passed 80, her conversation quickly deteriorated to a running complaint about how everything had changed and how everything she was familiar with was gone. She shook her head a lot and sighed, "it's so confusing, so confusing."

...The San Francisco Bay foghorn booming through a pea-soup fog, nuns in long black habits teaching English grammar to third graders, priests in any sort of identifying garb, telephone switchboards like the one at my college dorm where I had a work-study job, Red's Tamales, spumoni ice cream, Cherry-a-Let chocolate candy bars....

I'm not that old yet, but, like my mother-in-law I too have a sinking feeling that every year one more cultural eco-system that I grew up with, am familiar with, is disappearing.

Now, I'm not whining about how this or that "used to be cheaper." EVERYTHING used to be cheaper. And I'm not carping about how something -- let's say, fresh peach ice cream -- used to taste better. That, I suppose, is a matter of opinion.

What I am talking about is the complete and utter evaporation of certain Things, Places, Events, Practices. That are simply No More. Gone. Extinct.

We're glad to be rid of some of these things.

....Air raid drills, bomb shelters, leprosy, carbon paper, sanitary napkin belts, rubber girdles, Toni Home Permanents for Little Girls, iron lungs....

A few years ago I heard a story on the radio about a man who was living in an iron lung. As a young boy in the 1950s he had contracted polio and here he was almost 50 years later still being kept alive by a grotesque piece of hardware that is obsolete, that no one under the age of 40 has ever seen or even heard of. What an absurd fate to be living today with the consequences of a scourge that no one fears any more because it no longer exists.

...The hospital where I was born (which was turned into a Mall), my first home (which was shaken to the ground in the California earthquake of 1989), my high school (which was bulldozed to make way for a housing development), the fruit orchards between my town and Grandma's house in Santa Cruz (which got paved over and renamed Silicon Valley)....

Some of these losses are personal and only recalled by a select group. (There are probably some young people who even think Silicon Valley is a more attractive place now that it's not cluttered up with acres of apricot trees.) There are other losses that all of us of a certain age lament.

....Saturday afternoon kiddie matinees with news reels, serials, and cartoons, drive-in restaurants with carhops, white and brown saddle shoes, door-to-door milk delivery....

It's a New Year and everybody is making the annual lists of best dressed, worst reviewed, and most important. We all know that 2001 was an historical turning point and that we begin 2002 in an altered state of consciousness.

As the word goes out across the land that The World As We Know It is Changed Forever, I'm moved to compile a modest list of those things that have, during my own relatively brief stay on this planet, gone extinct...the Fuller Brush man, uniformed gas station attend- ants, eating fish every Friday, white dress gloves on little girls, tuition-free universities, house calls by doctors ...

Nita Micossi invites you all to contribute to this list at
micossi@earthlink.net

January 2002

10.
HEALTH, WEALTH, AND THE HEREAFTER

REPAIR AND MAINTENANCE. The reason most of life's achievements are by young people is that old people spend all of their time just trying to keep up with the repair and maintenance. Page 247

IN YOUR DREAMS. But after almost two decades of sweet breath and, god help us, cultural correctness, I must confess a dirty little secret. I still do smoke... in my dreams. Page 250

COULD BE NOTHING....: could be everything.... Dr. Maggie considers my chest pains. Page 252

BORN TO LOSE: I know, in my secret dark place, that I am constitutionally unequipped to make money in the stock market, that I am unworthy to be a Player. Page 255

SOLID WASTE DISPOSAL: Lest you think that your options are limited to a pine box, a furnace, or a gross anatomy lab, let's consider some creative ways not to waste that too, too solid flesh when you're no longer in it. Page 258

METAMORPHOSIS: Wrinkles and grey hair are birthday cliches; but nobody ever mentioned the bleeding gums, rheumy eyes, and dry nipples. Page 260

BORN AGAIN, AND AGAIN, AND AGAIN: Reincarnation -- it's something to look forward to. Page 262

TO THE BILLING MANAGER. I am nothing if not cheerful and prompt in my bill paying thanks to my mother who also insisted on flawless penmanship, blind hems, and the perfectly ironed French cuff. .Page 264

ON THE MAGIC MOUNTAIN. Except for childbirth, I've managed to avoid hospitals. But I made up for lost time over the past four months and have discovered, up and close and way too personal the grotesqueries of the American health care system. Page 266

MY LATEST WILL & TESTAMENT. being of as sound a mind as any fool who's signed up for elective surgery, I do hereby make, publish, and declare this my Latest Will & Testament. Page 269

REPAIR & MAINTENANCE

7:30A.M. THE ALARM CLOCK goes off and my brain synapses flash the alert: time to hop out of bed and begin a New Day! ... But wait. Not so fast.

I peel back the covers and do ten minutes of stretching on my back so that my sciatic nerve will not scream when I do make that hop out of bed. I then sit up very slowly in deference to my newly diagnosed Benign Paroxysmal Positional Vertigo and do a recuperative exercise in which I fling my head and upper body violently from side to side for ten minutes. The idea is to jog loose the microscopic crystals that are lodged in my inner ear causing the vertigo. The drill induces dizziness and makes me look like a puppet in a Punch'n'Judy show on the losing end of a mugging. My husband on the other side of the bed is propped up on one elbow laughing his fool head off.

Like with a tape deck or a toaster oven, as the warranty on a human body runs out -- sometime around age 50 -- the breakdown of random bits and pieces accelerates. A few of these bits, like a hip joint or cornea, can be replaced, but most of our parts demand ever more time-consuming repair and maintenance just to function at a minimum level.

7:50a.m In the bathroom, I brush and waterpik my teeth, then jump into the shower where I do a quick mammo check, gargle with warm salt water, and, since I've been working on a head cold, flush out my sinuses with a neti pot.

For those of you not yet hip to the charms of the neti pot, behold this miraculous invention by Indian Yogis that looks like a miniature genie lamp with a long slender spout. Fill it with warm salt water [warm salt water seems to be a universal curative] and, tilting your head ear-to-shoulder, jam the spout into one nostril and let a stream of water trickle up the nasal passage where it makes a loop-the-loop and exits through the other nostril. The sensation is akin to hitting the water after a swan dive off the high board; water floods all the cavities in your head giving you an instantaneous ear ache, sinus burn, and slight migraine over the Third Eye. But the neti pot does dislodge quarts of nasty mucous and, for about fifteen minutes, you can breathe again.

8:30a.m. I flip the coffee machine switch; strap on my heart rate monitor; pile on the gloves, scarf, and overcoat; and head out the door. It takes me about 45 minutes to make the three-mile circuit around the village which finishes the job begun in bed of loosening up my limbs.

Back home, I unload the outdoor gear and head into the kitchen for breakfast. My options are Special K cereal with half a banana, chopped walnuts, and a cup of one percent milk, or a five minute egg with dry whole wheat toast. I pour a cuppa decaf and enjoy.

Stomach now fully lined, it's able to withstand my morning dose of medications and supplements. I take Tapazol to help control a thyroid imbalance and Metformin to help control the side effects of the Tapazol. In addition, I take calcium and magnesium for my aging bones, Vitamin D to assist the absorption of the calcium, Vitamin C to sabotage head colds, a capsule of bioflavonoid to fight inflammation, and a B-complex for everything else.

10:30 a.m. I leave the house for an 11a.m. with the physical therapist I engaged two months ago to rescue me from a crippling back spasm, but who became a fixture in my week when my chronic sciatica went into overdrive. After an hour of hot packs, deep tissue massage, and electrical stimulation I head over to the ladies' gym for a half hour on the stationary bike, two rounds of circuit training, ten minutes of stretching [can't do too much stretching], and plenty of advice from the girls on the latest postmenopausal hormone therapy.

Then it's time for lunch: a green salad with water-packed albacore tuna, olive oil and lemon. Boldly risking a glucose challenge, I top off lunch with a single chocolate covered cherry that I furtively purchase at the Deli.

2:30p.m. I'm back at the gym for a Gentle Yoga class. And then a quick visit to the oncologist who's monitoring a lump on my right breast. All is well. So I celebrate with a protein bar and a cup of green tea at the Health Food Store.

5:00p.m. I have a bit of time before dinner so I sit down at my desk and pay the month's medical bills. This cycle I owe the endodontist who redid a failing root canal, the endocrinologist who readjusted my medications, the ear, nose, and throat specialist who diagnosed the vertigo, and the surgeon who did a biopsy.

6:00p.m. I start to cook dinner — poached Atlantic Ocean salmon, steamed broccoli, brown basmati rice, and a Greek salad. My daughter wants to know if there's anything on the menu that she'll eat. When I tell her what's cooking, she boils three hot dogs and brings a jar of peanut butter to the dinner table. I demure when my husband offers me a glass of pinot noir. It reacts badly with the Metformin.

8p.m. I spend a half hour soaking my feet and scraping plantar warts, contracted at a friend's pool, off the calloused soles. I then persuade my husband with false promises of passion [with my back, are you kidding?] into massaging my wrists that have been getting carpal-tunnel-like twitches lately.

9:30p.m. I floss and brush my teeth, wash my face, rinse my eyes with a special concoction I get from the ophthalmologist, and slather an ointment on the hives that pop out all over my chest every winter, caused, says the allergist, by insufficient hydration in my office.

10p.m. Last chore before climbing into bed with an ice pack on my left knee and my current reading material [STIFF: THE CURIOUS LIVES OF HUMAN CADAVERS by Mary Roach] is to weigh myself on the bathroom scale. Buck naked I'm up half a pound.

It was obviously that chocolate covered cherry.

January 2007

IN YOUR DREAMS

I QUIT SMOKING ON November 20, 1979. It was one of the hardest things I've ever done and I needed help. So every Thursday for five weeks I joined a dozen other addicts at the local hospital and we tried to convince each other that quitting was a good idea.

On week six, after one last blistering confessional, we retreated to the hall for a farewell smoke. One middle-aged waitress with the rhino wrinkles of a four pack a day user, was fascinated with my slim brown-wrapped Shermans (does anyone smoke these lovely things anymore?) and asked if she could bum one.

"Where have these been all my life!" she coughed, and snatched the rest of the box that I had, just moments earlier, pledged to throw in the garbage can. She disappeared into the bathroom and smoked every last one of those sweetly scented, slightly nutty tasting Shermans before returning to the group green around the gills, but clearly on a higher spiritual plane.

I don't think the waitress kept the faith. But I did. After that chilly November night (you remember the details of a really important event), not a single roll of tobacco passed between my trembling lips even though all my friends still chain-smoked and I suffered in their company.

I was armed with a piece of information that fortified me against temptation. For I knew, as surely as any honest alcoholic knows: there's no such thing as "just one." I cannot have a single smoke and walk away -- I tested that theory once while rooming with a recovering heroin addict who smoked two cigarettes simultaneously when she was *really* nervous. This reckless experiment landed me back in the clutches of a two pack a day habit and I had to go through that dreadful six week program all over again.

I am an addict and always will be. (Ma, who quit after Pop died of cancer, admits that, after all these years, she still can't drink a martini without yearning for a Lucky Strike.) And I know in my soul that if it wouldn't kill me or result in my anti-smoking-fascist husband divorcing me, I would take up the filthy habit again tomorrow.

250

But after almost two decades of sweet breath and, god help us, cultural correctness, I must confess a dirty little secret. I still do smoke... in my dreams.

Just last night I dreamt of a favorite saloon in the French Quarter of New Orleans where Madelon and I like to begin cocktail hour. In the dream we are matching vodka martinis and I am blowing blue smoke rings over the glowing tip of a Gauloise. Together, in our Bacallesque voices, we sing a husky chorus of "Am I Blue?" Hoagy Carmichael is at the piano and my hair cascades over one eye as I lean in close for him to give me a light.

Last Thursday I relived the girls' night out I had with my old pals when I was home at Christmas. In reality, of the five of us sitting around the table, only one is still a confirmed nicotine addict. In my dream, however, a pack of Nazionales senza filtro (the brand of collective choice during our college year in Italy) sits on the table. And though we all smoke ceaselessly, the pack is never empty. Now, that's a dream.

In these nocturnal escapades I occasionally feel a twinge of guilt or the need to conceal my behavior, as if, even my unconscious is not allowed this fugitive pleasure. But more often, I close my eyes, drag deeply, and enjoy every single puff.

My favorite smoking dream of late is the one where my mother and I are sitting at a plush mahogany bar in Manhattan. I am drinking a rye on the rocks, she a dry martini with three olives. A pair of carefree demimondes, we laugh gaily and take turns lighting each other's long, thin, ever so glamorous, highly illicit cigarettes with the stainless steel Ronson lighter my father used to carry when he was a bush pilot in Alaska.

It is 1940-something in this scene and, as the jazz trio in the corner plays "Smoke Gets In Your Eyes", even the Surgeon General lights up.

Call it a crazy pipe dream, but I'd like to believe that in heaven there's a red leather and wood paneled lounge where we can all smoke to our heart's content.

July 2008

COULD BE NOTHING....

"Could be nothing.... Could be everything." Not the sort of prognosis you want to hear from your doctor when you call to tell her about chest pains.

She couldn't see me till the following day at 11:15am. Eighteen hours. Quite enough time to unravel the threads of those diverging possibilities.

I had a hard time falling asleep that night especially since Dr. Maggie had grabbed the phone from the appointment desk nurse to add an afterthought: "If it gets worse between now and then go straight to the Emergency Room." Thank you, dear, I will.

I lay in bed trying to figure out a good metaphor to describe the taffy-pull that was occurring every 12 seconds in my upper chest.

Could be heartburn. Could be gas. Could be nothing. Maybe they'd have to keep me in the hospital for a week to run tests. The idea of seven days on my back with a stack of books, the remote control, and room service was not without its charm.

At the other end of the spectrum was the Could Be Everything conclusion which I reframed as the Other Shoe Is Finally Dropping Theory. Or Richard Dreyfuss' Infantile Paralysis Philosophy of Life. Once, when asked to explain how he, a man with everything good in this life, was involved in not one but two near fatal car accidents, Dreyfuss replied, "Well, it's like this: just when you've got everything together – a happy family, a nice job, enough money in the bank – Bang! God gives you infantile paralysis." To even things out? To teach you humility? Because it's Wednesday?

Not that my life has been perfect lately. It was in balance for about five minutes in January when I got a raise on a Friday afternoon. But I was fired the following Monday, so that sort of doused the celebration. Nevertheless, things have, in general, been on the ascendancy since my daughter was born five and a half years ago. After 18 nomadic years I now have a permanent street address. All but one of my student loans has been paid in full. And we all HAVE OUR HEALTH!

So naturally I've been waiting for the other shoe to drop or infantile paralysis, whichever comes first.

My brain, moving swiftly to the endgame, saw my slender self (for surely I would be sick for a while and lose a little weight) lying serenely in a white satin-lined casket. This image did not trouble me. What did trouble me was the thought that I'd miss a deadline after I'd finished all the sweaty legwork on the story. My family could really use that $1800 right about now, I thought sadly.

While sitting in Dr. Maggie's waiting room I mentally put my affairs in order. I made a note to tell my husband where to buy the black beans for Thursday night's low fat vegetarian quesadillas, what Dr. Seuss story I was scheduled to read to the kindergartners on Friday (since he'd have to fill in for me), and where to locate all our Important Documents – including Sofia's Key Bank DinoSaver Club passbook, my luggage keys, and the tax accountant's phone number since we, or at least he, would probably be needing an extension if... well, you know.

After taking my blood pressure (perfect), doing an EKG (exemplary), and listening to my lungs (clear), Dr. Maggie asked me if I was particularly stressed lately. Stressed? Well, two weeks earlier I had returned from a fabulous 18-day trip to Southeast Asia without the family. I'd picked up my pal Sharon in Singapore and we had gone to Bali where we picked mangoes off the trees and shopped till we dropped and then on to Borneo where we swapped tall tales and drank rice wine with a tribe of fun-loving headhunters.

"Was the trip relaxing?" asked Dr. Maggie.

"When I got back everyone said I looked ten years younger," I replied shyly.

"And what did you come back to?" she asked.

I dropped my head to my chest and recited a sorry litany: 97 e-mails, a stack of overdue bills, three story deadlines, a lawsuit (remember the motorcycle guy?), and a daughter who decided to punish me for leaving her alone with her father for 18 days by waking me up every night at 3:30am to extract compensatory acts of love and affection.

"When did the chest pains begin and what were you doing at the time?" asked the good doctor.

"Well, it was day before yesterday and I was driving over the bridge into Kingston to pickup the TV set into which I'd absentmindedly jammed a cassette earlier in the day that had to be extracted by a professional, and my car, into which I'd put a new radiator in January because the new radiator I'd put into it in September had been ripped to shreds by a fan blade gone mad, started to overheat. The child was in the backseat weeping because I refused to buy her an intercontinental ballistic missile."

Dr. Maggie told me to take two aspirins and call her in the morning. It turned out to be nothing AND everything.

March 2001

BORN TO LOSE

IT'S NOT LIKE I'M frittering away my discretionary income on Barbie collectibles. It's not like I don't want to see my savings double every Thursday afternoon. It's not that I don't envy my peers who have invested so prudently that they'll be playing golf between Caribbean cruises by the time they're 55.

I want to get into the stock market. I want to buy mutual funds. I want to be a PLAYER. How could I not?! They're giving money away down there on Wall Street.

It's just that I am bound by love and habit to a profession run by people who believe that the Work is its own reward. They do not wish to soil the sanctity of the scribe's vocation with anything as profane as money.

Thus, for years I've eaten rice and beans and prayed that one day I too would be in a position to toss a few coins into that bubbling pot of financial plenitude that spews forth unending wealth and peace of mind.

And whenever one of my affluent friends, my tax accountant, and every other radio talk show guest insisted that I absolutely must invest in the market (and they've been doing it since 1982), I screamed Yes! Yes! Yes!... as soon as my income is higher than my rent plus $10.

That day finally arrived last spring. I had a $2000 windfall -- a publisher actually paid me what he owed me -- and I put it straight into an IRA stock fund.

Please note, that in anticipation of this moment, I had, all these years, paid attention to the wise and high income tax bracket gurus. I know from load and no-load, growth stocks and value stocks, diversified portfolio. I may be a greenhorn, but I am an informed greenhorn.

Well, I can hardly describe the emotions that welled up in me as I wrote out that check to Fidelity Investments. I felt proud -- patriotic -- adult. I clutched a slice of the American Dream in my hand as I trod the path to fiscal nirvana. I was now a PLAYER.

I imagined watching my money grow with the same barely contained excitement that my little girl feels watching her parsley seeds sprout in a clay pot. My friend Joel had said that 20-25% increases a year in mutual funds were not uncommon. But I kept my expectations modest. I'd be happy with, say, 10%. Why that would be $200 a year! That's more than a lot of editors think a 2500 word magazine feature story is worth. I could live with that.

I didn't exactly spend the money in my mind, but I did project out a bit.... If I kick in a few hundred dollars every year, what with current growth index projections and earnings forecasts, my little nest egg might actually be worth something when I'm ready to retire. I could reinvest it in mortgage securities and intermediate-term municipals and, with the interest earned, add some extra bucks to my monthly social security income.... It was intoxicating.

You can imagine my shock, then, when the year-end statement arrived from Fidelity declaring that my $2000 investment was worth $1758.03.

"Good Lord! What happened?" I asked one of those radio talk show guests first chance I could. "I'd have done better if I'd kept my money stuffed in a sock under the mattress."

"Ah!" came the honey-toned reply, "why that's just the point now isn't it, dear? You take a Chance when you invest in the stock market, don't you?"

"But it's all going up, up, up!" I hollered. "Nobody else I know is losing money."

Then she explained it to me: It was all probably due to the "timing" of my purchase. I probably sent Fidelity my $2000 when the stocks were exceptionally high, now they were back to "normal". Who knew?

The truth is, I knew. For 17 years I watched everybody else being a big-shot PLAYER in the market, making a killing, buying Sub-Zero refrigerators and Manolo Blahnik sandals with their dividend checks.

I knew, in my secret dark place, that I am constitutionally unequipped to make money, that everything I touch turns to insolvency, that I am unworthy to be a PLAYER. Just look at my vocation.

But it's okay. I lead a full life. My family loves me. Friends have promised to say nice things at the wake. I count my blessings.

And I've written off the $2000. No blame. Che sarà sarà.

Still, there is this nagging feeling that I am the only one who cannot grok the sure-fire, fail-safe prosperity formula that everyone else is applying with such dazzling success. It's like working out at the gym four times a week for two and a half years and not losing a single pound. But that's another story.

> *As of the last quarterly statement, Nita Micossi's Fidelity mutual fund is worth $1702.25.*

June 1999

My Philosophy of Life, plus a few handy tips

SOLID WASTE DISPOSAL

I NEVER THOUGH THAT I'd be considering my physical remains post mortem as a problem of solid waste disposal. But thanks to Mary Roach the topic has been on my mind a lot lately. Lest you think that your options are limited to a pine box, a furnace, or a gross anatomy lab, Mary vividly describes in her book --"Stiff: The Curious Lives of Human Cadavers" -- an array of possible uses of dead bodies.

For instance, you – or, rather your empty old carcass – might serve as a crash test dummy for Buick, a flash-frozen slide specimen at the Harvard Brain Bank, or composted fertilizer in Sweden. For the exhibitionists among us there is the new science of plastination that replaces the water in a corpse with a silicone polymer turning the body into a permanent, art-gallery-worthy, version of itself. Go see one of the touring shows – Bodyworlds or Bodies: The Exhibition – for a preview of how you might entertain millions of nine-year-old boys as a flayed cadaver playing tennis or doing the tango with your spouse.

And for those who would do anything to continue looking fabulous after death, there is a company in Illinois called LifeGem that will transform cremated human remains into a diamond. My daughter could attend the memorial service wearing her parents as a pair of tasteful two carat stud earrings.

Like Ms. Roach, who spends the last chapter of her book contemplating what to do with her own body when she is no longer in it, I too have been wondering which of these intriguing alternatives would best serve me, the planet, and my grieving loved ones.

The question has become more than academic due to a housing shortage at my husband's family plot in Queens. His foresighted grandfather purchased a substantial piece of real estate at Mt. Lebanon Cemetery off Myrtle Avenue 80 years ago. A massive slab of granite bearing the family name rests on a hillock, surrounded by mature trees and on either side, in tidy rows, the gravesites of the man's multitudinous offspring. My husband and his sisters visit the site every September to visit the dearly departed and imagine whether that oak tree in the northwest corner will block their eventual view of the Chrysler Building. Problem is,

258

the family site is short two plots, and, unless the cemetery allows some double-decker arrangements, the mister and I will have to spend eternity on a different Carnival cruise.

My family offers no help since the ashes of my parents were surrendered to the Pacific Ocean some years ago and the California Current has, no doubt, deposited their grey bits on some remote atoll by now.

So we are on our own.

I'm okay with organ donation. But, frankly, who would want these tired old spare parts? Plastination is cool, but just my luck some goofball would exhibit me hot dogging on a skate board with my naked tatas swinging in the wind. Is this how I really want to be remembered through the ages? And as for the diamond-is-forever -- with a price tag of $40,000, I suspect that the kid would rather have the cash. I know I would.

After examining all of the options, Mary Roach has decided that in disposing of her solid waste she should not waste it. Organ donations, certainly; medical research, if she can get her squeamish husband to consent.

As for me, I've concluded that the most appealing choice is to be composted and spread around a fig tree near my grandmother's birthplace in Tuscany. The kids could come visit, sit in the shade, talk about the good old days, and eat some nice fruit.

February 2007

METAMORPHOSIS

I AWOKE ONE MORNING from uneasy dreams to find that brown freckles the size of raindrops had appeared suddenly on the back of my hands. Had they grown from tiny dots I'd never before noticed? Or had they popped out full-sized? And where had they popped out from?

The appearance of these unsightly freckles shocked me. I am too young to grow old, I whimpered, recalling the crushing lament of a friend who, on her fortieth birthday cried out in horror, My God! it's happening to me.

Something is clearly happening to me as well. And none of it looks good. Black hairs darken the corners of an upper lip that has always been lily white. Small hard pimples have erupted like grains of sand on my once smooth shoulders. And between seasons, the expanse of my back has mysteriously broadened. I've gained no weight, I swear, but the dorsum is indisputably two inches wider than my summer shirts remember.

I have, over the past few years, noted with resignation the occasional grey hair and, in the corner of each eye, the faint emergence of tiny crow's feet (who came up with that appalling metaphor?).

I fight the inevitable victory of pregnancy, nursing, and gravity over my once admired bosom with sweaty Nautilus exercises. And I anoint the creases between my mouth and cheeks with Nivea in what I know to be a futile ritual. About these failures of the flesh I have been warned. Wrinkles, grey hair, and pooped boobs are, after all, birthday clichés.

But there have been so many other nasty surprises that nobody even mentioned. Brittle toenails and bleeding gums, rheumy eyes and dry nipples. Delicate zones of pink flesh turned to muddy brown, rivers of lubrication becoming damp trickles -- why do the dry bits becomes wet and the wet become dry? And then there is that wrench in the lower back that screamed suddenly one morning as I eased into a yoga move that I've been doing for 15 years.

Why didn't you warn me! I shrieked at my mother who was too preoccupied with her swollen ankles to come up with a deft defense. Perhaps there is a tacit agreement among mothers to withhold the grim details of aging to prevent mass defection before the close of the breeding season.

Or could it be that the less visible signs of decline, like permanent horny toe calluses and chronic hemorrhoids, are simply eclipsed by the cruel public ones, like those deep trenches between nose and chin?

Or perhaps our elders, who should be guiding us through physical decline with wisdom, compassion, and a few helpful tips have forgotten what life was like with smooth skin, a strong back, and a full head of hair.

Forgetting does seem to be one of the more humiliating side effects of growing old. Words, for instance. It took me ten minutes and a trip to the medicine cabinet to jolt my memory into recalling the word "hemorrhoids." I can describe the symptoms and act it out in a game of charades, but damned if I could come up with the actual word.

I used to keep on my office wall a running list of "Glamorous Actresses Over 40" for inspiration and reassurance. I tacked up photos of great grandmothers, bright-eyed and limber, scaling the Himalayas and meditating in full lotus position at the summit. I listened with reverence to TV septuagenarians interrupting a tennis match to offer sermonettes on the joys of growing old gracefully.

Now that I have entered the zone of middle aged entropy, however, I scrutinize the liars for evidence of a hair transplant or an eyelift. I probe photos for airbrush artistry. I wonder if, like Oprah, they haven't stuck grandma's head onto Suzanne Sommer's body.

Only John, my 85-year-old neighbor, is completely honest with me on the subject. Growing old, he says, sucks.

So I buy facial hair bleach and keep it hidden behind the baby powder. I have abandoned braless comfort and doubled my upper body presses. I rub fading cream into those wretched spots on my hands and inspect daily for population expansion.

And although I try to take solace in knowing that I am not alone, the 20 year old trapped inside this freshly freckled skin is as bewildered as Gregor Samsa.

November 2000

My Philosophy of Life, plus a few handy tips

BORN AGAIN, AND AGAIN, AND AGAIN

IT LOOKS LIKE SHIRLEY MacLaine is finally going to get the last laugh. Dr. Ian Stevenson, director of the Department of Personality Studies at the University of Virginia has for years been collecting evidence to support the actual true existence of reincarnation and he's just published a tell-all book called "Old Souls".

Actually, Dr. Stevenson has been cataloging evidence for several lifetimes, but it took him 118 years to find an agent who didn't think he was totally loco.

I wish I'd heard of him sooner. You see, I've always suspected that there was something fishy going on. For instance, every time I put on a turtleneck sweater I have the strangest claustrophobic feeling. My sister used to joke that I'd probably been hung for my crimes in a previous life. I'd laugh -- and then wonder.

And what about my obsessive fear of beeswax facials? Was it, as I've always believed, caused by seeing Vincent Price in the House Of Wax at the drive-in movies when I was eight years old? Or did I actually experience a peculiar death – by bee sting? by facial? -- in some previous incarnation? Dr. Stevenson says that the one thing people most often remember from a past life is the manner of death, especially if it was violent.

So after I read a review of "Old Souls: The Scientific Evidence For Past Lives" I decided to do a little investigating of my own.

Dr. Stevenson declares that small children can easily recall details from former incarnations, so I asked my four-year-old daughter if she could remember anything from her previous lives. "Oh, yes," she obliged without hesitation, and started to rat on what she called her old "bad parents" and the nasty circumstances of their demise. Warming up to the exercise, she went on about her two wicked stepsisters and how they made her, a Real Princess, do all the dirty work around the house. "But the bad guys came and ate them up and I was able to marry the king and go to Disneyworld for our honeymoon."

Maybe little kids mix up the facts with their fantasies. So I asked my friend Sheila if she had any inkling about her past lives. "Absolutely," she replied. "I was Vivien Leigh."

"Vivien Leigh! How do you know?" I asked suspiciously.

"We have the exact same shoe size and we both hate anchovies," she said proudly. "Also, I always get hot flashes whenever I'm in Atlanta."

Obviously the subject brings out the giddy in people so I asked my husband, who doesn't have a giddy bone in his body. He mumbled something about being the deposed Prince of Vilna with a secret Swiss bank account – but he's been saying that for years.

I realized that I had to push this investigation to the next level. So, on the advice of my masseuse, I went to see a channel. Now for those of you who don't watch daytime TV talk shows, a "channel" is somebody who allows spirits from the beyond to use their bodies to annoy those of us in the here and now. Remember Whoopie Goldberg in Ghosts?

I didn't know what to expect, but Marge certainly looked spooky enough to be a channel. A six foot tall albino woman with white hair down to her waist, Marge spoke in a breathy Marilyn Monroe kind of voice and wore lots of American Indian jewelry.

She didn't say much as her Marge self though. Soon after I entered the room where she held sessions, she slumped in a chair, closed her eyes, and began to speak in a husky baritone. She or actually he, since the baritone introduced himself as Clive, rattled on a lot about my past lives. But since I hadn't been an Egyptian queen or a Renaissance painter none of it was terribly interesting. Until, that is, Clive mentioned my first husband, from this life.

"You have been together in many incarnations," he intoned gravely. "Sometimes you give the backrubs, sometimes you get them. You two have much left to work out on this plane of existence before moving on to the next."

"Good grief!" I cried, "You mean I have to deal with that jerk all over again in another life?"

This was not good news. The man not only drank, gambled, and womanized, he had regrettable personal hygiene habits. On the other hand, since I was the one who had to do all the income tax returns this go round, maybe I will luck out next time.

Reincarnation – it's something to look forward to.

February 2000

TO THE BILLING MANAGER

TO: HAZEL GRINCH, BILLING Manager

The Soggy River Bodily Fluids & Radiology Lab

Dear Ms. Grinch,

I have in hand your bill of $320 for the mammogram done on me last spring. As you know, my doctor made a typographical error on the original prescription and the insurance company refused payment on the claim. They asked you to resubmit the corrected claim and, despite exhaustive letters of explanation from me, my doctor, and the chiefs of oncology at three teaching hospitals in the tri-state area, you have refused to cooperate. Thus, I am left to pay the bill in full myself. And here I thought that coverage of yearly mammos was mandated by the State of New York.

Now ordinarily I would cheerfully and promptly comply, since I am nothing if not cheerful and prompt in my bill paying thanks to my mother who also insisted on flawless penmanship, blind hems, and the perfectly ironed French cuff. [Ah! Now those were Family Values.] But extenuating circumstances present a number of obstacles in this situation.

Let me explain. In the past nine months I have had two iffy surgeries, three nasty biopsies, and four months on my back trying to recover movement in my left leg. Although I thought I was out of the woods this summer, I was diagnosed with the cancer in August, and so have spent the past ten weeks undergoing the chemo.

I've always been a working mom. You might know what that means – 15 hours a day on your feet, seven days a week – making a living, transporting the kids, separating the dark laundry from the whites, chopping carrots for the chicken soup, arguing with the claims adjuster, and so forth. Alas, I am now down to about three good functioning hours a day. I need a lot of naps in order to stay upright.

All of these medical problems don't trouble me so much. I'm no quitter, I have confidence in my doctors, and I've already committed to hosting next year's annual block party.

However, I have stumbled into what is probably your average Red or Blue American's worst nightmare. My catastrophic health insurance company – to whom I've been paying premiums for 14 years, to whom I have not in all these years submitted a single claim, and from whom I received a confirmation and a mighty Hi, Ho, Silver before undertaking my first surgery – has decided that they, due to an obscure technicality [which needed a magnifying glass and seven lawyers to find], don't have to reimburse me for anything. Nada, niente, rien, nichts. Of course, I am fighting them, but they have a lot of money to fight back since the federal government just gave them $122.8 billion in "bailout" funds.

In addition to this setback, I am relentlessly assaulted by billing agents who want their money last July, collection agents who can do Threatening 27 different ways, lawyers who demand my eldest as a hostage, and.... well, you get the idea. Just opening the mail and answering their phone calls occupies most of my three good functioning hours a day. It is very disheartening.

Now to your demands. I have already received at least one menacing letter from you, so I know that you mean business. But a bill for $121,000 from one of the five hospitals I have been in since January sits on my desk. Their lawyers are bigger and meaner than your lawyers, so I must attend to them first.

I'm not sure how long it will take, but know that I'm running as fast as my little feet will carry me. For at least three hours a day.

Yours sincerely,
Patient #057091147XYB

November 2008

ON THE MAGIC MOUNTAIN

IT WAS ADVERTISED AS a straightforward elective surgery. But there were complications, which is why they make you sign that draconian disclaimer upon entering the hospital. So, instead of a quickie in-and-out, I spent two weeks in the hospital -- half of it in intensive care – had 10 blood transfusions, and, oh, yes, a second operation 15 weeks later to deal with "the complications."

Except for childbirth, I've managed to avoid hospitals. But I made up for lost time over the past four months and have discovered, up and close and way too personal the grotesqueries of the American health care system.

In short, Hospitals have nothing to do with Healing. In fact, the last place on the planet that you want to be if you are sick or recuperating from a major assault on your flesh and bones is in a hospital. Think about it. What does a body need to get better? Rest, nutritious food, and appropriate medications.

Let's start with the food. To their credit, the hospital I stayed in the longest will make you an egg salad sandwich on whole wheat bread if asked, and after a week I discovered that it was possible to special order fresh fruit and raw vegetables. But most of the choices on hospital menus are processed and packaged, loaded with salt, sugar, and red dye 40: jello, fruit yogurt, pudding, tapioca, canned soup, orange salad dressing, soda crackers, Cheerios, canned fruit, Wonder bread, and mystery meat. I did appreciate efforts like the chicken francese with lemon sauce and broccoli; but, alas, they cooked the bejezus and all nutritional value out of it.

Rest? Only if you're in a coma. Patients are interrupted once every hour or so to have blood drawn or vitals taken or fluids discarded, monitors recalculated or sheets changed or garbage dumped. Or a doc you never saw before and will never see again stops by and asks "how are you feeling?" Regardless of your reply, s/he will note something in a chart and later send you a bill for $300. I nodded off for fugitive minutes here and there, but I did not sleep for the first six days after surgery number one.

And then there are the meds. When did we become obsessed with indiscriminately over-prescribed drugs? After Ma died we hauled three garbage bags filled with pills out of her house. The woman was taking dozens of pills every day and she looked like hell. Didn't any one fool with a stethoscope think to ask if these were all necessary or, god help us, remotely compatible? Did the damn pills kill her in the end?

Every drug is freighted with at least a dozen unpleasant to life-threatening side effects. They teach 'em in med school to respond to a side effect with another drug, and another and another, until the patient is swallowing more pills than a Jacqueline Susann hussy.

Consider this: I'd been taking a drug called Metformin prior to the operation, although its value was marginal and mostly prophylactic. Early on in my stay in the hospital I complained of relentless nausea and was given two anti-nausea meds – one in the IV and a patch behind the ear. After a string of sleepless nights I asked if any of the meds might be the culprit. Sleep disturbance is a side effect of anti-nausea medication so they put me on sleeping pills. But the sleeping pills constipated me so they ordered a pill to loosen me up. And, just in case I loosened up too much, they prescribed some iron.

One morning, the nurse offered me a fist full of pills and I asked her what they were. Number one was the Metformin. At home I'd always taken the Metformin AT NIGHT because it made me queasy. I told the nurse to bag the Metformin. I didn't really need it anyway and I wouldn't need all the other pills because each one was there to suppress a side effect caused by another one.

When the nurse miraculously complied [a newbie? a hardened vet?] I discovered the secret of dealing with the medical establishment. You must take charge and be your own General Contractor. I had a surgeon, a medical doctor, a hematologist, an endocrinologist, nurses and technicians who changed shifts every eight hours, and a dozen assorted docs who looked in on me once and tried to prescribe another drug.

No one on this so-called team knew the whole picture because they never got together and discussed my "complications". I was the only one who knew the rises and dips of every vital sign and blood test, the ebb and flow of my sleep patterns, the timing of the aches, the responsiveness of the pains to what and when, the details of my bladder and bowel behavior. I didn't always know why, but I definitely knew who, what, when, where, and how. And listening in on the guessing games of all these drop-in medics, I was in the best position to eventually sort out the why.

In fact, I was the one who id'd the anti-thyroid drug [which I've been taking for two and half years] that caused the complications that baffled my medical team. Yes, I do read the side effects on those pharmaceutical websites.

Just as the plumber, electrician, excavator, and carpenter need one well-organized head dude to coordinate the process, so too a medical team – brilliant specialists all who don't know squat outside of their specialty – require a GC to keep the information straight and consistent. And someone to ask the uncomfortable questions. Who better than the one lying in bed with a vested interest in getting out of it?

During my four-month home confinement I've been reading Thomas Mann's The Magic Mountain. It's about a tuberculosis sanitarium in Switzerland before World War One. In this remote sanctuary, well people become sick and sick people die. The medical director prescribes a "cure" designed to weaken the paying customer and keep him tethered to the institution for months, sometimes years. When the book was published in 1924 the critics applauded Mann's droll sense of irony. But, frankly, 80 years later the tale hasn't much changed. Only now we're tethered to the corporate food processors and the drug companies.

June 2008

MY LATEST WILL & TESTAMENT

I GO UNDER THE knife in a couple of weeks and my husband suggested that perhaps I should update my Will sooner than later. He is a practical person.

I have every intention of being perky enough to host my annual Oscar Party on February 24th. But the hospital makes you sign a bone rattling disclaimer form exonerating the institution, its personnel, and their progeny unto the tenth generation for any of the grotesque mishaps that can go wrong under their roof. And I am a practical person.

So, being of as sound a mind as any fool who's signed up for elective surgery, I do hereby make, publish, and declare this my Latest Will & Testament.

FIRST: I hereby direct my executor – presumably my husband, since he's not having any surgery that day – to forego the expense of a fancy funeral since we've never agreed on burial plots anyway. A quickie cremation will do nicely, followed by a respectful scat-tering under the two sorry apple trees in the back yard that haven't gotten any compost in years. Tell them I apologize for all the neglect and that this is the best I can do under the circumstances.

SECOND: I direct my executor to empty my personal bank account and throw one stupendous party for all my pals. He should spare no expense to fly in the gang from California, Texas, and Louisiana and to provide a top-shelf liquor bar and a live rock'n'roll band. Tell them I apologize for the recent decline in the stock market, otherwise we'd hold the damn thing in Dublin.

THIRD: As regards my coveted stuff: To my brother Jim I give and bequeath my steel string guitar since he's the only one in the family who can tune it.

To my sister Carol I give and be-queath my mother's old fur coat since she was clearly sore when Ma willed it to me.

To my old friend Maddy I give and bequeath forty years of personal journals with a warning that after the first couple of years it's all pretty much repetitive and I really won't mind if she burns them, in fact, I insist.

To my beloved daughter I give and bequeath all of my jewelry since every time I wear it she asks if she's going to get it some day anyway, and my 27 family photo albums even though she doesn't know 90% of the people in them [it's your burden now, darlin]. She also gets my record and audio tape collection of Broadway Musicals, New York Cabaret Nights, and female jazz vocalists in the hope that she carries on the sacred worship of this music, passed down to me from my mother.

All the rest, residue, and remainder of my property, including my eight year old computer, ten year old station wagon, and 30 year old Pentax single-lens reflex 35 millimeter camera [think of them as antiques], I give and bequeath to my husband, and I go on record here that I don't mind if he sells the whole lot and moves to a Greek island because I sure would if the tables were turned.

FOURTH: To ensure that there is enough money for the party, my child's education, and my husband's recovery cruise to the Mediterranean, I hereby declare that no extreme and costly measures be employed to keep my organs artificially beating and burping if the aforementioned surgical procedure goes terribly amiss. How will we know if it's time to pull the plug? If I am rendered a drooling fool who fails to respond to offers of a dry martini, a corned beef sandwich from the Carnegie Deli, a full body massage, a six-figure book advance, or nasty sex with Patrick Dempsey – then it's time.

In witness whereof I have subscribed my name on this first day of January, two thousand and eight.

Ta ta and see y'all on Oscar night.

January 2008

www.ingramcontent.com/pod-product-compliance
Lightning Source LLC
Chambersburg PA
CBHW061634040426
42446CB00010B/1405